Human Energy

The Critical Factor
for Individuals and Organizations

JOHN D. INGALLS

LEARNING CONCEPTS
2501 N. Lamar Austin, Texas 78705 (512) 474-6911

ISBN 0-201-03202-3
CDEFGHIJKL-HA-79

To Malcolm S. Knowles

Who awakened me when I was least expecting it.

Contents

Preface

About two years ago I had the pleasure of meeting Alvin Toffler, whom I greatly respect both as a writer of exceptional skill and as an author who is able to pull together highly diverse materials and sources into a compelling story. I was then in the early stages of work on this book and I asked him if he had any words of counsel for one about to embark on a writing project of some complexity. His answer was surprising in its direct simplicity: "Pay close attention to craftsmanship and have a passionate theme." I have thought about these two issues frequently during the months I have been engaged in this project, and I am well aware that while writing skill develops through continued practice and experience, a passionate theme emerges from deep feeling and intuition. I sincerely hope the reader will find that this book has "a passionate theme."

After serving an apprenticeship of many years in the field of personnel management, primarily with business and industrial firms, I have come to believe deeply that the most difficult problems we face (and fail to face) are the human problems inherent in organizational life. I have reached the conclusion that many leaders of human organizations allow themselves to become preoccupied with technical and administrative tasks—those that deal primarily with objects, numbers, and procedures. These individuals seem to prefer the task orientation, finding it more simple and certain perhaps, and more satisfying, than the highly ambiguous needs and wants of what Douglas McGregor so aptly called "the human side of enterprise."

As a result of this task orientation, many managers and administrators fail to develop either an adequate theoretical understanding of the human issues in organizations or sufficient skill in the practical resolution of human organizational problems. It is also true, of course, that many organizational leaders find educational and psychological theory too complex and contradictory to be of much help in a day-to-day administrative environment. Most busy managers and administrators simply don't have time to do a lot of searching and synthesizing on their own. They need theory translated into a format that makes it adaptable to their immediate needs. In addition, many organizational leaders are also specialists, in fields such as engineering, finance, or law, for example. It is only natural for them to view the human organization and its problems from their specialized viewpoint, but if this viewpoint excludes psychology, education, philosophy, and perhaps also theology there is likely to be a radical misperception of situational reality.

I have attempted to create a book that will synthesize much current organizational theory and highlight those aspects of education and psychology that are most important in developing and maintaining effective organizations. I have also presented some models that I have found to be of great practical value in engaging and utilizing organizational energies for constructive purposes. In the process of writing this book it has been necessary to deal to some extent with theory. I sincerely hope, however, that the work has not become too abstract or too symbolic. While more illustrative material might have been helpful, it would not only have made the book too long, but also perhaps robbed the reader of what is now an ample opportunity to use active imagination in relating the concepts presented to his or her own past, present, and potential future experience.

The book has been written for a diverse audience—all those who are responsible in one way or another for creating, ensuring, or increasing organizational effectiveness. Because of the variety of roles and responsibilities and because of widespread differences among organizations, some needs will not be met. What may appear simplistic to some may to others appear quite sophisticated or complex. Nevertheless, both professionals in the field of organizational development and those who have not given much thought or time to these issues will, I hope, find much of value. And I hope too that this book will prove useful in classrooms and academic settings where future managers and administrators are being trained and developed. Though the book itself is far from academic, it is written in part for students who are tired of textbook dullness and are looking for something more "alive."

The overall purpose of this book is to describe the human energy forces at work in individuals and organizations and to show how human energies can be focused and balanced to bring about results that are fully human and constructive. Bearing in mind the writings of the late Abraham Maslow which have been a source of joy to me, I am looking into the "further reaches of human nature," enjoying a vision of that future day when individuals and organizations are more consciously aware of their potential and the actual ways to go about fulfilling it.

In addition to the primary goal stated above, this book has five basic objectives:

1. To build an overall philosophical framework for improving the practice of individual and organizational development

2. To provide comprehensive models that will help to integrate diverse theories of individual and organizational development

3. To give managers and administrators who are frustrated and perplexed at the apparent "irrationality" of much human behavior a better understanding of, and ability to deal effectively with, interpersonal and intergroup conflict

4. To promote a philosophy and practice of education that focuses on learning as a continuing lifelong experience—an experience that is often painful, as old structures break down before new ones, but always joyful when those new structures are created

5. To help managers and administrators achieve a balanced viewpoint between the world of things and the world of people, and to show that management does have a scientific basis and that effective management practice is a little-recognized but very real form of artistic expression.

I believe a book like this cannot be written by one person. I have been very fortunate in having been exposed through the years to a wide variety of individuals representing a rich combination of different backgrounds and experiences. All these individuals have had a real part in this book's preparation, and to them I say thanks. A special mention, however, must be made of those friends and close associates without whom this book definitely could not have been written. First are those in government service: Jim Phipps of the Social and Rehabilitation Service of the Department of Health, Education, and Welfare; Bob Philleo and Lou Vogeler of the National Institutes of Health; Bob Cox of the U.S. Public Health Service, and all of the many staff development and training specialists around the country (and in Puerto Rico) with whom I have worked closely over the past few years. In industry, I owe deep appreciation to Frank Conway, Don Johnson, Dick Corcoran, Bob Scofield, and Alan Komins of the New England Telephone Company, whose patient acceptance of my ideas and willingness to try them out has led to much continued learning on my part. In my consulting firm, my partner Joseph Krzys has been a constant source of helpful ideas and my associates Jim Barnes, Mike Cooper, Dan Hogan, Bob Lynch, and Dave Marion have been most supportive. Special thanks also must go to Joseph Arceri, whose enthusiasm for the work of Carl Jung led me in a new direction.

Finally, thanks go to Malcolm S. Knowles, to whom this book is dedicated. He is the one who found me in a dead-end street and pointed out the way to the park—a very nice change of environment. And to my wife Dee, who gave the book its title and in our years together has more than anyone else helped me to develop the thoughts that are expressed here, loving appreciation is given.

In the final preparation of the book I am also grateful for the helpful comments and suggestions made by Alan Bennett, Chris Argyris, Richard Hackman, Peter Yensen, Dugan Laird, Fr. Ernest Serino, Fred Steel, and Bill Walsh. My thanks go also to my manuscript preparers Nancy Buehler and Sally Funk, and especially to Valerie Sarles for her outstanding effort and excellence.

Arlington, Massachusetts   J.D.I.
June 1976

The Allegory of the Mountain

Centuries ago, there lived a tribe at the base of a mountain. The valley in which they lived was fertile, but being completely surrounded by mountains whose sides were for the most part sheer cliffs, it was cut off from the rest of the world. There was, however, an abundance of food and water and the tribe's cattle and crops flourished. Everyone seemed to be happy and life progressed quite peacefully. One mountain in particular attracted everyone's attention. It was awesome. Higher than all the others, it held a commanding position at the end of the valley. Its slopes were gradual but soon steepened, and it stood as a mystical giant guarding the exit from the valley below. One day someone said, "Let's climb the mountain," but the others just looked at him and let him know that not only were they uninterested in the idea, but they also thought he was a little bit crazy for suggesting it. The idea persisted, however, and soon became a most important topic of conversation. Everyone began to be seized with curiosity about the mountain. Some of the wisest members of the tribe began to say that exploration was a good idea because the valley was rapidly becoming overpopulated and that bad times surely lay ahead.

One day there was a buzz of excitement outside the hut where the high priest of the tribe lived. A strange-looking object stood there. The one who had first suggested a mountain-climbing expedition stood beside the object beaming with happiness. It seems he had fashioned four round discs from a fallen tree trunk. A pole connected each pair of discs through holes in their centers, and a platform on top, tied with ropes, kept the whole object together. "Now we can climb the mountain," he said proudly, and pushed the object forward, showing that heavy rocks on top of the platform could be moved with a fraction of the usual effort. The high priest of the tribe looked very displeased and mumbled that punishment would swiftly follow such audacity, but the tribal chieftain congratulated the inventor and invited him to dine with the royal family.

In a short time, a base camp was established a quarter of the way up the mountainside. By now the inventor had set up a school and some of his students created ingenious devices to assist the tribe in mountain climbing. Gears and pulleys, connecting rods, chains, sprockets, capstans, and blocks and tackles all appeared rapidly. The students in turn became the teachers, and the school developed several departments of specialized study that soon broke away and formed into separate but equal centers for transmitting the knowledge the tribe had acquired. One invention after another tumbled from the imagination of the students. They learned how to use fire to melt metal and form castings, and one day someone discovered how to wind a metal strip to create a regulated source of mechanical power. They began to tell time. A wise professor in the school observed that "every action has its opposite reaction," and also that a powerful force, which he called "gravity," caused people and objects to tumble down the mountain causing severe injuries and even death. The old priest shook his head with grave foreboding; never before had death and injury come to the tribe in such a violent and tragic manner. But still they pressed on.

Many years passed. The schools in the valley had now become universities. Buildings sprang up and specialists in all fields of knowledge enjoined one another in noisy arguments concerning whose knowledge was most important to the tribe. By now they were halfway up the mountain, and as expectations rose they worked harder and faster each day. Leadership positions went to those who got results and those who couldn't maintain the pace were quickly demoted. New sources of power were found everywhere. First coal, then steam, then oil, and then electricity appeared, and soon there emerged new devices called machines. The people of the tribe were enraptured with machines; there was a machine for keeping time, and one for printing books, and others for making articles of every description, some of which the tribe needed and many they did not. They eventually made an iron horse, a horseless carriage, and talking pictures. They experimented with mechanical birds, trying to make them fly with rigid wings, and they succeeded in making words fly through wires and through the air at great distances. Magic became less popular as it gradually became replaced by something called "reality."

People began to worship machines and compare themselves to them. One said, "Animals are like machines." Someone else said, "Man himself is the best machine of all." The tribe's doctors began to experiment with those who were sick and injured and soon found that pieces of their bodies could be taken out and replaced when they were broken or damaged. Some time before, the old priest who served as the tribe's conscience had died. A new, young priest complained bitterly about the modern developments that were taking place and threatened the tribe with damnation for its audacious behavior. This angered several of the more influential members of the tribe and they turned him out of his hut, which by now had become a palace, and refused to listen to him any more. The tribe gradually became more and more sophisticated and began to lose all of its primitive respect for the powerful and mysterious ways of nature.

The tribe eventually found it necessary to organize itself for greater efficiency. It divided into sections and groups and formed a great assembly for the final assault on the mountain. The tribe thus organized began to take on the characteristics of the machines that everyone admired. Each tribal member had a specialized part to perform. He worked only within the structure of his section and each section became a part of a larger structure called a unit. Units consisted of ten sections; ten sections made up a span. No one could talk to the tribal leader anymore, except the heads of spans. Each major group of spans had a leader who became an "assistant operator." Accordingly, of course, arguments broke out within sections and units or between spans. When this occurred, the "grand operator" simply took the oil of benevolent leadership and poured it over these frictions; for everyone knew that friction was harmful to machines and would prevent the smooth operation of the individual parts. When a part did not perform efficiently, it was pulled out, tossed aside, and a shiny new replacement part was installed in its place. Eventually storerooms were provided for broken and malfunctioning parts, and areas were designed to house those parts that did not pass the initial quality control inspection. It was only natural that these storage areas were left uncared for, and they soon became shabby and infested with rats. As the storerooms themselves became more and more crowded, and as more and more unusable parts piled up, they began to cost the tribe enormous sums of money for support and maintenance. But very few worried, as all active eyes were still eagerly fixed on the mountain.

Eventually the tribe became engulfed by conflict. There never seemed to be enough benevolent oil to go around. Units and sections that had been in friction with each other almost continuously now began to involve whole groups of spans in an ongoing struggle. Sometimes physical violence erupted, and many tribal members were killed or badly injured. Some of the deaths were discovered to be other than accidental and, as violence became justified if it "helped" in getting up the mountain, the tribe entered a new era. Assistant operators met in conference after conference, trying to resolve conflict, but they were unable to listen to each other. One would insist on having his part turned on, while the others had theirs turned off. This uneven operation placed great strain on the entire tribal mechanism, and as costs rose efficiency dropped.

When friction was at its worst and had become almost unbearable, a strange calm descended upon the whole tribe. The tribe's greatest day was actually going to be realized. All stood in awe as the top of the mountain was about to be reached. But suddenly, a grave foreboding came over everyone. "Once the top is reached, where shall we go?" people began to ask. "We shall have nothing to look forward to," others said. "We have always had a purpose since our ancestors first suggested that we climb the mountain. We have a need to climb because life without a goal is aimless and frustrating. If our mainsprings lose their tension, who will wind us up again?" But any thought of going back to the simple life of the ancient valley was useless; there was no way to go home again, no way to return to a life that was gone forever. The only choice lay before them. They could descend the other side of the mountain and enter the unknown! Suddenly they felt a rush of anxiety.

Introduction

Human energy. Everyone knows what human energy is. It is obvious by its absence in the tired, lethargic, or ill. It is exciting by its presence in great athletes, outstanding artists, and extraordinary public figures. Every field of human endeavor has its highly energetic people. And yet many questions arise when we consider the manifestations of energy in ourselves and others. Human energy is, in many ways, quite mysterious.

What is human energy? Where does it come from? Can we increase the energy we have, or are we allotted a fixed amount? What accounts for some of us having more energy than others? What part does human energy play in determining who will lead and who will follow? These and many other questions tend to arise when the subject of human energy is considered in any depth. We may say that human energy flows from life itself; we may call it a natural phenomenon or a human capacity. It is, of course, our most abundant natural resource.

How can we best tap the human energy potential? Can we come to understand our own energy capacity and how best to use it? How do we save it? How do we waste it? How is it that we throw ourselves into some things and yet have real difficulty in getting started on other things? If we were able to understand our own energy, could we use this knowledge to begin to understand how human energy ebbs and flows in human groups and organizations? Consider human energy from the standpoint of creativity and control. Human history is full of examples of creative bursts of human energy with controlled excellence. Irving Stone provided us with magnificent insight into the agony and the ecstasy of Michelangelo's experience and how his energy produced extraordinary creativity with incredible control and precision. Yet history also presents us other pictures, examples of control without creativity and creativity without control.

History is also full of examples of one group or nation exploiting the human energy resources of another. These examples testify to the terrible misuse and waste of energy that occurs under conditions of aggression and conquest. The creation of a condition of involuntary servitude by means of military power or aggression (such as the slave markets created by the rum merchants and plantation owners of early America) drastically reduces the energy level in the controlled group. As long as the control remains, the energy level remains low. The economic output of countries during periods of military occupation has nearly always been a bitter disappointment to the conquerors. The expectation of abundant fruits of conquest become forgotten dreams in the face of reality, while the conquered enjoy little triumphs with extreme satisfaction. When the controlled group is freed from both its physical and its economic bondage, pent-up energy is released; and it is not unusual to see dramatic growth and expansion in the recovery period. Witness the situation of Western Europe after World War II and the emergence of the new black consciousness (and competence) in the United States. It seems that the most effective utilization of human energy occurs in free societies. In free societies human energy can be expressed or released in natural and normal ways.

Human energy must also be controlled. And the best form of control appears to be internalized self-control. Groups or organizations composed of willing participants who have effective leadership and who believe in their own value and worth as individuals tend to yield the most productive and creative results. Uncontrolled energy of low or medium intensity leads to organizational dissolution and decay. When striving ceases, life is lived at low ebb and no one seems to care. Uncontrolled energy of medium to high intensity leads to social unrest, anarchy, or revolution. And when high energy is uncontrolled there is increased likelihood of violence and bloodshed. Every now and then we read of someone who has led an honest, hard-working life and suddenly, for no apparent reason, bursts into a destructive and senseless rampage of mass murder. We wonder: Why?

Human energy must be controlled. But control is not enough. Human energy must also be directed toward constructive and creative ends. In our time, we witnessed the Third Reich accumulate and release controlled energy of incredible intensity. The direction of this energy toward destructive warfare and genocide created indescribable horror for a civilization that prided itself on its attainment of "rationality"; and yet one cannot say that the perpetrators of this destruction were not willing participants in the action, nor that they were unaware of what they were doing. The controlled efficiency of Hitler's military and police organizations was truly remarkable, made all the more so because the members of these organizations were, for the most part, quite fully committed to the values implicit in their assigned tasks. Perhaps the only fortunate aspect of this destructive burst of human energy lies in the fact that it occurred just before the development of the so-called new technology. The capacity for destruction in today's atomic, chemical, and biological weapons would, if unleashed now, make World War II pale into insignificance.

Will massive warfare and genocide occur again? Can we find the solution to the puzzle of human energy in time? Can we resolve the enigma of creation and destruction, of control and freedom, into an equation that will enable us to perceive the actions necessary to maintain balance and at the same time ensure forward movement? Can we find out how to order relationships among individuals, organizations, and whole societies so that the appropriate balance between internal and external control is achieved that will provide guidance toward continuous creative development?

The answers to these questions are complex. They require the simultaneous combined wisdom of many separate fields of inquiry: psychiatry, medicine, biology, anthropology, religion, sociology, economics, history, psychology, law, and philosophy. The answers also require a deep appreciation of the arts and the artistic influence on human life. Of course it is not possible to deal here with all of these multifaceted, enormously complex subjects. They are the contents of human experience. What is possible is to comment on, and examine in some depth, the *processes* of interaction that occur with individuals, organizations, and societies; the processes of energy build-up, transfer, and release. It is these processes that give insight and direction to the emerging field of management, not in the narrow sense of business administration and control accounting but in the broad sense of determining direction and implementing actions that give shape to the future always emerging before us. Management ability is needed everywhere. Families, businesses, churches, schools, government agencies, associations, foundations, labor unions, and health-care institutions all need effective management, as do groups fostering awareness and action to improve community life in general. Effective management requires knowledge and skill in guiding any human enterprise toward the achievement of creative and productive outcomes. It requires an understanding of how human individuals and human organizations function (and malfunction) and above all it requires an understanding of human energy. And having management ability does not simply mean knowing how to use techniques of guiding and directing organizations from outside, like a master puppeteer making the spectators laugh at the antics of the marionettes as their strings are jerked and pulled. The ability we seek is that of being able to guide an organization from within; to interact rather than to manipulate, to negotiate changing roles and responsibilities, and to actively seek the growth and development of all of any organization's members. And no longer is it possible or even practical to simply restrict one's cares and concerns to one's own organization. In a world shrinking daily under the impact of mass communication and transportation technologies there are no longer any isolated parts. We must now be concerned with integrating organizational systems, and with the qualities of organizational interaction. One might say that a kind of organizational statesmanship is now called for on the part of leaders everywhere.

Daily living in the twentieth century has seemed to increase in complexity and frustration. Organizations have grown to such enormous size that they appear to be reaching (or may have already reached) a stage of unmanageability. We hear increasingly frequent complaints that organizations are dehumanizing. A feeling of powerlessness follows the feeling of depersonalization. From the feeling that "no one really cares about me" in this organization arises the belief that no one is likely to care in the future. A predictable result of this attitude is a lessening of care for the organization itself; care required not only to maintain the quality of services or products but also to develop satisfying relationships with those with whom we come in contact in our daily interactions. We appear to have mastered the techniques of mass production; now we must learn to rediscover the means to ensure a life of high quality for all.

As a result of the increasing complexity of organized society, many of us long for a simpler day and find an irresistible charm in stories about frontier life. Even the physical hardships and the threat of death from outlaws or from the Indian wars seem oddly preferable to and more appealing than the prospect of dying in one's automobile on a crowded highway or becoming the victim of a fire on the thirty-fifth floor of a glass, plastic, and concrete skyscraper. Yet we know that this is our time. We do not live in a bygone age; we live now. So our task, as with those before us, is to come to terms with the present reality and make of it what we can. All of us must of necessity engage in the artistic enterprise of life by using the materials and situations at hand. While many have chosen to turn off and tune out, others see the ability to cope effectively with the complexity of our social, organizational, and individual problems as a twentieth-century art form, a major vehicle for the creative and expressive use of human energy and imagination.

In the past, living required a great expenditure of physical energy. Today it requires less physical energy and greatly increased psychic energy. Everywhere we see people exercising to make up for the lack of physical energy needed in today's sedentary occupations. Public jogging is increasingly evident and health clubs and local exercise spas are often found next door to the supermarket. While physical exercise is essential to the building up and maintaining of appropriate muscular tension, we must also find the appropriate level of psychic tension for present-day living. As this level appears now to be too high, we need to learn how to "exercise" to achieve psychic relaxation while working. It is no accident that many business executives in the United States are now practicing yoga and transcendental meditation during their lunch hours.

In the past, people who were required to perform much physical labor learned how to pace themselves. They learned how to store up energy and how to release it for the most constructive results. One could ill afford to become physically exhausted, lest some sudden or unexpected crisis require an extraordinary physical response. Today, we need to learn more about psychic energy and how to store and release it. We need to know more about how human energy, particularly psychic energy, affects organizational life and how it often gets blocked, resulting in frustration that sometimes causes the release of aggressive and violent reactions. We need to know more about how blocked energy in organizations may be a predisposing factor in heart disease and other forms of illness and how effective control of energy can increase individual productivity and creativity and health.

Human energy is the bedrock that underlies all theories of motivation. Many who seek to understand motivation theories may have been confused by the contradictions that appear between *external* theories and *internal* theories. External theories of the carrot-and-stick variety are radically different from internal theories of the development or growth variety. An analysis of the energy forces in humans tends to clarify discrepancies and contradictions among internal and external theories and to move us closer to a general theory of motivation that has great applicability for improving the quality of life and work.

Another of the major problems faced by all of us today arises as a consequence of the dramatic specialization of knowledge. So many of us are so well educated, in one technical or specialized area or another, and some of us are even well educated in several areas. But even so, when we try to speak to each other as backyard neighbors, the intellectual fences erected by our Ph.D.s and M.D.s and Sc.D.s and LL.D.s are so high that we are quite effectively blocked off and separated from one another. In attempting to build the tower of our civilization, we are frustrated by the babel of technological jargon in its many and varied forms. In addition, we like to believe that our own specialty grasps the totality of the situation more competently than do the specialties of others. *We* could solve the problems if *they* could only understand. The energy that it takes to acquire specialized knowledge represents a personal investment of great value. How frustrating it is when we experience situations in which we cannot communicate or share the knowledge we have, especially when we know how much it could help. What kind of process is needed, then, to help us transfer the stored-up energy of specialized knowledge from one person to another? What is the function of energy in education? Can a more effective use of energy accelerate learning?

We are still plagued with the two-headed dragon of competition and collaboration and its progeny of power, control, influence, position, and wealth. We would like to collaborate and yet we often find ourselves betrayed as someone seeks to gain unfair advantage. We willingly accept the challenges of competition and we do compete aggressively, but we find that we cannot achieve ultimate successes until we learn to collaborate effectively with others. Given the defensive and reactive mentality of "Nice guys finish last" and "Don't give a sucker an even break," many of us have built an ethical defense for competitive and aggressive behavior as justifiable protection against an anticipated attack. A recent slogan makes the point, "Just because you're paranoid, doesn't mean they're not out to get you!" Another slogan, "Don't look back because they may be gaining on you," may also seem to be wise counsel for one who is intent on "winning the race no matter what the cost." But what are we racing for, and what have we got when we "win"? While competition often seems to call forth superior effort, failure to value collaboration and to build social and organizational norms and structures for its realization is tantamount in a nuclear age to signing the death warrant for our planet. We no longer can afford win/lose strategies; present circumstances call for strategies that allow everyone to win.

Today Western civilization is being effectively challenged by the rising consciousness of the new East and by the emerging consciousness of the Third World. One hoped-for result is perhaps a new world civilization that will emerge out of necessity in the face of incredibly disastrous alternatives. This new civilization will be built, if it can be built at all, upon a respect for pluralistic cultural values and traditions, because we are beginning to realize at last that cultural values and traditions do not dissolve in a mythical melting pot. They remain as concrete manifestations of human experience. Cultural values become historical facts.

What now seems necessary is a map for exploring strange territory in an uncertain future, because many of the old maps in which we have placed our trust no longer meet the needs of our present situation. This book attempts to provide such a map, and while it may be as limited and inaccurate as the ancient parchments used by the early seafaring explorers of the fifteenth century, it will at least provide some indication of a direction for sailing. It will by no means be a certain guide, nor will it have the benefit of verification by extensive research (although that may come at a later time). The early explorers did not have a certain guide either, but they did have a sense of direction and a resolute purpose. In their day, they didn't pause forever to examine the splinters on the decks of their tiny wooden boats nor did they conduct endless arguments about the purposes of sailing; they put out to sea, faced the unknown bravely, and found something. They didn't always find what they were looking for—Christopher Columbus sailed four times for the Far East. By sailing West, from southern Europe, he did not achieve his objective; thus by some standards of evaluation today he would have to be considered a failure. To take such a posture, of course, would be ridiculous, but it is disconcerting nevertheless to observe the tendency of some to insist on being told exactly where a planned voyage of discovery will lead. If you knew, it probably wouldn't be worth the trip.

The map I now set before you will, I hope, be useful. It is a map of energy forces or influences that stimulate individuals and organizations. It has two hemispheres: one in the field of action (the external world of everyday), the other in the field of consciousness (the internal world of personal and subjective awareness). The two hemispheres are described and a number of issues and questions are then raised that may lead to the desire for further personal exploration. This map points out some directions for conducting such exploratory activities and also some areas in which "gold" may be found if sought with creative effort. This is not simply a map to look at; it invites you to actively explore and discover. But you must lead your own expeditions and I seek to serve only as your guide, and only for as long as that may be useful. Let us, then, unroll the parchment and look at some new "signs" and "symbols." Perhaps when you have seen the map, you will want to start right away in your efforts to discover, and then unlock, the treasure chest of human energy that is present in your own unique situation.

1 The Action Matrix

A man climbed the steps of a tower, unpacked several high-powered rifles from the bag he was carrying, and quietly and deliberately opened fire on people walking innocently along the street below. A young woman, walking in New York's Kew Gardens, was attacked and murdered by a knife-wielding assailant while many people watched from their apartment windows across the street, listened to her screams, and did nothing. The well-known incidents of the University of Texas shootings and the murder of Kitty Genovese give rise to a troublesome question. The Texas sniper was a bright young college man with a good family background and excellent potential. We may have observed that he was a war veteran who had just returned from active duty in the Korean conflict. But frankly, we don't know why the tragedy occured; the man himself is dead and cannot tell us. The Genovese case is perhaps more disturbing. How could those people watch her die and do nothing? No one even called the police. Could we say they didn't want to get involved; could we say that each of them assumed someone else would act? If we found ourselves in the same situation tomorrow, would we have any confidence that someone would come to our aid? And do the people themselves know why they adopted such frightening passivity?

Robert Kennedy lay dying on the floor of the hotel kitchen, Martin Luther King fell mortally wounded on his motel balcony, and John Kennedy slumped back in the seat of his Dallas limousine with his head hopelessly shattered. We watched with horror and each time struggled to find explanations and answers. The "work of madmen," some said. "Maniacs," "it was a plot," "deliberate and calculated," said others, while still others rationalized by observing that "political assassinations are part of our American culture." Perhaps most people feel "you'd have to be crazy to do something like that." But what is crazy and what is sane? Again we are confused and perplexed. Can we say that all killing is abnormal behavior? If so, is warfare made normal simply because it is planned and organized killing that has been given social and political approval? When we first heard about the incident at My Lai, the story affronted our senses with a contradiction. Does "good" killing (killing enemy soldiers) turn to "bad" killing when the victims are unarmed women and children? If so, were Hiroshima and Nagasaki really war crimes? Why didn't we drop the bomb in a desolated spot, or in the water, to prove its power to the Japanese, thus allowing them to choose surrender to avert the massive destruction of unarmed and unprotected life in two heavily populated cities? These are difficult questions to answer. They tend to trouble us deeply. And we are aware also of much destructiveness in our society that does not result in death but results instead in personal injury and property loss.

Any look at human destructiveness may be contrasted with a vision of human creativity. Countless creative and constructive activities are carried out daily. A realization of the effort and energy it has taken to develop our civilization from its earliest beginnings in ancient Greece staggers the imagination. What we have today is the result of centuries of accomplishment and we often fail to appreciate how much we have had given to us. We tend to single out some individuals and point to them as examples of extraordinary ability or even genius; and rightly so, because the great men and women of every age are those who have seen the inherent potential in a situation and have effectively used their energy to bring their extraordinary intuitions into actual fulfillment. They have had to work with the "givens," the constraints and difficulties of the age in which they lived, and they have risen to overcome them. These outstanding individuals have in many ways created their own opportunities. What is the process of outstanding creativity, we may ask, and how does it occur?

In the Introduction, I raised a question about creativity and control. It appears from everyday observation that individuals who are being controlled (or who feel controlled) by someone else or by an organization have their freedom of movement diminished and experience a simultaneous diminishment of energy. To the extent that individuals are able to increase their autonomy in a situation, their freedom of movement increases and their energy levels rise. There is an observable sense of freedom, joy, and exhilaration, and an increase in spontaneity.

Let us also look at the other side of the coin. If an individual is trying to gain control over another person or is trying to maintain control in order to hold an organization together, the experience of impending loss of control raises that individual's level of energy until either a crisis is reached or there is a relaxation of effort. Any attempt to increase control is generally accompanied by an increase in categorical thinking of the good/bad, right/wrong variety, and is typified by attempts to fix responsibility or place blame on the other person rather than oneself. In these situations, tension tends to rise eventually to the point where either "fight" or "flight" will occur.

It appears that much of our thinking about human issues or events involving such things as creativity, destructiveness, energy, passivity, activity, potential, and fulfillment has been overly constricted or obscured by a too-narrow or too-limited point of view. We are accustomed to thinking in categories such as good or bad, right or wrong, and true or false. We separate and divide into black and white and not gray; it's got to be "this" or "that," we say, an *either/or* situation. It is now perhaps time to open our minds to a bigger picture.

The most difficult and complex problems can often be reduced to quite simple terms if we create an appropriate framework within which to view them. Complexity arises when issues are jumbled together, when competing needs and passions obscure our attempts to understand, and when limited categories of judgment are erected like fences to prevent free and direct access to our experience. And if we think of *experience* as simply touching or seeing objects or things that engage our attention, we also have to consider *relation*, the direct awareness of persons and nature, which we cannot fathom, master, or ever fully comprehend. While our experience of things is concrete and specific, our relation with others, and the world, always lies open before us. And relation cannot be grasped or defined: all words are inadequate.

Let us look now at a field on which all human action takes place. This *field of action* can be characterized by four simple terms that, when paired, form two sets of polar opposites. A vision of this field may show us our true selves and enable us to choose an alternative mode of play or a new direction for our own game of life. Deep awareness of the field, and of our actions on it, may even enable us to raise our experience of life to a higher level and stimulate within us both the capacity for and acceptance of the responsibility of significant creative effort.

Most of us wish we could improve our understanding of ourselves and learn to achieve better relationships with others. The widespread interest in recent years in such subjects as transactional analysis (I'm OK—You're OK), transcendental meditation (TM), encounter groups, behavior modification, assertiveness and effectiveness training, and interpersonal communications, provides ample evidence that many of us wish we could be more effective in developing and maintaining effective relationships with others. There are many new approaches, but as yet none seem to provide a sure and simple foundation either for understanding human behavior in any situational context or for deciding what to do to bring about situational improvement if one wants to. It now appears that there is a key that might unravel the human mystery. That key lies in understanding the operation of the human energy field and its two hemispheres of action and consciousness. To reach such an understanding it is first necessary to refer briefy to a theoretical foundation.

A BASIC ATTITUDE

In recent years three compatible theories of human behavior have emerged from ongoing research in the field of social psychology. We may refer to them as the *theory of cognitive balance, the theory of social comparison*, and *the theory of attribution*. Upon inspection they appear to be closely related.

Perhaps more importantly, they are easy to identify in day-to-day situations because they represent commonplace, factual behaviors. We can describe these theories and their behavioral characteristics as follows.

Cognitive Balance or Consistency

We constantly seek to organize the world we live in to make it meaningful to ourselves. We strive to make sense out of any situation in which we find ourselves, to bring order out of chaos. If things are mixed up, we attempt to straighten them out. In short, we all try to act in a logical and rational manner. To help ourselves achieve cognitive balance or consistency, we work hard to determine what is true or false and what is correct or incorrect. In addition, we are not satisfied until everything within our field of vision, or experience, has a name or a label. If we don't know what something is and can't name it, we often tend to avoid it in confusion. Sometimes we apply different labels to the same person, place, or thing, but the effort is the same: to identify, to organize, to make consistent.

Social Comparison and Evaluation

We constantly seek to determine our standing in relation to others. To do so, we make social comparisons or evaluations such as, "I'm smarter than she is" or "He's stronger than I am." While some of these comparisons are harmless, others may be very judgmental and quite unfair; nevertheless we seem to have a need to make judgments and comparisons more or less constantly. When our judgments could get us into trouble if stated openly or directly, we tend to keep them covered up or to share them with third parties as a way of seeking confirmation or agreement. When we get the confirmation we are seeking we feel satisfaction, but we are also uneasy that our confidence may be betrayed and our true feelings may be made public and bring us embarrassment or worse.

Attribution or Assignment of Motives

We constantly seek to understand why other people act or behave as they do. In the absence of certain knowledge about the acts of others we will actually make up or invent motives and attribute them to the behavior we observe: "He did that because he was jealous" or "She ran out of the house because she hated her father." These assumptions usually remain unchecked or unverified. We tend to attribute motives to others very frequently, and unless we receive information that discredits our attributions and assumptions they soon become part of what we see as reality. We forget quickly that our initial attribution was, after all, based only on assumption. Because attributions are usually not made directly and openly it is often difficult to find out what someone really think or believes about you.

For purposes of simplification we may group these three behaviors together as a set and call them Type A behaviors. It is fairly easy to see how all three are related and are manifestations of the basic tendency we all have to find out what's going on and how one is both actually and potentially affected by it.

There are two interesting characteristics about these Type A behaviors. First, they are normal. In general, it is clear that the behaviors described above are part of our everyday accepted pattern of relating or responding to one another. We do not perceive these ways of behaving as bizarre, odd, neurotic, or psychotic at all; they are, in fact, the very basis of rationality for they support and give daily testimony to our deep-seated belief in the scientific axiom of cause-and-effect relations—the principle of causality.

The second notion is a bit startling, especially in light of the recognition that the Type A behaviors are normal. Recent research has demonstrated that the normal behaviors described above can be directly responsible for the disruption of social and organizational relationships and for breakdowns of interpersonal understanding and trust.

The idea that normal and rational behavior may cause interpersonal misunderstanding, human conflict, and mistrust may come as a shock to literate men and women. We have believed so deeply, and for so long, that logical, calm, and rational behavior will reduce conflict and lead us toward stability and peace. We place our faith and trust in systems of order and control and tend to pride ourselves on our ability to overcome irrationality and excess emotion. We have implicitly believed for a long time that human conflict occurs because of abnormality (or human weakness) and that the achievement of normality will eliminate conflict or reduce it to manageable proportions. We have also believed that somehow abnormality began at the dawn of human history with what theologians are accustomed to calling original sin. The idea that normal rational behavior may itself be a major cause of human conflict is new and different. It is also quite disturbing.

It is not hard, however, to see just how these three Type A behaviors can cause conflict and misunderstanding. All of them seek to eliminate discrepancy and to establish fact. They seek to distinguish what *is* from what might be or could be. And they are loaded with moral imperatives. In judging what is true and good there is the implication that their opposites are wrong and bad. Indirectly, then, Type A judgments can create feelings of guilt and unworthiness. When such feelings are repressed they tend to build up energy; when they are expressed they may come out as attacks and stimulate defensive counterreactions. Let us look more closely at how this occurs.

If I proclaim a fact (in Type A style), we will have no conflict unless you announce another fact that contradicts mine. If I also back up my fact with strong feelings (in other words, I feel that my fact is very important to me and represents some of my basic values) and you back up yours with the same emotional strength, we are well on the way to a deep-seated disagreement. Now, if I go on to attribute meaning and motivation to you as a contradictor of me (for example, "You are dumb, stupid, and your facts are based on very superficial and ill-developed logic and what's more, you are simply trying to embarrass and provoke me"), and you in turn attribute meaning and motivation to me as a proclaimer of my fact ("There he goes again on another ego trip, always trying to show everyone how smart he is, he's really stupid and anyone could poke holes in such a dumb argument"), we may be well on the way toward physical violence. If, however, you were my boss and I was deeply concerned about the security of my job, would I not perhaps be tempted to contradict myself, withdraw my fact, suppress my feelings, humor you, and emerge from the discussion being seen as a good soldier or team player? Would you, with a sense of personal competence, go on to point out to me how erroneous my conception was, in light of your broader experience and knowledge? Would I be very careful in my attempts to dissuade you from your convictions, even though I felt or even knew them to be erroneous? Under such conditions I would probably experience feelings of diminished self-worth and increased dependency on you. If the conflict between us remained unresolved, however, you might begin to feel that I was lacking in competence and integrity and possibly seek to terminate my employment or have me transferred. I, on the other hand, might resign.

Chris Argyris, formerly professor of industrial administration at Yale University and now a professor at the Harvard University Graduate School of Education, conducted a field action research project several years ago, the results of which support the above contentions (Argyris, 1969). The findings show that in typical organizations there is an overriding "tendency toward minimal expression of feelings, minimal openness to feelings, and minimal risk-taking with ideas and feelings." In addition, they confirm a high degree of concern in the groups and organizations studied for the maintenance of norms of conformity. Argyris's research demonstrated that Type A behaviors tend to function as primary social and organizational norms and values. In our society people often make negative and feeling-laden judgments about one another, make arbitrary decisions or assumptions, and do not tend to share feelings openly with the person being judged. Instead they tend to share feelings and judgments with third parties, which reduces openness and authenticity in interpersonal relationships and creates suspicion and mistrust, thus undermining organizational effectiveness. Unfortunately, perhaps, the Type A pattern is deeply embedded in our families, schools, churches, industrial and business organizations, and governmental bureaus and at bottom seems to be the cause of many organizational and social problems.

Type A behaviors are the behaviors of control. As such they tend to diminish freedom of movement and also the level of energy and spontaneity in those being controlled. Type A behaviors can be, and very often are, the cause of lowered morale and lowered productivity on the part of individuals and organizations. *Some* control, of course, is required in order for organizations to exist and function; the question is how much and of what variety?

AN ALTERNATIVE POSTURE?

The dilemma posed by the existence and prevalence of Type A behavior is *that our normal and necessary tendency toward logic, structure, order, and rationality brings with it a tendency to create conflict and alienation.* Fortunately, there is a way out of this dilemma. Experience and research show us that there are three other behaviors that tend to offset the potentially negative or destructive dimensions of Type A behaviors. These behaviors, which for convenience we will call Type B, are also normal but they tend to bring about closer interpersonal relationships and improved collaborations and social cohesion. Let us examine them in some detail.

Openness to Experience

We all have the capacity, to a greater or lesser extent, to temporarily suspend our search for cognitive consistency and remain in a state of imbalance or uncertainty. We may say, "I do not yet know the answer." We may seek to explore conflicting viewpoints and seek to gain more information about them. We may also recognize that different people see things differently because of differing backgrounds and experience. To remain open to the experiences of others and to accept differing points of view, even if they are inconsistent, is a normal and reasonable way to behave. This is especially true if we anticipate that new information, soon to be obtained, can clarify a disputed claim and lead to resolution of any potential disagreement—we do not have to start off with a logical or rational solution.

Descriptive and Nonjudgmental Assessment

As an alternative to making good/bad, right/wrong judgments, we may depict a scenario of events or occurrences. We are able to say, "This is how the situation appears to be" or we can describe from a positive posture how we personally feel about an event or set of circumstances. From this descriptive stance, we are also able to affirm differing perceptions of others as *relatively* valid depending on the personal orientation of the reporter, and we can affirm the integrity of the reporter by accepting the description given as a valid and verbatim report of what he or she actually saw. We can, in fact, suspend judgment, if we wish to.

Questioning Inquiry

Although we may have acquired the habit of doing so, there is no reason why we must constantly make decisions about the motives for others' behavior when these decisions are based purely on our own assumptions. We may instead develop a posture of questioning inquiry. "Why did you do that?" or "Do you know why he might have done this?" Perhaps people tend not to ask such leading questions because they are not prepared to receive the answers they might get. It may after all feel much safer to operate on the basis of covert or unchallenged assumptions: for example, if we find out that the person's real motive was stimulated by something unpleasant they thought or felt about us, we may find ourselves in an uncomfortable situation. The human capacity to question, to inquire, to explore, and to experiment is the capacity to risk uncertainty and to tolerate the potential for error, mistake, or personal failing as an unavoidable cost of discovery, growth, and progress.

In looking at Type B behaviors we can easily see why they lead to interpersonal union and improved collaboration. First, instead of seeking to reduce discrepant perceptions and to establish fact, by having the capacity to remain open to experience we allow discrepant views to hold equal value (or to exist temporarily value free) and we reduce the chance of win/lose confrontations over choices between mutually exclusive propositions. Openness to experience is thus the *sine qua non* of coexistence. Second, the ability to be descriptive affirms the *subjective* value of individual perception and tends to temporarily set aside the requirement for dealing with *objective* facts. When moral judgments are also withheld, tension in interpersonal relations is reduced. No one feels obliged to behave defensively or to create a favorable image when the right/wrong, good/bad orientation is removed. Third, the desire to question and inquire allows new sources of information to flow into a discussion or a problem situation. Thus potential antagonists become increasingly aware that new facts or data can bring about changes in anyone's position, and their need to hang onto any position with bulldog-like tenacity is greatly decreased. Finally, an orientation toward discovery creates an aura of excitement and expectation that can act as a powerful bond in uniting individuals in collaborative effort. Type B behaviors can create conflict, however, if another individual has a deep need for structure, logic, or certainty and cannot tolerate the Type B modality for any appreciable length of time.

Unfortunately, where Type A behaviors predominate, those who behave in Type B ways are often regarded as incompetent or inefficient by those in senior positions of power and authority. Positive and logical behaviors are valued in most organizations and managers are often rewarded for having

The Need for Certainty Type A (Normal)	The Toleration of Ambiguity Type B (Normal)
The search for cognitive balance or consistency (logic)	The capacity for remaining open to experience (acceptance)
The tendency toward social evaluation and comparison (judgment)	The ability to be descriptive (nonjudgmental assessment)
Attribution and the assignment of motives (assumption)	The willingness to question and inquire (experiment and exploration)

Figure 1.1

"good judgment" (especially if the judgment conforms with that of the boss). Type B behavior is much less prevalent in our society and in our organizations than Type A. A ratio of 8 to 1 (of A over B) would not be surprising if a comprehensive survey could be devised.

Now let us look at the Type A and Type B behaviors side by side and see if we can reach some tentative conclusions about them. First, it may be useful to identify each set of behaviors more clearly. If we take the three Type A behaviors together we may assert that they represent a basic human need—this is *the need for certainty*. If we take the Type B behaviors and group them in a set we may say that they represent a human *capacity for tolerating ambiguity or uncertainty* (see Fig. 1.1).

CERTAINTY AND AMBIGUITY

Thus *certainty* and *ambiguity* become the first two simple terms for describing the field of action. They form the first pair of opposites. However, perhaps we might inquire if these two behavior sets really represent two different types of behavior at all? Are they really *different* behaviors? Further, why is Type A stated as a *need* and Type B stated as a *toleration?* Does not our experience also speak to us of the reverse order; of a need for ambiguity and a toleration of certainty?

Let us again look at the two sets. What clearly emerges is their oppositeness or reciprocity. Not only do they offset one another, *they lead away in different directions;* they are, in fact, mutually exclusive. You cannot say, "This *is* right or wrong," and "This *may* be right or wrong" simultaneously. It is inconceivable to think of being judgmental and nonjudgmental at the same time. Attribution tends to fix or pin down while questioning or inquiry releases or opens.

While in a generic sense there is only one basic behavior (that is, human), the A and B types represent polar or reciprocal modalities. One might say that Type A stands for or represents the psychological posture of *answer* while Type B represents the psychological posture of *question*. In addition, the Type A behaviors possess the characteristics of stopping the action (time limiting), while the Type B behaviors possess the opposite characteristic of keeping the action moving, creating a sense of timelessness.

Let us look at the questions of toleration and need. In our *need* for certainty we can see the necessity for making the world of our experience meaningful to ourselves. We must all try to organize our own situation, to make sense out of our lives, and to ensure that we will go on living. Our need for certainty is directly related to the general human will to live and to our own safety and survival. While we also have been reminded since biblical times to "Judge not, that ye be not judged," who among us can refrain from making judgments? Making judgments seems to be a requisite for prudent and responsible action, and even making moral judgments about others appears inevitable if we would adhere to, or support, any moral code.

Furthermore, why do we have a need to attribute meaning and motivation based on our assumptions? I believe it is because we can seldom get all of the answers we need for choices and decisions we must make. We therefore need to make assumptions as practical foundations for action. If we waited until all the facts were in, we would never act and very little would be accomplished. On the other hand, it is potentially harmful to forget what our assumptions are, or have been, and it is important to keep in mind that they are in fact only assumptions.

Now let us look at toleration. There is a limit to the amount of ambiguity anyone can tolerate. We have learned that various forms of torture and brainwashing, such as forced isolation, interrupted sleep, physical distress, and other strategies of disorientation and cognitive dissonance, create an ambiguity so unbearable as to lead to mental imbalance and insanity. But moderate and normal amounts of ambiguity must be tolerated for healthy and normal growth and development. If no one could tolerate any ambiguity, children would not mature, problems could not be solved, difficulties of all kinds would not be overcome or surmounted, and everyone would still be huddled against the walls of caves seeking security against the dangers outside.

It is also clear that the reverse of the above situation exists. While there is a limit to the amount of ambiguity we can tolerate there is also a limit to the amount of certainty we can stand. All of us need some degree of novelty, surprise, and excitement in our lives and there are very few of us who could stand having every event of our waking lives totally prescribed and structured. If we have too much certainty we feel controlled, manipulated, or bored. It would appear, therefore, that while both certainty and ambiguity are needs and neither are absolutely tolerable, it is the need for certainty that forms a secure foundation for human activity while the degree of ambiguity tolerable determines the appropriate level of personal risk. The degree to which ambiguity can be tolerated determines the amount of difficulty the individual can, and is willing to, meet and overcome in coping with the problems of human life and in taking advantage of the opportunities life has to offer.

Since the ability to tolerate ambiguity varies from person to person and is changeable over an extended period of years (it normally increases as a function of maturation and growth from childhood to adulthood), it is a dimension we must investigate if we would seek to find a satisfying explanation for individual differences. Once we can find how individuals differ, it may then be possible to discover a methodology for resolving differences, accepting them, and solving problems of both interpersonal and organizational relations.

To approach this task it may be useful to construct a matrix that shows certainty and ambiguity as two poles at each end of a continuum and displays the two types of behavior, A and B, as dominating the two halves of the field of action. This matrix is illustrated in Fig. 1.2.

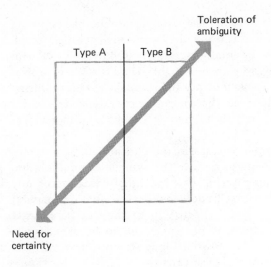

Figure 1.2

Thus ambiguity and certainty represent two of the four poles in the field of action. We may suggest at this point that certainty represents the dimension of control and ambiguity the dimension of creativity. Great artists typically operate at extremes of both dimensions; they have extraordinary control or certainty with their instrument or medium and yet take great risks and engage in highly innovative and ambiguous exploratory efforts of artistic expression. Consider, for example, the history of European art and music from the period of Raphael and Rubens to Pablo Picasso; from Mozart and Handel to Dimitri Shostakovitch. During a span of roughly three centuries the general level of ambiguity in both forms increased significantly; in painting there occurred a movement from realism through impressionism to cubism; in music the basically diatonic harmonies of the early Germans gave way before the much richer fabric woven by Debussy and Ravel, Tchaikovsky and Richard Strauss, for example, which in turn gave way before the frenzied chromatic figures and whole-tone scales typical of Stravinsky and Prokofiev. As the levels of ambiguity increased audiences were progressively challenged to keep up with the rapid development of the artists themselves. It is small wonder that many individuals cannot yet tolerate either modern art or modern music.

Other examples of control and creativity may be found in our recent social history. The creative explosion of knowledge and technology in recent years has brought about much ambiguity and change. Many individuals in positions of power and authority have begun to feel that they have lost or are rapidly losing control and they seek to reestablish it firmly. Others feel they are already overcontrolled and seek further opportunity for creative expression and more rapid human development. It is inevitable that opposing tendencies of such magnitude will clash and that some violence will erupt. It is significant that the Type B orientation of many followers of Martin Luther King and of the many individuals who sought to end the Vietnam War probably prevented even more massive violence than actually occurred during that difficult time. It may be observed that more violence tended to come from those seeking control than from those seeking change or a more creative solution.

One may also interpret attempts to assassinate political figures as a tendency on the part of a lunatic fringe to remove the symbolic representation of the force they feel is controlling them. Thus potential assassins of any leader may emerge, no matter what that leader's political persuasion or point of view may be. If a leader is strong and effective he or she may be a target until that time when physical violence is no longer felt to be an effective means of exercising control. Such a day may be a long way off, however, and thus it is both wise and necessary to provide safeguards.

OBJECT AND RELATION

Let us now look at the other poles of the matrix we have just constructed. We all live in a world where work or tasks must be accomplished and where we must interact (collaborate and compete) with others in the course of their accomplishment. Robert Blake and Jane Mouton (1972) demonstrated effectively that a relationship exists between an individual's concern for work (task accomplishment) and his or her concern for people (building and maintaining effective collaborative relationships with others). Their book *The Managerial Grid,* first published in 1964, was received with enthusiasm by those interested in human organizations, and the resulting practical application of grid-oriented strategies for both management and organizational development represented a high-water mark in the 1960s for the acceptance of social science and behavioral theories by both government and industry as a whole.

The notion of the dichotomy between things and people goes much deeper than Blake and Mouton's managerial grid, however. The existentialist Martin Buber (1958) plumbed the depths of the concept of human *relation* and came up with two simple yet profound categories that tower above the judgmental and logical categories emerging from the Type A behaviors described above. Buber's two categories, I-It and I-Thou, form the basis for the second pair of opposites in the field of action. This assertion may require a brief explanation.

Buber claimed that all men and women see the world as twofold in accordance with a basic twofold attitude. He claimed that we all adopt a psychological posture in relation to two primary words that are spoken silently by all of us in the depths of our being. These two primary words are not single or separate, but rather are two sets of combined words. The first part of each combination is the word *I*. While the term *I* appears to be the same in both combinations, examination proves that it takes on a different characteristic depending on its second combination word.

The first primary word (or combination set) is *I-It*. The second primary word (or set) is *I-Thou*. In the first set, the term *It* may be replaced by *He* or *She*. Whenever the word *I* is spoken it is always spoken with or joined to either one or the other of its connectives. That is to say, the second word in the combination may remain unspoken but it is always present by implication. The primary words, according to Buber, do not signify things in themselves; rather they intimate relations. The I-It relation is that between *I* as a knowing subject or conscious being and any *object* or *thing*. The replacement of It with He or She simply indicates that I may often treat other persons merely as objects or things. When we use the first combination, we tend to screen out or obliterate the other primary set, I-Thou. I-Thou is the primary word that signifies human *relation*—the relation between two knowing subjects or conscious beings. The I in the combination I-Thou enhances the life of its utterer by joining it with that of the Thou. The I in the combination I-It restricts the life of its speaker to the realm of the objects referred to. Buber's insight cuts to the heart of an important matter. Objectivity or I-It relations, without subjective acceptance and affirmation of I-Thou relations between persons, tend to create meaningless situations: "Work for the sake of work," and so on. If a person's own primary subjective existence has been violated, objective facts alone will not be sufficient to set any human problem straight. No amount of explanation, rational clarification, legal argument, or appeal to common sense will suffice when humanly meaningful relationships are denied or obliterated. It is only when the initial violation of I-Thou relationships is corrected that order will be brought to any situation and that conflict and its

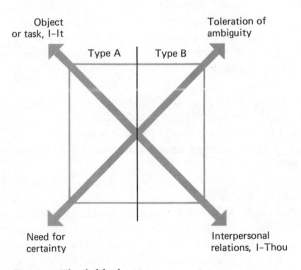

Fig. 1.3 The field of action

resultant confusion may be dispelled. Progress in human problem solving comes about when the objective and subjective realms are joined, when both I-It and I-Thou relations stand together (Buber, 1958).

Now we may perhaps see the nature of the second set of polar opposites in the field of action. The I-It relations we can visualize as *object*. Object in this sense may also mean any task, purpose, or effort directed outward toward the world of objective facts or experience. The I-Thou relation we can visualize simply as *interpersonal relations*, and by this we mean the subjective awareness of persons, their feelings, and their relative acceptance of each other in any situation whatsoever.

It now may also be obvious that the Type A behaviors referred to above apply especially to the domain of object or task (I-It) while the Type B behaviors fit comfortably with the I-Thou domain of interpersonal relations. In Fig. 1.3 we reconstruct our matrix to show this additional set of polar opposites.

AN ENERGY ACCELERATOR?

We may now begin to draw some important inferences from the two sets of polar opposites in the field of action that will apply to all organizations of every description. It is because these four concepts may be applied universally that we can begin to see patterns of behavior and of organizational performance and come to understand them more clearly. There is also a benefit to be gained from utilizing a matrix model. The matrix is ideally suited for describing situations of relative difference or variation. The outer dimensions of the matrix are changeable, for in individuals and organizational behavior there are no absolutes; relativity is the expected condition.

The four poles of the field of action—ambiguity, certainty, object, and relation—create, as it were, a magnetic field. A tugging or pulling of energy occurs because of the inherent psychological properties of these four factors and also because of their reciprocal and complementary relationships. All four poles are fundamental and basic to life itself. They represent the bedrock foundation of the human energy system.

Let us now look further and inquire how the polarities in the field of action affect human energy. In this exploration we need to consider more explicitly the relationship and interaction between these four poles (or rather, our interaction with them), and we also need to ascertain just how human energy is stimulated and engaged.

For simplicity we may first look at the relationship of the individual to the field of action. This relationship is illustrated in Fig. 1.4.

Human life is a dynamic process. While life exists there are periods of relative rest but no cessation of activity. All physiological and psychological processes are constantly ongoing, even while we are asleep. Likewise, no individual can escape any of the four poles of the field of action. He or she must confront them all and come to terms with them more or less continu-

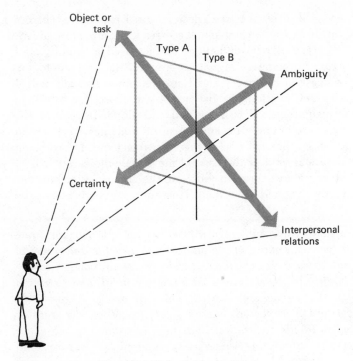

Fig. 1.4 The individual and the field of action

ously. In other words, everyone must make decisions. All decisions or choices we make call forth response and engage psychophysical processes. In fact the very process of making choices or decisions is itself a psychophysical process involving energy expenditure. Human life must be lived actively. Purely passive behavior is a radical diminution of life itself; active living requires the full utilization of human energy.

Let us look at the process in its simplest terms. An object appears before me. It is curious, different, and appealing. I am attracted to it by its ambiguity. I have never seen anything like it before. As it is growing on a tree and it is within easy reach, I pluck it, examine it, smell it. It looks appealing. More ambiguity is experienced. I bite it. It tastes good. It is juicy and sweet. I am now certain that I like it and I am satisfied. I give it a name. I call it a peach. I want to tell others about it and share my discovery with them.

Such a scenario may well have been enacted in some ancient age and to a real extent it is reenacted constantly by all newborn infants discovering the world of objects around them. But there are many variations to the story. What if I try repeatedly to reach the object to which I am attracted and it eludes my grasp? Eventually I become angry. I try harder and I fall and hurt myself. I grow angrier, the ambiguity intensifies. I struggle to find different approaches to attain the object. These succeed or fail. If I become angry enough I may even try to destroy the tree and its fruit. I experience success eventually, or I give up. If I experience many successes I become more inventive and creative in the face of new difficulties or increased ambiguity. If I constantly fail, ambiguity becomes a signal to stop trying. If I go to my friends to share my success or discovery and I am welcomed and affirmed, I feel a sense of belonging and relationship. If I am told my discovery is boring, mundane, useless, or insignificant, I feel rejected and alone. Instead of the certainty of belonging, I experience the ambiguity of loneliness. I summon my energy to go and seek other friends. If they too reject me, I may begin to reject myself and others as well. If they accept me, I feel whole and well.

Simple stories like the above serve to illustrate the energy principle contained in the polarity of the field of action. This energy principle may be stated as follows:

The perception of ambiguity with regard to either an object or an interpersonal relationship creates a gap that stimulates both psychic and physical energy to bring about closure. Energy increases in direct proportion to the extension of the ambiguity in the situation. At a relative point, as frustration increases, anger (high energy) emerges to the point of destructiveness. As the potential for destruction is passed, energy slackens. When the state of ambiguity is accepted with the realization that the gap cannot be closed or that closure is not worth attempting, anger is supplanted by passivity and attention is directed elsewhere. If the gap is closed successfully, the energy subsides to a normal state of rest accompanied by feelings of satisfaction.

It seems clear upon reflecting on personal experience that the ambiguity/certainty continuum in the field of action represents an energy accelerator.

TENSION AND RELEASE

Let us once again look at the characteristics of Type A and Type B behaviors. We have said that Type A dominates or holds sway over the left side of the field of action while Type B dominates the right. Each behavior set has its own domain or, we might say, its proper place.

Let us first consider the Type A or left side of the matrix. This is the side that predominates for task and object accomplishment and for I-It or person/thing relationships. The primary orientation here is toward certainty and control and also toward closure. The A side is vitally important for increased competence or mastery over the world of objects or things. It is a necessary condition of achievement and accomplishment. It is perhaps for this reason that so many high achievers are very much oriented toward Type A behavior and task accomplishment (the I-It relations).

Now we must look at a very curious phenomenon. Type A behavior is necessary for mastery, control, and certainty yet it dramatically increases psychological and interpersonal tension. The movement toward the control of things leads simultaneously toward a loss of control in the interpersonal domain. Type B behavior, on the other hand, decreases interpersonal tension and leads toward I-Thou union but *simultaneously* brings about increased ambiguity in the domain of objects or things and leads to increased tension and increased desire to achieve control or certainty. Thus lovers who try to possess one another are constantly frustrated because all interpersonal relationships must of necessity remain ambiguous, and managers are frustrated because complete control and certainty always eludes them. The I-Thou relation is characteristically uncertain, and *the absence of certainty or control is the fundamental basis of any authentic interpersonal relationship.*

Now things become even more complex. Martin Buber's observation that the I-It or I-Object category may also contain I-He and I-She makes clear that persons can very easily be reduced to objects, or things, and treated in utilitarian fashion. In other words, when the Type B side is ignored and denied, human relationships are diminished or destroyed and people may be used as the means to achieve certain ends to which they are not committed by choice. Under these conditions human energy is usually engaged and exploited by the invoking of the ambiguity of fear, and tends to be drastically diminished or employed defensively (and often destructively) instead of creatively.

On the other hand, the I-Thou category (the category of relation) allows for openness, shared experiences, and free choice. In societies that would profess to be "free" it is crucially important to recognize the value and validity of the Type B domain. When the ambiguity contained in issues of interpersonal relations has been made manifest and acceptable through the exercise of Type B exploration of individual human needs and concerns, commitments can begin to be made and sufficient interpersonal trust established so that the ambiguity inherent in any problem or task may be faced and dealt with as an issue of common concern.

Typically individuals and organizations in our society do not understand the human energy implications in the field of action. As a result the energy field becomes or remains continuously disorganized and many polarizations exist or develop, leading to unresolved conflict, ineffectiveness of performance due to partial problem solving, blocked or thwarted effort, and great inner frustration and psychological stress. There is little wonder that coronary heart disease is such a problem today. One team of medical researchers attempted to alert us to the physical danger inherent in organizational stress with an interesting book entitled *Type A Behavior and Your Heart* (Friedman and Rosenman, 1974). Understandably these medical researchers did not dig deeply into the underlying causes of Type A behavior in social psychology and organizational theory and their use of the term *Type A* appears to be purely coincidental, as if it were a reference to some kind of a virus. They did, however, clearly identify the symptoms inherent in the Type A orientation from a medical point of view and they quite effectively pointed out the dangers of unrelieved psychological tension and stress in a variety of situations.

Now we may see that the human ideal for any situation involving the accomplishment of tasks with others requires a balancing of the four poles in the field of action and a recognition of the tug and pull of the human energy forces present. As these forces tend to vary from person to person and from situation to situation, it is most useful to practice and learn both sets of A and B behaviors and also to develop the ability to move appropriately from one set to the other as circumstances change.

Let us now turn our attention to the wellsprings of human energy, for what occurs in real-life observable behavior is generally prepared in the privacy of individual consciousness. It is a fact of no little significance that human history emerges from inside human consciousness.

2 *Human Consciousness*

A powerful ruler had a strange and troublesome dream and upon waking could find no one to help him discover its meaning. Someone then remembered that a prisoner, who was also a slave, seemed to have a strange ability to interpret dreams and foretell the future. The slave, named Joseph, was summoned to the royal court and predicted that seven years of plenty would be followed by seven years of famine. The ruler gave Joseph dominion over the land of Egypt and trusted him to gather wheat and corn into the country's barns to prevent the expected disaster. The famine came as predicted and Joseph's ability to foretell the future from a dream saved the people from starvation. This Old Testament story from Genesis sounds very strange to us. Would we today summon a prisoner from San Quentin to interpret the dream of a president of the United States? And would we then give the prisoner the power to formulate his interpretation of the dream into a plan of action? We have traveled a long way down the road of rational certainty and we are now much more skeptical about the interpretation of dreams and the plans of dreamers and visionaries. And perhaps rightly so. History is filled with disasters perpetrated by dreamers and idealists and yet history also gives ample testimony to the incredible capacity of many human dreamers and idealists to create, to invent, to discover, and to solve riddles of tremendous complexity. Where do great ideas come from? What is the process through which creative discovery emerges? What is genius? And are geniuses born or made? Or both? These are perplexing and vitally important questions, for in a civilization that has already discovered the power to destroy itself, time may be running out. And, when we look at many of the plans and programs perpetuated by organizations of every description we see an alarming lack of creativity and awareness.

In Chapter 1, I described the characteristics of human energy on the field of action. It is on this field that the drama of life is played. It is on the *field of consciousness* that the drama of life is conceived, staged, and rehearsed. Many of us prefer perhaps to concentrate on the observable facts of human experience, but by doing so we may miss a vitally important part of the human story. In looking always at external events we may gradually come to believe that only what is observable is real. Our inner life is just as real, however, and all human events are external manifestations of inner experience. What is inside us has a way of coming out, sometimes with surprising results. And the intriguing fact is that our inner life proceeds largely unseen.

As we explore the field of consciousness, I wish to pay particular attention to two primary issues. First is that of raising consciousness or increasing awareness; second is the linkage between consciousness and action. Many tragedies, both great and small, have occurred throughout human history because both the victims and the perpetrators of tragedy have been insufficiently aware of their thoughts and actions and the relationship between them. The connection between psychic energy (consciousness) and physical energy (action) is a frontier for research in both education and psychology and further study in this area holds great potential both for helping us understand how to accelerate the rate of human learning and for helping us learn to resolve social problems and conflicts of every description more effectively.

We have been plagued for centuries by the belief that body and mind are separate realities. In fact, René Descartes "proved" that mind and body are separate and that nonmaterial, psychic, or spiritual forces or properties cannot be thought of as connected with material, physical, or earthly beings or things. It now appears that the Cartesian viewpoint was too limited. If we adopt a strictly Type A mentality, Cartesian thought is rational, logical, and perhaps unassailable. When we look at the question of relation, however, the capacity of the I in both the I-It and the I-Thou categories is that of a consciously aware human person. It is only when we begin to explore the dimensions of human consciousness and the influence of psychic energy that we begin to see the inherent ability of consciousness to melt into or fuse with physical reality. This is nowhere more evident than inside ourselves. Our bodies are enriched and energized with conscious awareness.

As we inspect the field of consciousness we will find it to be a realm of intense darkness and brilliant illumination. It is a world of personal adventure and private discovery. It is the raising of conscious awareness that is perhaps the primary broad aim or purpose of us all. The restless searching and seeking of human consciousness is the lodestone that attracts and leads forth human activity like a magnet attracting iron. The interaction between conscious awareness and human action is thus the primal force that stimulates both the actualization of the human self and the evolution of the human race.

FOUR FUNCTIONS OF CONSCIOUSNESS

The world within was first explored in depth by Sigmund Freud. Freud proved that humans were not simply the passive or static receivers of external stimuli that many had assumed, but possessed in fact a dynamic and active inner life. While Freud approached his work with a spirit of questioning inquiry, he was quite slavishly devoted to the rational and analytical scientific method of the nineteenth century. He quickly turned his exploratory questions into judgmental answers and proceeded to dissect or analyze the human psyche piecemeal. Because Freud also chose to study abnormal manifestations of behavior and particularly sexual aberrations, his work was overburdened with examples of the results of repressed sexuality. He concentrated on the bizarre and as a result the inner world of consciousness, regarded by the ancients as dark and mysterious, began to acquire a bad name. What was at first suspected now appeared to be confirmed by "respectable" science. Consciousness was seen as the deep well from which all manner of vices had sprung. The human psyche became, for the nineteenth-century Freudian, Pandora's box of malicious evils.

This mistaken notion of consciousness may take a long time to disappear. Freud's analytical approach prevented him from seeing a total psychic picture and got him mixed up with a variety of fascinating and intriguing details. Even so, he made an enormous contribution to human knowledge and laid the essential groundwork for what was to follow. A much fuller disclosure of the nature of human consciousness was left to Freud's brilliant but much younger contemporary, Carl Gustav Jung. While Freud dug deeply to unearth psychic artifacts and details as befitted his nineteenth-century scientific approach, Jung approached his own work from a totally different orientation. Jung sought to discover the total psychic story and to build a holistic conception of consciousness. To do so he turned to original sources, to ancient mythologies and religious beliefs from antiquity. As he built up a constitutive picture of mankind's mental universe, he carried on active experimental studies in psychology and sought to further the development of psychoanalytic theory. In so doing, he kept his theoretical formulations grounded in practical real-life experience, fusing his own increasing awareness with experimental activity. Jung, like Albert Einstein, belongs wholly to the twentieth century. In fact the well-publicized conflict between Freud and Jung might well be characterized as a clash between the nineteenth- and twentieth-century psychoanalytical viewpoints.

Many of us are as yet unaware of the great gift Jung has left us as our inheritance. In order to present some of Jung's key ideas I owe a great debt to Joseph Campbell, whose extraordinary scholarship and editorial skill enabled him to compile a comprehensive selection of Jung's writings into a small volume entitled *The Portable Jung* (1971). Campbell's work made Jung's writings much more accessible to me.

Jung (1960) says that our consciousness possesses four functions, or four separate but related ways of inducting information from experience and achieving internalized understanding. These four functions are *sensation, thought, emotion,* and *intuition.* All external information flows into us through one or more of our five senses. Sensory information provides the first "message" of outside or external experience; sensation is the first source of awareness.

Sensory data remain as only concrete or specific facts, however, unless we are able to transform them into internalized understanding.

The second source of awareness is the function of thought. This function consists of the capacity to compare and differentiate and to abstract, specify, and generalize. It is assisted by stored prior experience, which we call memory. This source of awareness is analytical; it thrives on rationality and logical order and it is the foundation of the Type A modality. Thought is the prin.ary organizing function of the human psyche. It is the function of thought to take sensory information and organize it into meaningful relations.

The third source of awareness is that of feeling or emotion. The sensory information, clarified by analytical thought or recognition, may evoke or call forth emotional phenomena known as *feeling-tones*. These feeling-tones cannot be adequately described because they are not part of the external, objective world but are rather a part of our internal, subjective world. We can describe feelings with analogies, or with terms such as warm or cold, or with expressions of revulsion or passionate attraction. We are aware when others experience feelings similar to our own, particularly if the feelings are extreme, such as in situations involving da ₁ger, violence, sexual attraction, or love, but we cannot tell another person *exactly* how we feel.

The fourth source of awareness is that of intuition. Intuition is the antithesis of analysis. Jung tells us that intuition is *the perception of the possibilities inherent in a situation*. Intuition is outside the domain of rational analytic thought. It is a way of seeing; it is the achievement of deep insight where a prediction or expectation of events is perceived apart from the process of causal connection or reasoning. Intuition is also picture thinking. This notion is derived from a sense of the interaction between the foreground and the background in a picture. Intuitive awareness comes about when a problem situation is perceived pictorially. Some elements are primary and are in the foreground. Other elements form a supportive background. The nature of intuition is that of receiving a flash of insight that enables you to see new or different relationships among these figure and ground elements, or a new element among them unseen before. Real intuition is thus quite different from imaginative notions or hunches. The new situation, or set of relationships, presents possibilities previously unrealized. This figure-ground way of perceiving has been called *holistic*, and is also often referred to as a *gestalt*.

Following Carl Jung's lead we can now construct another matrix, this time for the field of consciousness (see Fig. 2.1). Now we may see emerging a pattern of similarity between the fields of action and consciousness. What occurs in the world of external events is mirrored in the world of our own consciousness. Sensory awareness of the external world around us is analogous or related to the task or object pole in the field of action. All tasks require sensory contact or a physical touching of the external world of objects around us. Analytical thought is likewise related to the need for certainty; the thought function of consciousness is in fact the psychic expression of the need for certainty. Sensation and thought are thus in more or less direct con-

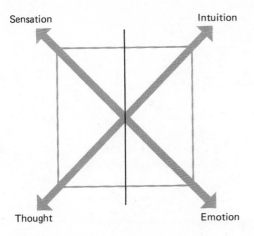

Fig. 2.1 The field of consciousness

tact with the outside world of observable events, while emotion and intuition are more interior, more subjective, and in a way more intensely personal than the other two.

Emotion is the hallmark of the I-Thou relationship; it is the bond of feeling that makes interpersonal relationships possible. Intuition belongs analogously to the pole of ambiguity because it is the function of intuition to grasp the hidden meaning in ambiguous situations and to achieve insight into or a vision of a new possibility or creative structuring previously unseen. See Fig. 2.2 for a pictorial representation of the relationship between the fields of action and consciousness.

It is both appropriate and legitimate to postulate the existence of two modes or states of consciousness that are analogous to the A and B sets of behavior referred to in Chapter 1. Thus we may visualize a Type A consciousness of a sensory/thought character and a Type B consciousness that is typified by an intuitive/emotional modality. These four functions of consciousness all need to be well developed and appropriately balanced in the fully functioning person. Unfortunately they seldom are for a variety of cultural, historical, and educational reasons.

We may see the emergence here of grounds for repudiation of the sexist bias that emotion and intuition are weaker and, because they seem to predominate in women, women are the weaker sex psychologically as well as physically. In this view, sensory contact and thought, being stronger, would be considered more properly the property of men and men would be encouraged to develop these capacities and deny the other two. But the fact is that all four functions of consciousness are, of course, *intrinsically human* and an overbalance of any one function or combination of functions may lead to serious problems, as we shall see in a moment. The current trend toward women's liberation may be a trend toward increasing sensory and

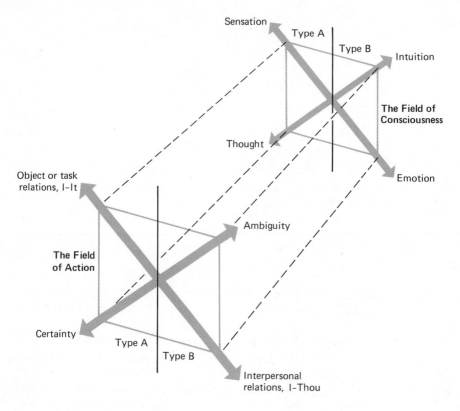

Fig. 2.2 The relationship between the fields of action and consciousness

thought contact and involvement in the world, and we may shortly see a parallel trend for men who wish to develop greater emotional and intuitive capacity without being judged by their peers as adopting effeminate tendencies. Likewise, women who seek more involvement, responsibility, participation, power, influence, and control need not be judged as aspiring to masculine roles. All four of these capacities are, as we have said, intrinsically human. It is, I believe, cultural bias and stereotyping that has tended to separate the sexes and make each less human in a reciprocally opposite way.

We may reflect at this point that it may not be possible to adopt authentic Type B behaviors (see also Chapter 1) without first having an awareness of the processes of interpersonal relations, a sufficient capacity to tolerate ambiguity, an awareness of one's own emotionality or feelings, and some capacity for intuitive understanding. The reverse of the above would also be true with regard to the development of authentic Type A behaviors if one happened to be overdeveloped on the B side or underdeveloped with regard to clarity of analytical thought and task effectiveness (Type A).

Let us now turn our attention to the process by which the human psyche contacts the world of external reality and influences it in turn. This naturally brings up also the subject of education.

INDUCTION AND EXPRESSION

The Socratic educative method of stimulating the human emotions and intuition through the use of questioning inquiry (Type B) was superseded in the early 1700s by the English philosopher John Locke's "empty vessel" theory. In Locke's reasoned judgment the human infant's mind at birth was a *tabula rasa*, an empty slate. Experience, flowing in through the five senses from outside, would "write" on this slate, making deep or shallow grooves depending on the degree of repetition or emphasis. One recalls the phrase, "repetition is the mother of study." The educated person was thus one whose mind was filled to the brim with factual knowledge that had been drilled into him. It is quite easy to see how this reinforcing approach to education also reinforces the Type A orientation. Facts became more important than feelings. One who lacked facts was taught to rely on logic, judgment, or the attribution of assumptions. Emotion and intuition were considered to be positively detrimental and potentially misleading. Imagination and fantasy were discouraged as idle, while dreamers and romantics were sternly disciplined. Poets, musicians, and actors came to be regarded as increasingly odd or bizarre.

The assumption that the newborn infant's mind or brain was a tabula rasa was never questioned. But let us pause to reconsider for a moment. Could any human infant born with the heritage of millions of years of evolution ever be considered "empty"? It is true, I believe, that only those who have learned to live "within" can fully experience life "outside." The ancient Greeks and Romans knew this well and their approach to learning and living was that of discovering the within. The ancient term for education was *educare*, meaning "to lead forth" or to draw out from within. Somewhere during the beginning of the machine age this notion of *educare* got lost and the term *education* in our day has come to mean "indoctrination," "drill," "instruction," and "reinforcement." As a result education lost excitement for many of us. The fascination of discovery was replaced by a graphic and direct show-and-tell reality and this trend has reached its culmination today with the advent of television, while imagination and fantasy have taken a back seat. Intuition and emotion, on the other hand, appear to have remained unwanted exiles from the territory of modern-day education.

It is what is already within that we need to draw out, cultivate, and allow to grow through experiment and experience. While it is a basic function or purpose of education and educators to provide or allow for information from outside to flow in, in the true sense of *in-form*, information is of little use if we are poorly developed or ill prepared to use it. Educators must therefore create environments for learning that stimulate consciousness and help the learner to forge exciting new structures or possibilities from the fertile ground of his or her own imagination. The learner must be turned on to learning and must achieve excitement from creative expression. As we shall see, learning requires a combination of an inward flow of information and an outward flow of creative expression. This process is analogous in many ways to the natural biological process of breathing.

It is my contention that we do not achieve full internalized understanding of any situation or event until we experience it fully through all four of our functions of consciousness, until we "breathe" it in to the fullest depth possible. Let us now take a closer look at the process of induction and expression and see how and why this may be so.

First let us describe the induction process. As information bombards our senses, some of it is perceived and some of it is blocked or screened out. We may call this stage 1. Stage 2 occurs almost simultaneously as the thought function selects certain information from that presented by the senses and engages it. Thought occurs and the memory is brought into play along with the concrete capacity to recognize and the abstract capacity to compare and differentiate. Stage 3 is emotional involvement. Stage 3 does not occur unless the receiver of the information gets in touch with or experiences the feeling-tones stimulated by the sensory and cognitive processes that have occurred in stages 1 and 2. If the feelings generated or stimulated are realized, there is a curious enrichment of the information; objective data now become subjectively important to the individual as well; he or she is "affected" by the data and generally a surge of excitement (or a build-up of energy) occurs. It is my belief that this building up of energy or enrichment of information is what is required to propel us into the realm of intuitive understanding, which we may label as stage 4. This fourth stage is what the late Fritz Perls described as "awareness per se." If a blockage does not occur in any of the three prior stages it results in the emergence of a new way of seeing, a new understanding or a solution previously unperceived. This is the hallmark of creativity and it is present with all great discoveries. Figure 2.3 shows the process of induction. I would now like to describe how this process reverses itself and flows outward into creative expression, also shown in Fig. 2.3.

The achievement of the gestalt experience of stage 4 releases energy in the form of a new insight or understanding of a situation (stage 5). This released energy then flows back into the emotional or feeling area. If emotion does not block or inhibit the release of energy, either instinctive desire or intentional volition (or both) accelerates the energy flow and releases it further to the cognitive area of analytical thought. The person now wants to create, to implement or express his or her intuition. This is stage 6. Stage 7 occurs as a decision to act or not to act, and serves as the addition of intellectual assent to the volitional commitment. At this stage practical judgment is utilized, in the decision as to when and how to move into action. Finally (although this entire process may occur in a fraction of a second), stage 8 is reached as directly expressed activity or human action.

Two further blocks can occur at stages 7 and 8. At stage 7 the energy flow may be inhibited by an inability to decide among two or more alternative

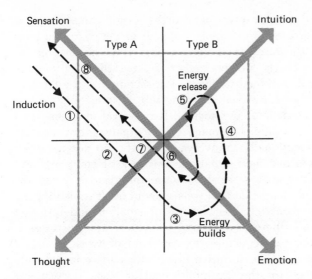

Figure 2.3

courses of action or whether to act or not. At stage 8 the behavioral expression may be inhibited as a result of a sudden input of new information or a restraining force.

Reflection on this process of induction and expression shows that there are eight stages at which internalization of understanding and appropriate responsive expression may be blocked or released. Whenever a blockage occurs (except of course at stage 1, where the incoming information is simply disregarded), frustration and anxiety can be expected to rise, leading to an increase of internal energy without appropriate outlet or release.

If the ambiguity inherent in frustration is accepted and tolerated, it increases psychic energy or tension. This increase of psychic energy or tension can sometimes be valuable because it heightens the level of the feeling-tones and makes them more accessible, thus triggering stage 3 and enabling the person to become more emotionally involved. This increase of emotionality occurs in the expression as well as the induction process, when one goes back for deeper insight into a problem that is only partially resolved or not yet ready for release. As the level of ambiguity rises and psychic energy increases, the level of excitement increases also. When a gestalt, or breakthrough, is achieved energy rushes outward toward expression, ambiguity is resolved into certainty, and excitation returns to a state of rest. When there is too much ambiguity, too much energy, or too much excitement, frustration or blockage occurs and the natural process of induction and expression is aborted, leading to a sense of failure or disappointment. Much or continued disappointment leads also to an unwillingness to experience further ambiguity or emotional involvement.

In many cases the induction/expression process is not completed. For example, if the induction process stops (or is stopped) at the cognitive level of analytical thought and the receiver of information either has no feeling about it or does not get in touch with his or her feelings, the resultant behavior is expressed simply as a thought/sensory transaction and the receiver is not emotionally or intuitively involved. This incomplete induction/expression process is quite characteristic of our society. It is typical in buying and selling. Many of the jobs or positions in many of our organizations also are filled by people who are emotionally uninvolved and who do not use their emotions or intuition to improve their situation. This lack of emotional and intuitive involvement is analogous to very shallow breathing and is the source of much of the boredom and disinterest that we see about us. It is also typical of many classroom environments. In the absence of emotion and intuition in an educational experience, there is a general lack of creativity, interest, excitement, and enthusiasm. Consequently, in any kind of work or study environment that lacks emotional or intuitive involvement there is a drastic reduction of available energy for the accomplishment of tasks, particularly if the tasks are assigned. In addition, when the incomplete induction/expression process is combined with blockages of emotional or intuitive expression, there is a simultaneous combination of disinterest and frustration, which may lead further to apathy and indifference.

Another characteristic of an incomplete induction/expression process is that of hyperactivity: a frantic racing to complete mundane tasks or to meet artificially set schedules or deadlines. The hyperactive person, like the hyperactive organization, fails to achieve full potential precisely because emotional and intuitive capacities are seldom engaged and work proceeds with a shallow superficiality.

It has been observed that the greatest rate of learning occurs in humans from birth to about age six. At that point learning slows dramatically. One may also observe that the natural learning process involves all four functions of consciousness and that all normal human infants behave very naturally at birth and continue to behave naturally in a healthy and happy environment. No one has yet been able to discover the intervening variable that dramatically slows the rate of learning at about age six. Could it be possible that this variable is school? We all know that school presently requires an excessive concentration on the sensory and thinking functions of consciousness. Do we unintentionally begin to distort and warp the development of our children at the start of their sixth year of life?

THE TRANSCENDENT FUNCTION

So far we have explored the ordinary domain of consciousness. We are now ready to begin our exploration of regions of great depth and incredible potential and possibility, regions that can only be found by raising consciousness and expanding awareness.

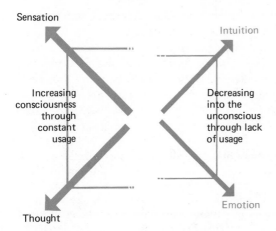

Figure 2.4

Jung points out that the characteristic behavior for most of us is to adopt one of the four functions of consciousness as an individual, preferred way of knowing (Jung, 1960). We then support the favored way with a second function that we tend to use in a kind of back-up capacity. For example, we may choose analytical thought as our preferred mode and back it up with sensation. As a result we may unintentionally allow the other two functions to atrophy from disuse. The more one develops the primary and secondary preferred modes, the more the third and fourth modes tend to disappear into the unconscious; it is as if they ran the other way at exactly the same rate that the first two advance or develop (see Fig. 2.4). This notion of running the other way Jung calls *enantiodromia*, a term taken from Heraclitus, who intuitively saw at the dawn of Western history the tendency of all things in time to turn into their opposites—a fundamental reciprocity that exists throughout nature.

The notion of reciprocity between the pairs (or dual functions) of consciousness is the key to increased potential for growth and development. It is also the signal that warns of psychic danger. We need to develop all four functions of our consciousness simultaneously. If we unintentionally neglect or even repress one-half of our conscious capacity and allow it to lapse into our unconscious, we are heading inexorably toward eventual disaster. We may at such times seem to be making dramatic progress and heading toward great success. But the further we develop one side of our consciousness without also developing the other, Jung tells us, the more we are creating a tension that will eventually call forth its opposite. Furthermore, if the contents of our unconscious are blocked, they can be expected to burst through at some point with unwelcome and potentially disastrous results. An outburst of destructive rage, therefore, may well be expected to come from one who has suppressed emotional expression for a long time.

What is needed, then, is a balance between the reciprocal functions of our consciousness that allows the contents of our unconscious to flow into creative expression. Jung claims that the capacity for this balance is present in all of us: he has named it the *transcendent function*, or the *fifth function of consciousness*. It does not exist independently of the other four functions but arises as the union of two paired functions of consciousness with their reciprocal opposites.

Joseph Campbell (1971) makes an astute editorial observation:

> Jung's concept is that the aim of one's life, psychologically speaking, should be not to suppress or repress, but to come to know one's other side, and so both to enjoy and to control the whole range of one's capabilities; i.e., in the full sense, to "know oneself." And he terms that faculty of the psyche by which one is rendered capable of this work of gaining release from the claims of but one or the other of any pair-of-opposites, the Transcendent Function, which may be thought of as a fifth, at the crossing of the pairs of the other four.

The activity of resolving opposite or reciprocal pairs of conscious and unconscious functions dramatically fosters and accelerates individual development. The exercise of the transcendent function also enables us to reach out to others, for it tends to free us of the rigidities and oddities that cause other people to dislike us or avoid us. As we become less eccentric, rigid, and closed and more flexible and open, we become more able to tolerate external ambiguity and we develop a stronger inner sense of certainty and security. Use of the transcendent function of consciousness increases or stretches the amount of psychophysical energy available to us as individuals and also increases our conscious awareness. Failure or inability to achieve the transcendent function can produce psychic inbalance and can eventually bring about the destruction of the human personality. Figures 2.5 and 2.6 show the operation of the transcendent function graphically.

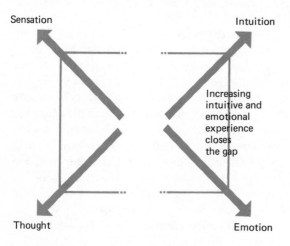

Fig. 2.5 Getting to know one's other side

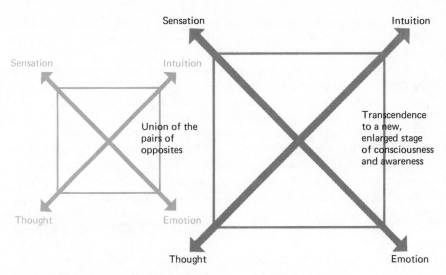

Fig. 2.6 The transcendent function

Use of the transcendent function of consciousness calls forth the contents of the unconscious and makes them available for active use. One may wonder if this is desirable or if it is perhaps dangerous. Anxiety in this regard may well arise as a result of stories and portrayals of abnormal and unhealthy people. The unconscious as we have said has become identified with bizarre and tragic elements and has acquired a bad name, largely as a result of Freud's somewhat morbid interests and thanks to generations of fiction writers. What Freud discovered, however, was the negative effects that occur when the contents of the unconscious are blocked or distorted. When unconscious elements cannot flow into the light of consciousness and out into the world of events they tend in a sense to become stagnant or rotten. Later they may come out as insidious or poisonous manifestations or as intrinsically evil or destructive acts.

THE DUALITY OF CONSCIOUSNESS AND THE SPLIT BRAIN

Jung's insights have given rise to the speculation that human consciousness possesses a hitherto unrecognized duality. Recognition of the transcendent function and the process of overcoming the dualistic tendency of human consciousness to split and lead away in different directions enables us to see clearly how it is possible and in fact probable that a gap or split would tend to occur as a result of individual educational development at one level and cultural development at another. Unless the split or gap is overcome and/or large-scale corrective measures are taken, our civilization may well be on a collision course with psychophysical disaster. The signs are already present in abundance, although fortunately there are other signs that indicate that the impending disaster may be avoided. I will elaborate on these notions further in a moment. For now it may be useful to consider some new findings in the field of neurophysiology.

In recent years there has been renewed interest in the possibility that humans (and animals as well) have two brains and not one. The structure of the brain is clearly binary; it is divided into two hemispheres, left and right, and joined by the corpus callosum. There is much evidence to suggest that the right and left hemispheres perform different mental functions and numerous schemes have been developed to distinguish the characteristics of each. In addition, surgical operations requiring the severance of the corpus callosum and the removal of one hemisphere have proved that the remaining hemisphere provides full mental functioning. Thus it is possible to assert that man has two brains and not one as is commonly accepted. As we have two eyes, two ears, two arms, and so forth, two brains would not necessarily be unnatural.

The great problem with the notion of two brains is that it runs headlong into one of the great beliefs of Western civilization, the unity of the individual. A way out of this dilemma is posed by Joseph S. Bogen (1969), who expresses the assertion that "the individual with two intact hemispheres has the capacity for two distinct minds." He goes on to say, "in the human, where *propositional* thought is typically lateralized to one hemisphere, the other hemisphere evidently specializes in a different mode of thought, which may be called *appositional*." In simpler terms, the two brains (or two hemispheres) think differently.

Bogen's view, which has considerable support from many quarters, heralds the emerging belief that the human brain, hence consciousness, is in fact dual. Bogen quotes a variety of interesting sources to illustrate his assertion further:

> André Gide averred: "There is always a struggle between what is reasonable and what is not." It is perhaps because we live in a society in which rational thought is held in particularly high esteem that the "other" is often considered to be base or undesirable even when it is un-named. More likely, this evaluation is not cultural in origin, but arises from the fact that the hemisphere which does the propositioning is also the one having a near monopoly on the capacity for naming. C. S. Smith (1968) recently remarked on "the curious human tendency to laud the more abstract." He went on to suggest that scientists are becoming increasingly aware of the need for a simultaneous and synchronous use of two points of view, "one, intellectual, atomistic, simple and certain, and the other based on an enjoyment of grosser forms and qualities." In a recent presidential address to the American Association for the Advancement of Science, D. K. Price . . . goes so far as to suggest that today's cosmopolitan rebellion" reflects not so much a generation gap or a racial problem, but rather a confrontation between two "processes of thought," one of which he terms analytic, reductionist, simple, or provable, and the other he describes variously as synthetic, concrete, and disorderly.

In Chapter 1, I expressed the duality of behavior in the field of action, represented by the Type A orientation grounded on the need for certainty and the Type B orientation that floats with a relatively changeable level of toleration of ambiguity. Earlier in this chapter we looked at the duality of consciousness. These two behavior sets were shown to be mutually exclusive of and reciprocal to one another. The evidence from neurophysiology suggests that there is in fact a supportive and reciprocal relation between these two modalities in the human brain as well as in the fields of action and consciousness. Type A consciousness appears to represent the objective functions of thought (analysis) and sensation (perception) and involves direct contact with the certainty of real events outside the human psyche. Type B consciousness may represent the subjective world of our own inner reality. The functions of emotion and intuition create, as it were, a world of their own that is personal and real. The dual brain appears to synchronize these two modes of consciousness, with Type A generally predominating in the left hemisphere and Type B generally predominating in the right. These two hemispheres appear to be equal at birth and develop through usage, although the development is usually not equalized because of our cultural conditioning. According to Bogen (1969),

> The hypothesis of an appositional mode of thought implies that in this regard the hemispheres are equipotential; and as the ability to propositionalize tends to dominate the activity of the left hemisphere, the appositional mode is made free to exploit the intellectual capacities of the other side. The extent to which appositional ability develops must depend on the nature and extent of environmental exposure, just as the development of propositional capacity is highly culture-dependent.

If it is true that we have two brains as well as two types of consciousness, and that these differences are manifested in two types of behavior or two characteristically different ways of acting in the world, is it surprising to find that we contain within ourselves the sources of misunderstanding, conflict, and interpersonal confusion that we see all around us? Is it possible that while you, for example, are acting Type A behaviors and I am acting Type B, or that while you are thinking B consciousness and I am thinking A, we are passing each other like freight trains in the night with no possibility for relational communication? If this is true we apparently must learn to identify, recognize, and use both sides; we must come to possess both sides of our consciousness with equal intensity and develop the ability to move appropriately from one side to the other depending on the value that each offers for resolving problems and enjoying life. In addition, the simultaneous and balanced development of both brains will most likely put us directly in touch with the transcendent function referred to by Jung, and thus it appears that developing one's other side opens the path for greatly accelerating human growth and development.

EAST AND WEST—POLARITY AND UNIFICATION

Now let us take a cultural perspective. When we looked at Type A and B behaviors in Chapter 1, I indicated that Type B behaviors were not very prevalent in the United States. The Type B orientation is, in fact, that of the ancient Far East. The intuitive modality of openness to experience, emotional acceptance of the other person, nonjudgmental and descriptive picturing of reality, and questioning inquiry is fundamental to Eastern or Oriental thought and action. The fullest expression of Type B consciousness can be found in the philosophy of Confucius and Lao-tzu and in the religious practices of Zen and Karma. It is also apparent in the I Ching or Book of Changes and in the Upanishads.

In looking at the polarity of Eastern and Western cultures one cannot help but observe the fundamental passivity of the East and aggressiveness of the West. We can see this same pattern of passivity and aggressiveness in Type A and B behavior and consciousness. The primary goal of the Eastern mystic is to achieve Nirvana—the complete emptying of self into nothingness. The opposite goal in the West can be seen by the value placed on self-development, self-fulfillment, and the achievement of the personal salvation of Heaven. The East is oriented inward, the West outward.

Type B behavior is also characteristic of the culture of the flower children of the 1960s and the followers of Hare Krishna today, and is a notable characteristic of communal living as well. Type A, on the other hand, has been the hallmark of the military/industrial ethos of which the guiding mentality is that everything can and must be controlled and reduced to order and certainty.

The English poet Rudyard Kipling once observed that "East is East and West is West and never the twain shall meet." In his day it appeared that the vast differences in thought and action would never be overcome. In the twentieth century, however, we are now witnessing the cultures of East and West overflowing and fusing into one another.

Looking at the East we can visualize a centuries-old pattern of the acceptance of ambiguity: a passivity that is only now beginning to wane in some places that are yielding to Western influence or developing a greater Type A orientation. The loss of human life in the East due to inadequate food distribution and medical care, and that resulting from natural disasters such as typhoons and tidals waves, is staggering. The apparent cultural inability of Eastern peoples to develop positive and active programs to cure and prevent these disasters is tragic indeed. On the other hand, the West has given ample evidence of pursuing a path that when followed to its logical conclusion could result in physical annihilation of the human race. Unbridled competition and the win/lose conflict between superindustrial states over limited resources make continuing war seem inevitable. Perhaps an antidote for the excessive Type A behavior of the West is a tempering of this orientation with that of Type B. And perhaps the East needs a stronger Type A developmental focus to balance its heavy Type B emphasis.

We appear to need both Type A and B action and consciousness if we would propose to modify and modulate the overorganization of A and the lack of organization of B. We also appear to need the ability to achieve harmony between Type B's spiritual orientation toward acceptance of nature and life and Type A's determination to achieve and create order. The existence of a wide geographical and cultural division between the two great principles of knowing and being has resulted in the past in a failure of both Eastern and Western cultures to fulfill the potential of which the entire human race is capable.

If Bogen is correct and the development of the right versus left hemisphere of the brain (or brains) is culture dependent, could it be that Western civilization developed the left-hemisphere function while Eastern civilization developed the right-hemisphere function as a result of cultural forces or emphases? One is reminded here of the intriguing Whorfian hypothesis. Benjamin Lee Whorf (1965) proposed that the entire development of Western civilization was dependent on the structural foundation of the Indo-European language. The verb *to be* and the predicate *is* began the process of attribution, logic, and judgment. In Chinese there is no predicate, there is simply symbol: Man, Dog, Bite. It is the arrangement of symbols that gives meaning or creates humor. Man Bite Dog. One's emotion and intuition are thus left free to flourish with imagination. The connection between the properties of language and the A and B duality is clear.

Furthermore, if Jung is correct and the widening gap between the Western Type A consciousness and the Eastern Type B consciousness was brought about by the duality of consciousness, a movement in the direction of cultural fusion could bring about a new balance and result in the achievement of the transcendent function on a worldwide scale. The result would almost inevitably be the emergence of a new world civilization and there are in fact signs that such a civilization is now emerging.

THE UNCONSCIOUS—A PRIMAL SOURCE OF ENERGY

Let us now look at the mysterious realm of the unconscious and see whether it is such a den of iniquity as may have been supposed. First we might well inquire as to the nature of the unconscious mind and of its function. Again we turn to Jung (1960), who says: "To my mind there is no doubt that all the activities ordinarily taking place in consciousness can also proceed in the unconscious."

It is puzzling to think of a duplicate for consciousness that we are unaware of. It is also somewhat disturbing to think that a part of our psyche of which we are unaware can and does affect our life and our behavior, and it is natural to wonder about its normality. One also may wonder what *proof* there is of the unconscious, and if and how the unconscious could ever be contacted. Jung also states:

> In my practical work I have been dealing with dreams for more than twenty years. Over and over again I have seen how thoughts that were not thought and feelings that were not felt by day, afterward appeared in dreams, and in this way reached consciousness indirectly. . . . The dream belongs to the normal contents of the psyche and may be regarded as a resultant of unconscious processes obtruding on consciousness.*

The unconscious is contacted through dreams, and for the most part normal people have normal, healthy dreams and normal states of the unconscious.

In light of the above statements one might also speculate whether the unconscious does not have its own dreams also, dreams that emerge from a much deeper "beyond" that transcends the limits of individual human experience. Fundamental similarities in the content of dreams of many people whom Jung studied led him to discover the *collective unconscious*. This discovery led Jung to encounter the deepest dimension of the world within. The collective unconscious is the psychic bond that unites all members of the human race throughout all human history, and is the source of human symbols and myths. Jung says:

> This proof [of the collective unconscious] seems to me of great importance, since it would show that the rationally explicable unconscious, which consists of material that had been made unconscious artificially, as it were, is only a top layer, and that underneath is an absolute unconscious that has nothing to do with our personal experience. This absolute unconscious would then be a psychic activity which goes on independently of the conscious mind and is not dependent even on the upper layers of the unconscious untouched—and perhaps untouchable—by personal experience. It would be a kind of supra-individual psychic activity, a *collective unconscious*, as I have called it, as distinct from a superficial relative, or personal unconscious.

Thus we each have a personal unconscious and each of us is also joined together at the deepest level through participation in the collective unconscious. The discovery of the collective unconscious gives structure, meaning, and purpose to all human existence. In recognizing that symbolization and mythologization linked all humanity in the depth of the human psyche, Jung resolved the ancient problem of the one and the many: the problem of uniqueness and diversity. We are thus all members of the same human family

---

* This and subsequent quotations are from Jung, C. G. (1960), *The Collected Works of C. G. Jung*, ed. by Gerhard Adler, Michael Fordham, William McGuire, and Herbert Read, trans. by R. F. C. Hull, Bollingen Series XX, vol. 8, *The Structure and Dynamics of the Psyche* (copyright © 1960 by Bollingen Foundation and © 1969 by Princeton University Press), reprinted by permission of Princeton University Press and Routledge and Kegan Paul: short quotes from pp. 144, 148, 157, 158.

and yet each of us has our own unique difference. All races of all colors, primitives and moderns, are inexorably joined together for all of human history—past, present, and future. It is through the collective unconscious that the great ideas of mankind from all ages have survived as myth motifs. Jung calls these *archetypes*. He says:

> The [collective] unconscious as the totality of all archetypes, is the deposit of all human experience right back to its remotest beginnings. Not, indeed, a dead deposit, a sort of abandoned rubbish-heap, but a living system of reactions and aptitudes that determine the individual's life in invisible ways—all the more effective because invisible. It is not just a gigantic historical prejudice, so to speak, an *a priori* historical condition; it is also the source of the instincts, for the archetypes are simply the forms which the instincts assume. From the living fountain of instinct flows everything that is creative; hence the unconscious is not merely conditioned by history but is the very source of the creative impulse.

Now we can begin to see that the nature of the creative process lies in freeing the contents of our personal unconscious to allow what is within to flow out and adapt to the changing circumstances and new situations we encounter in our daily experience. Far from being dangerous, our personal unconscious is a vital source of our life and growth. We ourselves, however, must be mentally healthy to realize the full benefit of this source of energy and power.

The stage of life on which our own personal drama unfolds provides a fertile background against which we can write, direct, enact, and watch our own story take place as we in our turn become figured in the foreground of the human events we experience. The sources in the unconscious for our own creative acts are incredibly rich and filled with vibrant emotional and intellectual content. It is up to us to choose what we wish to use and how we wish to use it. Jung continues:

> All the most powerful ideas in history go back to archetypes. This is particularly true of religious ideas, but the central concepts of science, philosophy, and ethics are no exception to this rule. In their present form they are variants of archetypal ideas, created by consciously applying and adapting those ideas to reality. For it is the function of consciousness not only to recognize and assimilate the external world through the gateway of the senses, *but to translate into visible reality the world within us.* [Italics mine]

How do ideas and feelings get in and out of the unconscious? Can they be summoned forth at will? Do they signal us, telling us they want to come out? Jung tells us that the answer to these questions lies in understanding the psychic energy system. He says:

> I define the unconscious as the totality of all psychic phenomena that lack the quality of consciousness. These psychic contents might fittingly be called

"subliminal," on the assumption that every psychic content must possess a certain *energy value* in order to become conscious at all. The lower the value of a conscious content falls, the more easily it disappears below the threshold. From this it follows that the unconscious is the receptacle of all lost memories *and of all contents that are still too weak to become conscious.* [Italics mine]

The meaning of *educare* now becomes clearer. In order to release the contents of the unconscious and free what is within, the level of psychic energy must be raised. Thus raising consciousness means raising the *energy level* of consciousness. This is obviously an issue of astounding importance for individual, organizational, and social development. We will consider the above ideas in more detail in Chapter 7. Now let us turn to some very practical considerations about living and working in real-life organizations.

3 From Conscious Awareness to Action

From the previous two chapters we may derive further confirmation of what is already common knowledge from everyday experience. Human individuals are tremendously diverse in terms of their ability to tolerate ambiguity and their needs for certainty, and the problems we face daily usually involve the resolution not only of extremely complex tasks but also of difficulties in interpersonal relations.

All of us who seek to achieve greater effectiveness and competence must be able to find our way through the diversity and complexity of our own life situation and move successfully from awareness to action. What appears to be needed is an approach to problem finding and problem solving that enables us to sort out and organize our own individual tasks, roles, and responsibilities and form them into integrated effort with others. We need a process that identifies both task-related and interpersonal obstacles and brings buried and hidden emotional and intuitive elements to the surface. If we can generate sufficient information about a difficult situation we tend to become more aware of what the real problems are and increasingly effective in resolving the difficulties we face. Unfortunately many organizations, as well as individuals, tend to deny and suppress emotion-laden issues, and intuitive insight is less favored than statistical analysis.

We also need to realize that most problems contain unresolved conflicts. Conflict is highly ambiguous. It is disorderly and chaotic. Yet paradoxically we must engage it and enter into it—be disturbed by it—if we would achieve resolution. In other words, conflict cannot be effectively resolved from outside. Many of us, unable to tolerate the ambiguity inherent in a conflict situation, seek to avoid it. We often pretend that conflict is not present or that it does not have to be dealt with constructively. There are millions of excuses. "If we do nothing, perhaps it will go away," we tell ourselves hopefully. But it seldom ever does; it grows worse instead. We might recall a primary symbol of conflict avoidance for our age. Does anyone still remember the dignified man with a black umbrella who went to a meeting in Germany for reassurance? He returned from the meeting and in turn assured us that everything would be all right. The year was 1939. But the unresolved conflict the English prime minister Neville Chamberlain sought to avoid soon burst open with full fury as World War II, and millions encountered death and destruction. A much earlier intervention to deal with the sources of this conflict might have reduced its extent dramatically. When it finally did erupt its consequences were so devastating and so far reaching that it could well have destroyed us all, especially if that war had continued into the atomic era.

When human conflict reaches the enormous magnitude of a world war, it is raging out of control like a forest fire. Social scientists endeavoring to understand the phenomenon of human conflict are trying to learn how conflict ignites whole communities and engulfs whole societies and nations. Perhaps one way to confront this question is to look first at how individuals and organizations can handle small amounts of conflict effectively. When we can effectively extinguish small campfires of conflict we may then be able to deal with forest fires.

As human energy is the fire that burns within each of us, it is important to look at how we handle our own energy in relation to the field of action described in Chapter 1. We might think of ourselves as having within us an internal field of action that is comparable to a matching external one. Thus we have an internal need for certainty, an internal capacity to tolerate ambiguity, an awareness of ourselves as a physical object occupying space, and a concept of ourselves as a person capable of relating to others and the world.

We might call this relationship between our inner self and the outer world of our experience our primary gestalt. We are the figure in the foreground of our own picture; the background is composed of the multiple environments in which we live out our lives. In order to "live," we must step into the picture and play our part in the drama of life enacted upon the stage of our situational experience (see Fig. 3.1). How well we do is determined to a large extent by the choices we make from among the alternatives available to us. While we are making these choices constantly during every waking moment (and when we are asleep we are reviewing them), we are often unaware that we are playing such an active part. Much human tragedy could well be avoided if we realized that any choice to not act is an active choice. "Not to decide is to decide."

While we experience and are aware of conflict in others it is not only this conflict that we must deal with. All of us also experience conflict and tension within ourselves. We are often unsure about what we should do or how we might best proceed if we have decided on a goal or objective. Some people, in the face of the ambiguity and uncertainty of their life or work situation, seek certainty by simply resigning themselves to always being told exactly what to do and how to do it. By developing an attitude of resignation, they hope thereby to purchase safety and security. Some adopt a "show-me" attitude that places the burden of responsibility on someone else and usually

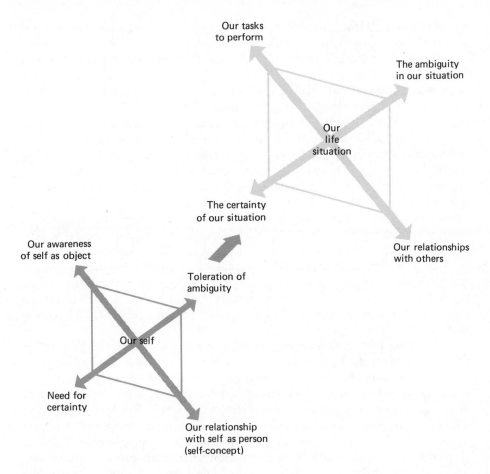

Figure 3.1

brings out intense anger in the person to whom it is displayed. And some take the bull by the horns and move ahead completely on their own, creating chaos that tends to belie the value that many place on self-reliance, individualism, and assertiveness.

It appears that to be effective in problem finding and problem solving we need to achieve a moderate capacity for resignation and acceptance simply in order to get along with others and be a part of the organized activity of our social situation. Yet at the same time we need to retain enough individuality and sense of purpose that we can provide the necessary leadership and give direction to whatever action we undertake. There is, however, a cultural impediment that tends to block our achievement of an appropriate balance.

With the pervasive tendency toward Type A behavior in our Western culture, we often rush into problem solving without fully finding out what the problem is. Hence we often find ourselves with solutions looking for problems and answers that produce questions. We typically find ourselves overreacting and engaging in painful explanations of surprises. We want to leap whenever a problem asserts itself, often before we look. It frequently appears unreasonable, unnecessary, or a waste of time to explore the ambiguities inherent in possible alternative solutions, or to involve others whose support and commitment may be needed now or later. The anxiety about lack of time, and the tendency to disregard the necessity for securing commitment and support from others, is a clear manifestation of a rampant Type A orientation. I will attempt to make clear in this chapter that Type A behavior is not very useful for problem finding. Type A behavior is for *answers*, not for questions. It is the language of certainty and solution and, when used inappropriately, it either produces conflict or it blocks conflict, preventing it from emerging appropriately. Type B behavior, on the other hand, creates a supportive environment in which conflict can emerge and be examined for what it is. Type B is exploratory. It is the language of ambiguity seeking acceptance and clarification. Type B extinguishes the fire. Type A ignites it. In a moment we will look at these assertions more closely. First, however, I must introduce a concept and a term that is much misunderstood and debated. The term is *management*.

Effective problem finding and problem solving is both the bedrock task and the ultimate goal of management. Many managers and administrators have expressed concern that there is no general science of management, no set of operating principles or foundational axioms such as those found in other fields like engineering, music, or chemistry, for example. While managers and administrators base a lot of their decisions on the scientific or practical axioms of related fields, such as accounting, engineering, economics, finance, and law, there seems to be lacking a basic foundation for the practice of management itself. Many managers and administrators appear content with "flying by the seats of their pants," using hunches and impulses as guides and picking out what they will do and how they will do it from a motley assortment of managerial techniques and styles. And the managerial culture tends to reinforce itself. Managers learn to manage by watching others do it; by adopting traditional practices and beliefs and by imitating those who manage them. I am now going to describe a process of problem finding and problem solving that is *management* in the best sense of the term. Anyone who uses this process, in any situation, may be said to be "managing" and to be a "manager," whether or not he or she is specifically given this title. This process of management is not traditional, however, because the first part (problem finding) calls for a Type B behavioral orientation that is not common to our typical Western practice. It is hoped that Western task-oriented managers will see the usefulness and practicality of the Type B approach to problem finding as a way of both enhancing task accomplishment and improving interpersonal relations at the same time.

The problem-finding, problem-solving model I am proposing here consists of seven steps or stages. They are:

Climate setting ⎫
Mutual planning ⎬ Problem finding
Assessing needs,
interests, and values ⎭

Forming objectives ⎫
Designing ⎬ Problem solving
Implementing ⎭

Evaluating ⎬ Problem finding

The first three steps comprise the process of problem finding, the second three represent the process of problem solving, and the seventh step involves a return to the problem-finding mode to prepare for a new round or a second-level effort. Problem finding, when effectively conducted, increases awareness. Problem solving moves us into action.

THE PROCESS OF PROBLEM FINDING

The first phase of our seven-part model encompasses climate setting, mutual planning, and the assessment of needs.

Climate Setting

Much has been said about organizational climate by many authors of management texts and articles. In summary, I have come to the conclusion that it is first necessary to identify what the climate is before attempting to set or establish a climate for effective problem finding and problem solving. Climate identification is the process of discovering and highlighting those elements in any particular environment that are "communicating messages." Marshall McLuhan (1965) and Harold Adams Innis (1951) have done much to help us all understand the pervasive influence of environmental messages. McLuhan's concept in *The Medium Is the Massage* is quite convincing with regard to the idea that our five senses are constantly being massaged, stroked, rubbed, or abraded by environmental influences of all kinds. Obviously, then, conducting an assessment of the environmental conditions of the moment is essential for getting in touch with how people may be feeling and what they may be thinking.

I have found it useful to assess work environments from three perspectives simultaneously. While other perspectives may also be important, I have found that looking at a threefold combination of physical, psychological, and organizational factors provides most of the basic information needed to make an assessment or to identify any climate or situational environment in a preliminary way.

Physical climate. If people are too warm or too cold, if the chairs are too hard or too soft, if the noise level inside or outside of a room in which you are working is too great—in short, if there is any significant physical discomfort—people will be distracted or unable to work as effectively as they might otherwise. While we humans are a resilient bunch, and we seem to be able to tolerate rather extreme conditions of discomfort for limited periods of time, the discomfort does tend to take away some of the energy available for working on a task, diverting it instead to coping with the discomfort. This energy diversion causes a lowering of the levels of perception and participation on the part of individuals and groups in organizations. One organizational group with which I am familiar works in a large office that occupies half a floor of a high-rise building. The buzz level is high, the area is overcrowded because the group has expanded to meet service demands, and there is a great deal of physical movement in the room, not to mention the clatter of typewriters and other office machines. In working with this organization, I heard much concern expressed about both the level of productivity and the opportunity for personal advancement. This very compact, high-density working environment may contribute significantly to the problems this group is experiencing. Furthermore, poor physical climate has a deadening effect; we have the capacity to get used to poor conditions so that we may cease to realize the effect they are having on us. A fresh eye or ear can often identify depressing physical factors that have long ceased to be noticed by those who live continually with the poor conditions. As Fritz Steele (1973) has said, "It's essential to get into the world of the user;" we must experience any physical climate to appreciate it and to assess its effect on us.

Psychological climate. More subtle and harder to identify, psychological climate is often more potent than physical climate as a drain on human energy. The term *psychological climate* can be defined as *the relative level of ambiguity present at any given time.* We can identify a band or wavelength of tension or amibguity that is appropriate for healthy human functioning in any situation. This wavelength has inner and outer limits, and exceeding these limits in either direction leads directly to operational dysfunction and a loss of energy. For example, a certain level of tension must be maintained in an organization to prevent the development of a country club atmosphere. A tensionless organization will tend to experience a rapid deterioration of both work quantity and quality. On the other hand, too much tension brings about a condition of prevailing anxiety in which everyone and everything operates under crisis conditions. In this situation there is barely enough time to cope with emergencies, which are rampant, let alone deal with the regular work or activity of the organization. The need for certainty calls forth more reports, more statistical analyses, and more explanations. Under these circumstances work efficiency tends to deteriorate rapidly, error rates rise, and physical health and safety are threatened. It is not uncommon under these conditions to hear complaints of overwork and understaff. While a staffing analysis may reveal that the group experiencing these symptoms is not understaffed at all, the anxiety or tension level is so high that the members accomplish very little and find themselves falling further and further behind. Three critical questions emerge with regard to psychological climate. What is the appropriate level of tension? If tension is too high what can be done to reduce it? If tension is too low what can be done to increase it?

The level of psychological tension (or the ambiguity/certainty level) can vary within groups and organizations. It can rise dramatically when a real crisis occurs and drop again when the condition is corrected. It can be affected greatly when group membership or leadership changes. For example, it is not unusual to find one person who is very tense or nervous (perhaps for reasons totally unrelated to the group's work) adversely affecting the performance of an entire group. If that person leaves the group, the entire climate may change and productivity may increase dramatically. Another factor of importance is the level of formality or informality in the work environment. Environments that require rigid protocol and highly formalized interpersonal relationships are environments of high psychological tension. Everyone must be on their toes to make sure they do the right thing at the correct time. One might say these environments are too *certainty* oriented. On the other hand, informal relationships may lead to a lack of necessary discipline and too little tension, leading to a tolerance for or acceptance of sloppy or unprofessional performance. Too much *ambiguity* can be disastrous. Unless the level of psychological tension is maintained at an appropriate level based on the needs of the situation, much available human energy may be lost or wasted.

Organizational climate. Organizational climate emerges from a combination of physical and psychological climate factors plus an additional factor, that of organizational identity. All organizations have a sense of identity, which can be thought of as analogous to the self-concept of individuals. Organizational identity concepts are perhaps difficult to identify precisely, but they can be assessed in general terms; they involve what it *feels like* to be a member of this or that organization. Does the organization express a clear sense of its purpose or mission? Does the leadership give evidence of providing positive and constructive direction and guidance? What kind of an organization is it and how well does it handle internal conflict? If the organization is polarized with a consuming struggle between two giants, say the vice president of marketing and the vice president of finance, who each hold conflicting views about goals, purposes, policies, and procedures, the organization may well be severely damaged by an emerging organizational identity crisis before the president or anyone else can bring it under control.

Organizational climates also vary widely with differences in density, size, and location. Some large manufacturing organizations may employ thousands in a series of buildings located side by side. Others may have manufacturing plants scattered around the world. Some of the largest government agencies or retail chain stores, on the other hand, may have a large organizational membership scattered over a wide geographic area, grouped together in small units or offices. Small organizations have a different climate altogether. The top leadership is usually present and accessible, and policies and procedures are usually more flexible and adaptable to the needs of special situations.

As changes occur in any organization's structure, in its tasks, functions, or its processes (ways of operating), there will most likely be a change of organizational climate. This difference in climate can be observed along the ambiguity/certainty continuum. Organizations are either increasing their toleration of ambiguity while developing an orientation toward greater creativity, experimentation, improved interpersonal collaboration, and higher levels of risk and trust, or they are responding to the felt need for increased certainty by stimulating greater discipline, less risk, lower trust, interpersonal conflict (if they don't produce, fire them), and a general tightening or centralizing of control in the face of any perceived crisis. Too much ambiguity leads to chaos; too much control or certainty leads to paralysis. The ebb and flow of movement from centralization to decentralization and back again, a characteristic of so many large organizations, may be viewed as a manifestation of an attempt to resolve the polarity between the dimensions of ambiguity and certainty. In actual fact, this polarity cannot be resolved without courting disaster. Each domain is necessary for competent organizational performance and if one succeeds in dominating the other for any extended period, negative effects are certain to follow in due course.

Finally, an organization's climate can be assessed in terms of the observed gap between its expressed goals and ideals and its actual performance. This gap between the real and the ideal is always present. To successfully bring about a change in climate, we must try to help an organization and its members achieve a raised level of consciousness of the existing gaps. As factors that lead to poor climate are usually found to exist in the discrepancy between expectation and fulfillment, we may well conclude that poor climate is most often the result of an inability of individuals or organizations to ameliorate, cope with, or accept this discrepancy. While any individual's level of expectation may be unrealistic, poor climate is always a manifestation of internally experienced disappointment. Climate can only be improved when the sources of such disappointment are identified and corrected or when individuals are helped to see that their expectations are unreasonably high.

Setting climate (or creating a more positive climate where a negative one exists) requires first identifying the present physical, psychological, and organizational climate characteristics, deciding what can be changed and what can't be changed, and gaining acceptance by an organization's members so they will participate in bringing about changes that are possible. Setting or changing climate in any organization must always be done from within. I do not believe groups or organizations can be changed from without as all groups tend to react to external pressures, defend their territory and boundaries, and maintain their status quo. If we would seek to bring about constructive organizational change, growth, and development we must enter into an organization (see Chapter 5 for an effective entry method), gain membership (albeit on some occasions a temporary or part-time one), and work with those inside who are also dedicated to achieving constructive results. To gain membership we must "buy," so to speak, the organization's idealized goals, norms, and values, and work to make the real situation conform as closely as possible to the ideal.

Obviously if we would seek to change any human or organizational situation we must first conduct a checkup on our own internal climate. Climate, as I have said, is always a "within" proposition; to be effective in changing or developing human organizations it is necessary to develop the capacity for forming open and honest relationships with others and for continuing the never-ending search for increased personal maturity. In this effort, Type B behaviors are crucially important, as is the capacity to remain neutral in the face of many attempts by factions to prove to you that their side is right and the other side is wrong.

Mutual Planning

Mutual planning is potentially the most easily misunderstood dimension of the problem-finding process. There are a number of significant reasons for difficulty with mutual planning and foremost among them is that mutual planning calls for group, rather than individual, action. Also significant is the fact that mutual planning implies asking and seeking, rather than telling and directing. Many managers prefer the simplicity and disciplined order of an authoritarian and directive stance. They like to be in the driver's seat, preferring to trust their own instincts and competence over those of their subordinates. Many managers also prefer the privacy of one-to-one relationships to the sometimes ego-bruising give and take of group effort. Building effective and efficient planning and action groups in organizations is a difficult process for all involved, and why wouldn't it be? Anything is difficult if one has not had much experience with it and hasn't taken much opportunity to learn or practice developing the requisite skills. Also, I think we have all become disenchanted with groups at one time or another because they didn't go anywhere. The well-known phrase, "A camel is a horse designed by a committee," questions the value of adding complexity to a situation by involving additional opinions, especially if there is an increased risk that the final product will be bent out of shape, distorted, or further confused in some manner. This risk is felt even more acutely when there is a limited amount of time available in which to come up with a solution to a pressing problem, and it is most acute when we are in the middle of a managerial crisis.

Another issue that questions the value of mutual planning is frequently heard expressed in one corporate corridor or another. It goes like this, often accompanied by a knowing wink: "Everybody knows democracy's a wonderful thing, but let's not practice it around here. Ho! Ho! Ho!" This statement reflects the attitude that one had better not question the authority of the boss if one expects to keep one's "head," and there is also an implication that dictatorships are more efficient, which is, of course, open to question on a number of grounds. Dictatorships, in addition to violating the integrity and rights of the individual, have a tendency to generate very high energy output followed by a disaster or a burnout; that is to say, they tend to have a short period of brilliant success culminating in drastic failure. What I believe may be closer to the point is that democracies, although inefficient, require continuous hard work and practice if ongoing improvements for the benefit of all are to be achieved; democracies can work if we work at them.

Why is mutual planning necessary and valuable? I think there are basically two reasons: greater involvement and increased objectivity. First let us look at involvement. It is now clear both from research on decision-making processes and from practical experience that to the extent that persons are involved in making decisions on issues and events that are important to them, to that same extent will they be committed, and motivated, to carrying out the actions implied by those decisions. Of course some issues are more important than others and there are relative degrees of involvement needed, depending again on the actual situation. Therefore I conclude that it is necessary to involve all of the key people (those responsible for conducting an activity) in the mutual planning of how any activity can best be carried out. As any group moves forward, it then becomes necessary to involve successive layers of peripheral people in the mutual planning of how the activity can best be carried forward *as these peripheral people in turn become central to the action.* This process must allow for redesign and redirection of a project or program to occur when (and if) negative feedback or resistance is encountered. If feedback is not incorporated, energy that is needed to push a project forward will tend to be turned against it, and resistance will build till all forward movement stops and regression begins.

Secondly, mutual planning is necessary if we are to achieve objectivity. All of us are bound by our subjective perceptions of any situation; we all see the world through our own eyes. What we see is inevitably colored and filtered by the rose-colored glasses of our prior experiences, our technical expertise, our present emotional state, our perception of ourselves in the situation (remember that only a little child who was not self-conscious was able to see and say clearly that the Emperor had no clothes), and many, many other variables. While we all strive to attain objectivity, it nevertheless remains true that our subjective perceptions steer our actual behavior. That is to say, we act in accordance with what we *believe and want* a situation to be and not necessarily in accordance with what it is. While intense personal subjectivity cuts us off from reality and blinds us to the significance of events occurring around us, there is great value in openly sharing differing subjective perceptions.

If we allow ourselves the opportunity to explore problems from the standpoint of the shared subjective perceptions of informed people, we stand to gain a much greater approximation of objectivity than if we try to make decisions in isolation. Ultimately, the leaders of any organization may have to make the final decisions on major policy issues, but the more correct and balanced is the information they have on which to base those decisions, the more likelihood there is of optimal success in the organization as a whole.

While subjective perceptions don't always yield correct information, they very often raise questions that when followed up with research generate vitally important facts that might well have gone unrecognized until too late. Getting at differing perceptions as a part of the problem-finding process is another way of engaging the human energy system and allowing available human energy to flow into constructive organizational effort. People who feel that their views are considered unimportant tend to withhold effort and save their energies for those activities in which their input is valued. Here again Type B behaviors may well encourage more openness and honesty as well as more involvement.

Another problem is encountered when the boss will entertain only those subjective notions or ideas that are congruent with his or her own assumptions. When this is the case discrepant information is suppressed, and mistakes are often made that could be averted or opportunities are missed that could be realized. Some bosses even want to punish the bearer of bad news. This tendency has ancient roots, and one can hardly blame prospective messengers for failing to deliver bad news under these circumstances.

Another tendency can be observed with managers who sometimes don't really want to get any information from others because they have already decided what they want to do and how they want to do it. This takes the classical form of the *hidden agenda*. In these cases, of course, the results must stand on their own merits. Occasionally a brilliant intuitive idea enables one person to see the way ahead with great clarity. However, even under these conditions it still pays to get as much information as possible before proceeding. When involvement and objectivity are achieved through mutual planning, the available human energy resources are well mobilized to provide an effective and efficient push forward.

Finally, mutual planning may break down because certain individuals may not trust the designated leader in an organization. While the leader may attempt to engage members in mutual planning and shared leadership, members may withhold their efforts and take a judgmental stance with regard to the leader, hoping or waiting for him or her to fail. As long as a situation of internal competition exists, the group will not achieve the level of performance of which it is capable. The leader in this situation has two simple choices: either to raise the level of ambiguity in the situation by raising the question of conflict, or to increase the amount of certainty by issuing directive commands or taking unilateral action. Either approach will alter the status quo and tend to facilitate the emergence of an authentic and open discussion of the real interpersonal issues involved.

Assessing Needs, Interests, and Values

Needs* tend to emerge quite naturally, both during consideration of the climate factors in any situation and during mutual planning as people's perceptions of a problem unfold. A comprehensive assessment of needs tends to form a model applicable to any system under study. That is to say, needs can always be viewed from three perspectives: that of the individual (microsystem), that of the organization or a component of an organization (system or subsystem), and that of the community in which the organization is imbedded (macrosystem).

The needs of individuals, organizations, and communities are sometimes in harmony; often they are not. It is unrealistic to expect an organization to succeed in meeting all of the needs of all of its members all of the time and under all conditions. Yet to the extent an organization does not meet most of the needs of most of its people it will tend to be relatively ineffective. Apathy and indifference on the one hand, and overt or covert acts of aggression on the other, are significant indicators of unmet needs.

Looking at this same issue from the perspective of the organization/community interface, one can see a similar force in operation. Consider the community needs (macrosystem) of the United States as a whole, interpreted by our elected representatives in Congress. The process of constitutional government is based on moderating and negotiating competing and conflicting community needs. Thus we have seen in the past the passage of such laws as those prohibiting child labor, those ensuring pure food and medicines, and those guaranteeing the right of labor to organize and engage in collective bargaining. Lately we have seen the passage of civil rights legislation and, most recently, we have received new safety and health laws. These reflections of community needs, when perceived and acted upon by the representatives of the community, have an impact on nearly all organizations in one way or another. We often see patterns of either passive or active resistance to social or protective legislation, stemming from a perception that implementation will be inimical to the needs of individual organizations. Gradually, however (with enforcement required in some cases), organizations adapt themselves to new circumstances and bring about the internal changes required to meet the new

---

* A reasonable distinction can be made between needs and wants. A person may want something and yet not need it. The existence of a need, on the other hand, tends to indicate a situation in which deprivation is psychologically or physically harmful. If an individual cannot make the distinction between wants and needs one is obliged to question his or her level of maturity. To avoid treating adults like children it may be assumed that expressed wants and needs are identical until proven otherwise during the problem-finding/problem-solving process described above.

situation. Of course if government regulation becomes too extensive, the capacity of organizations to function will eventually become impaired.

Needs, then, tend to arise naturally and are a reflection of the diversity and complexity of our social situation. Conflicts among competing needs emerge within individuals, organizations, and communities and also at the juncture between different systems and between the different components of each system. It is vitally important for any system to maintain a balance among competing needs if it is going to function effectively. The system of checks and balances among the executive, legislative, and judicial branches of our government is constantly under strain as a result of conflicting and competing needs. In recent times the enormous growth of the bureaucratic departments of the executive branch at both federal and state levels has created a situation where the needs of those who have access to the executive power base are often fulfilled independently of the will of the people as expressed through the legislature. This kind of imbalance leads directly to social and political conflict because, again, unmet needs form the foundation of social and political unrest.

There is an important distinction to be made between the assessment of needs and the decision to act (or perhaps not act) on what has been assessed.

An assessment of needs may be conducted quite simply or entered into with a great deal of complexity. Practical considerations dictate the extent to which needs can be assessed before an attempt is made to formulate objectives. I was working once with a group of government agency training supervisors who were participating in a training-of-trainers workshop. One of the participants asked, "Why is it so difficult to translate needs into *objections?*" Amid the laughter, we all realized the inadvertent wisdom in that slip of the tongue. In fact, the emergence of *objections* instead of *objectives* is a clear indication that all of the situational needs have not yet been identified and the organization is not, in fact, ready to leave the problem-finding phase and enter into problem solving. If critical needs remain hidden at this stage, they will tend to emerge at a later point where they can be extremely detrimental to the achievement of desired program or project objectives. As with electrical energy flowing through a wire, blockages in the human energy system lead to increasing heat and, finally, to short circuits and blown fuses.

Sometimes, of course, it is impossible to resolve the conflict between mutually exclusive needs. It then becomes necessary to take both the heat and the conflict. This situation has occurred often in the area of civil rights enforcement, with opposing forces speaking in two different "languages" expressing their needs in different terms, so that there is never a dialogue between them). While legal sanction and police action are sometimes necessary in these cases, it is vastly preferable to involve community leaders and residents in planning for change in advance of expected conflict. In this way, real needs and issues can often be brought into the open where they can be dealt with. Unfortunately the skills for resolving social conflict are often not present in the community, and there is still a pervasive tendency to spend vastly greater sums of tax money on controlling social unrest rather than on mounting sufficiently large-scale programs to effect economic improvements and to simultaneously develop community skill in preventing social conflicts from erupting in the first place.

A word must also be said about the importance of maintaining an appropriate balance among the three sets of needs. Typically there is a tendency in many organizations to overemphasize the importance of organizational needs at the expense of the needs of individuals or the community. Practically speaking, when it is the organization that is footing the bill (or providing the paycheck) the organization's needs must be satisfied and the job must get done. What I am suggesting, however, is that we *raise* the importance of individual and community needs to the same level as those of the organization so that we can learn to avoid some of the more familiar self-defeating strategies that provide us with short-run profits and longer-run losses. While we all want to look good as we move up in organizational hierarchies, the era of unlimited human or material resources has apparently ended and we must now develop strategies and plans based on very realistic assessments. If we concentrate on meeting only the needs of special organizational interests we may find ourselves one day in an insoluble mess where need satisfaction is no longer possible for anyone.

It is also important to say a word or two about interests and values. Many organizations make the mistake of trying to involve their members in performing tasks in which they are not really interested. This is particularly true in so-called voluntary organizations like churches, for example, whose members are paid only by having membership in the group and by serving. When committees are formed, individuals often feel that they must join in and show an interest or their membership may be questioned. Much time and wasted effort could be saved in such organizations if a climate could be developed in which a frank and open discussion of interests and of needs for belonging and serving was held. In some organizations this would reduce membership to almost zero; however the new and much smaller organization could then begin to get some real work accomplished when it was free of the dead weight of nonproductive members. Perhaps another way would be to provide for a legitimate nonactive status, so those members who did not want to work could continue to look good and possibly contribute financially.

In organizations where membership involves paid employment it is also important to consider individual interests when assigning work. It is amazing how many supervisors and managers assign people to jobs or tasks in which they are really not interested on the assumption that *somebody* has to do it. Often there is someone else immediately available who would prefer to do the task in which the other is uninterested, but to find this out the supervisor must open up the assignment process to mutual planning. If no one is interested perhaps the unwanted task may be rotated so that no one has to do it for too long a period of time. But if people are really not interested in what they are doing they won't do it very well.

It is also important to consider that individual values differ when we are trying to do effective problem finding. Individuals are unlikely to choose voluntarily to do something that violates their sense of values. Values indicate commitment to patterns of choice. When we speak of values, it is perhaps more helpful to look at the ways in which people choose values—the *process* of valuing—rather than trying to list a series of different values that persons may or may not have. Raths, Harmin, and Simon (1966) have developed seven criteria for clarifying values. They point out that a person who wishes to be really certain whether he or she values something can apply these value criteria as a reality test. If any one criterion is missing, it can be said that the item is not truly valued.

The Seven Valuing Criteria

1. *Choosing freely.* If something is in fact to guide one's life whether or not authority is watching, it must be a result of free choice. If there is coercion, the result is not likely to stay with one for long, especially when out of the range of the source of that coercion. . . .

2. *Choosing from among alternatives.* This definition of values is concerned with things that are chosen by the individual and, obviously, there can be no choice if there are no alternatives from which to choose. . . . Only when a choice is possible, when there is more than one alternative from which to choose, do we say a value can result.

3. *Choosing after thoughtful consideration of the consequences of each alternative.* . . . Only when the consequences of each of the alternatives are clearly understood can one make intelligent choices. . . . A value can emerge only with thoughtful consideration of the range of the alternatives and consequences in a choice.

4. *Prizing and cherishing.* When we value something, it has a positive tone. We prize it, cherish it, esteem it, respect it, hold it dear. . . .

5. *Affirming.* When we have chosen something freely, after consideration of the alternatives, and when we are proud of our choice, glad to be associated with it, we are likely to affirm that choice when asked about it. We are willing to publicly affirm our values. . . .

6. *Acting upon choices.* Where we have a value, it shows up in aspects of our living. . . . In short, for a value to be present, life itself must be affected. Nothing can be a value that does not, in fact, give direction to actual living. The person who talks about something but never does anything about it is dealing with something other than a value.

7. *Repeating.* Where something reaches the stage of a value, it is very likely to reappear on a number of occasions in the life of the person who holds it. . . . Values tend to have a persistency, tend to make a pattern in a life.

Input:	Choice:	Prize:	Action:	Output:
The question asks, Is this a value for me?	Freely accepting alternatives after carefully considering expected consequences	Enjoying and feeling pleasure and being willing to affirm it publicly	Implementing the choice openly and repeating it continuously	The answer states, This is or is not a value for me.

Fig. 3.2 Value clarifying

A systems diagram of the value clarification process appears in Fig. 3.2. While our values do change as our life experience changes, we can recheck them at any time by using this quick method of clarification.

Raths, Harmin, and Simon advance the notion that a great deal of apathetic, flighty, uncertain, or inconsistent behavior stems directly from the lack of clear values. They believe that *drifters, overconformers, overdissenters,* or *role players* are all people lacking value clarity, and that value clarification can achieve positive results in resolving behavior difficulties of this type.

Finally, one last issue may make a critical difference in the process of problem finding. Jerry B. Harvey of George Washington University has identified this problem as the *Abilene paradox* (Harvey, 1974). Harvey claims that inability to manage agreement may be, and often is, much more likely to produce disaster than the inability to handle or resolve conflict.

Harvey tells a gorgeously descriptive story of a hot and dusty afternoon in Coleman, Texas (population 5607). It's 104 degrees and the family is playing dominoes and drinking lemonade. Suddenly Harvey's father-in-law says, "Let's get in the car and go to Abilene and have dinner at the cafeteria." Although Jerry didn't like the idea of driving fifty-three miles in an unairconditioned 1958 Buick, when his wife chimed in that she'd like to go he decided to join the majority. As a last chance of avoiding the unwanted effort, however, he said, "I just hope your mother wants to go." "Of course I want to go," blurted Mother, so into the car and off to Abilene they went. Some four hours and 106 miles later, after a terrible meal, hot, exhausted, and covered with fine Texas dust, they were back at the kitchen table in Coleman. After a period of deep and penetrating silence, Jerry said, "It was a great trip, wasn't it?" The next period of silence was deafening—all sound seemed to stop. Jerry's mother said she really didn't enjoy it but then she hadn't wanted to go in the first place. She only went because she felt pressured into it. Jerry couldn't believe his ears. He knew he hadn't wanted to go but he just wanted to please his father-in-law and his wife. His wife proclaimed that she only went to please Jerry and her parents and finally her father entered the conversation. "Hell," he said, "I never wanted to go to Abilene. I just thought you might be bored."

Harvey states the Abilene paradox as follows: "Organizations frequently take actions in contradiction to what they really want to do and therefore defeat the very purposes they are trying to achieve."

The Abilene paradox occurs frequently in organizations because many individuals are reluctant to express their real feelings or needs. This reluctance is related to their inability to tolerate the ambiguity or risk of disagreement, negative fantasies about dire consequences that might follow nonconforming behavior, and the fear of separation or loss of membership in the group to which they belong. The failure or unwillingness to accept the ambiguity inherent in an open and honest disclosure of one's true feelings is to enter on a trip to Abilene. The resulting conflict after the trip is over may well produce all of the real negative effects previously anticipated. These negative effects might, on the other hand, never materialize if they are effectively confronted and sufficient ambiguity is tolerated before the decision to act is made.

Identifying and setting a favorable climate, fostering mutual planning among key participants, and carefully assessing individual, organizational, and community needs, interests, and values is the foundation of effective problem finding. When those participating in problem finding utilize Type B behaviors—by accepting the viewpoints of others, being descriptive instead of judgmental, and seeking (or validating) information through questioning inquiry—there is a movement toward opening up any situation and engaging the energy of others. Type B behavior lowers defensive resistance, builds interpersonal relationships, and prepares the way for realistic and well-grounded problem solving.

Type B behaviors also enable us to begin to bring to the surface some of the deep-seated emotional elements inherent in difficult problem situations. Interpersonal conflicts, racial antagonism, labor/management disputes, and hidden personal agendas all have emotional elements that hide beneath the surface of cognitive rationality and sensory awareness. These emotional issues must be engaged realistically rather than being denied, ignored, or avoided. The Type B orientation enables us to engage emotions without becoming defensive or creating defensiveness in others. Situations of scarcity, inequalities of wealth and power, educational disadvantage, and other such barriers to the development of democratic and participatory problem-solving effectiveness can be stripped of much of their destructive power if we consciously seek to remove the Type A judgmental orientation that many have toward these issues. After careful negotiation has clarified what may be done to move us closer toward any ideal situation, we can begin to enter into problem solving. Now we come to a very important issue.

Figuratively speaking, there appears to be a psychological river that flows between the stages of problem finding and problem solving. When we are working with a problem-finding group, we must all assemble on the river bank and prepare to cross over together when we are ready to move forward from problem finding to problem solving. I have observed and experienced the existence of this river of energy enough to be convinced that it is real. The river "cannot be pushed," to use an idea advanced by Fritz Perls (1969), "it must be allowed to flow by itself." Thus we must learn to allow nature to take its course when we are trying to resolve problems and social issues. This requires a combination of patience and acceptance that is characteristic of the Eastern world view and is hard for Westerners to develop. On the other hand, we must not become so comfortable with the Type B mode of problem finding that we fall asleep on the river bank. When we are ready to move from problem finding to problem solving we must get into our psychological boats and row across. Sometimes the going is difficult; we may encounter swift currents, sharp rocks, or even alligators.

Forming goals and objectives, designing strategies for alternative courses of action, and implementing action programs effectively appears to require a conscious effort that calls for the use of Type A behaviors. Whenever we set out to *do* anything we are in effect trying to bring order out of chaos and to create a more logical or coherent situation. We must make some practical *judgments* whether the effort we will expend will result in something good or worthwhile, and we must make some *assumptions* about what may or may not be possible. Therefore, crossing the psychological river involves a behavioral shift from Type B to Type A. Moving from problem finding into problem solving is moving from *question* to *answer*. It is the act of putting closure on an exploratory effort; of moving from *being* to *doing*. Closing in on a decision to act and implementing an action plan also imposes time constraints and summons forth accountability. There are some significant additional insights that flow from a recognition of this shift from Type B to Type A when moving from problem finding into problem solving.

First, we may now go a long way toward clearing up a problem that has plagued many organizations. Some people seem to overdevelop either the B or the A sets of behaviors and tend to use one or the other mode predominantly. We are well aware of the highly task-oriented person who wants to get moving and get the job done, even if it means stepping on some toes. This is our Type A problem solver and he or she is highly regarded (and richly rewarded) in business and industry. We are also aware that others seem to take forever exploring problems, issues, and concerns and may seem to care little about productivity or results. Here is our Type B problem finder and he or she is highly regarded (and often not so richly rewarded) as a minister or priest, a research scientist, or a teacher, for example. While we should not overgeneralize from these insights, it also appears that the Type B person tends to be more intuitive and imaginative while Type A is more of a cognitive clarifier and a "hands-on" practitioner. Type A is more of a doer; Type B more of a creative dreamer. A discussion of these modal differences sometimes produces a humorous response. In a discussion of these insights with some telephone company executives who were very much oriented in the Type A mode, the sudden realization of the Type B mode and its characteristics provoked a "Good Heavens, so that's what's the matter with Bell Labs!" The point is, of course, that we need to develop the capacity to use both modalities and to learn how to move back and forth appropriately from B to A and vice versa.

Another dimension of the discovery of the Type A and B phases of problem finding and problem solving is that the B-oriented person can apparently tolerate higher levels of ambiguity than the A type, who seems to have greater need for certainty. Thus in problem-finding sessions the B-oriented people are likely to be quite happy and content, while the A types will be champing at the bit and wanting to move ahead. On the other hand, if A types hold the power and call the shots, the B types will feel pushed and shoved into problem solving well before they are ready to move on their own. This inadvertent pushing and shoving, this recalcitrance to move forward, and this anxiety about holding back, are usually evident whenever we attempt group problem finding and problem solving. Thus we need to develop skills in identifying these tendencies and helping others to identify them and come to terms with the feelings associated with them. Doing so can increase the competence and efficiency of any group dramatically.

Polarizations in the field of action lead directly to conflict, disruptions of interpersonal relations, resistance, withdrawal, and attempts to dominate. These polarizations occur when there is a lack of competence in utilizing Type B behaviors and a lack of knowledge and awareness of when to use B and when to switch to A. The diagram in Fig. 3.3 shows the area of conflict in the field of action. Conflict is usually encountered whenever opposing posi-

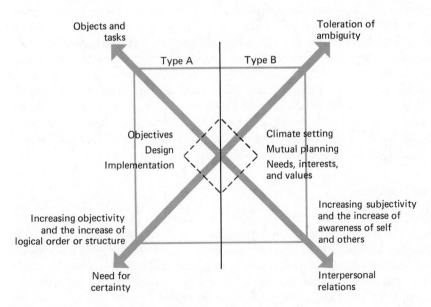

Fig. 3.3 The area of potential conflict in the field of action

tions are taken on opposite sides of the river, or when A or B stages are used at inappropriate times, or further, when there is a requirement to move from one side of the field to the other, to move from a discussion of needs to the formulation of objectives. Paradoxically, it is necessary to first increase subjectivity and the awareness of self and others (problem finding) before there can be effective movement toward achieving increased objectivity and structural order or control (problem solving). This is often difficult to realize when we are confused by the existence of conflict, which (in Type A fashion) we may attribute to irrationality, emotionality, stubbornness, or just plain stupidity. As frustration increases our capacity for both subjective and objective assessment deteriorates.

The dashed square in Fig. 3.3 indicates the area where we may expect to encounter conflict, interpersonal discomfort, resistance or withdrawal, or struggle for power. When working with other persons in groups or organizations, that is, where collaborative effort is required, we must move carefully whenever we are making a transition from one position in the field of action to another. When a group becomes skillful in the process of problem finding and problem solving, crossing the river becomes easy.

THE PROCESS OF PROBLEM SOLVING

When climate factors have been identified and needs have been assessed through mutual planning by the key members of any project or program team, the initial process of problem finding is usually complete. At this stage, it may become clear that more information or support of one kind or another is needed before a project or program can be moved forward. If so, it may be useful initially to establish only some *tentative* objectives, a *tentative* design, and some *tentative* plans for implementation. Sufficient openness can be maintained to allow for revision or updating if new facts or new information should arise. If appropriate, the group may decide to temporarily suspend its activity at the problem-finding stage and go after any additional support it needs prior to attempting to move ahead. Such a detour at the initial entry into problem solving is sometimes necessary to allow for proposal writing or for gaining the approval or concurrence that is often necessary in large organizations.

Forming Objectives

The proliferation of books and articles on management by objectives and goal setting are clear evidence of the preoccupation many managers have with the need for forming clear, specific, and measurable objectives. This sudden surge of interest in setting or forming objectives led one well-known psychologist to pointedly ask the question, "Management by whose objectives?" (Levinson, 1973). It is a crucially important question!

Planning is a complicated process, yet many large organizations are able to make fairly accurate predictions of outcomes three to five years hence by forming assumptions based on a knowledge of past, present, and expected future events. It would be interesting, however, to discover the extent to which any plan for the future influences behavior in the present—the extent to which any plan, or the planning process itself, places limits on accomplishment or on performance improvement.

Some of us have a great deal of respect for the military model of efficiency. It may indeed be stimulating to watch military units pass in review or to watch marching bands and drill teams conduct complicated maneuvers at sporting events. It may be highly satisfying to watch well-disciplined football teams carry out their objectives with blinding precision, and we may wonder why our organizations can't carry out their objectives in the same way. The idea of having orders given crisply and carried out efficiently is attractive, but many of us may fail to recognize that this type of efficiency is also programmed; it is practiced and learned by rote memory. Management decision making in an organizational setting is a vastly more complicated psychological process than marching on, around, and off the field in accordance with the programmed plan. Still, some organization leaders believe that programming managerial performance is an acceptable path to efficiency. I think it is the growing awareness that programming doesn't work nearly as well as we would expect that has helped us better understand that if we want to obtain effective results (output) we had better concentrate on the *process* of forming, clarifying, and communicating objectives (input), instead of simply issuing directives or commands and judging the reactions in stimulus/response, "knee-jerk" fashion. Developing and using a planning system and performance objectives requires a very different kind of drill and discipline than that required to ensure the success of a half-time show at the big Saturday game.

There are, of course, a number of alternatives to developing a system of management by objectives. Management by fiat, management by fear, management by crisis, and management by vacillation are all familiar styles practiced with varying degrees of consistency or variety depending on the penchant of the particular manager for dealing (or not dealing) with any problem at any specific point in time. I think many of us have grown accustomed to waiting for the boss to decide what he wants, responding as completely and effectively as we can without questioning his issued directive, and waiting again for his judgment on the value or effectiveness of our results. But it is precisely the *lack* of results experienced with this simplistic type of boss/subordinate relationship that led a few years ago to a great emphasis being placed on the importance of following up and following through. This type of activity often led further to the discovery that communications problems existed. But what precisely was the problem? An analysis of the communications involved frequently led to a confession of misunderstanding of instructions by subordinates. "Oh, is *that* what you meant?" After much apology and backing and filling, it often became painfully obvious that the subordinate really didn't want to (or couldn't) carry out the instructions at all. What happens when this time-consuming sequence has run its course and the problem still remains? Do we perhaps call a meeting and get everyone together so we can get to the bottom of things? Having attended a number of those kinds of meetings, I can assure you that the solution to the stated problem must be looked for elsewhere. Situations of this type tend to develop when the boss doesn't engage in any problem-finding activity before he starts to issue directives and commands. Thus the typical Type A manager often finds himself hoisted on the petard of his own assumptions. It might be helpful if looking into the mirror in the executive bathroom he could discover, "Lo and behold, *I* am the problem!"

As we have intimated above, one primary difficulty in forming objectives lies in the assumption that objectives are "objective." In other words, simply verbalizing an objective does not guarantee that those hearing it will accord it the same weight or value, interpret the means to attain it in the same way, or even agree with it as an appropriate choice among possible other alternatives. As we have observed before, we all see the world through our own eyes. It is for this reason that objectives must be helped to emerge naturally from needs, interests, and values, and not be imposed from without as commands. Again, this is not to deny the validity of, and necessity for, discipline and order; it is simply to provide a guarantee for the development of an *internalized commitment to command,* which cannot be assumed to follow blindly and unthinkingly from the employment contract or from the supervisor/subordinate relationship. The general (remember the fate of Mark Antony) whose troops left him standing alone on the desert sands had long before lost that internalized commitment to command that is the basis of all power.

It is also important to recognize that objectives form a hierarchy of their own. At the top we find a general statement of philosophy or overall purpose. At the next level we find general operating goals, then program or project objectives, next group or team tasks, and finally behavioral units or actions that need to be accomplished by individuals within task groups or teams. A diagram of the hierarchy of objectives is shown in Fig. 3.4.

The hierarchy of objectives, as we can see, assumes the shape of an inverted pyramid. Those objectives at the top of the hierarchy usually involve the total picture. They tend to be very global, while those at the bottom become quite detailed and localized. In many organizations there is a considerable distance between those individuals who formulate the overall philosophy or purpose of an organization and those who are responsible for implementing the day-to-day activities required to actualize the organization's general purposes. This distance or gap accounts for much of the confusion or misunderstanding that causes many plans and systems of objectives to fail. The people at the top often do not understand the complexity of the details and the

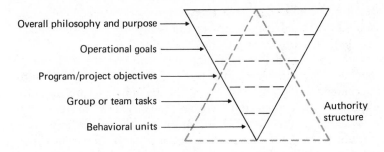

Fig. 3.4 The hierarchy of objectives

people at the bottom often do not see how their part is vitally connected to the whole. If we are to gain internalization of commands or commitment to objectives within the hierarchy, we clearly must have an acceleration of information processing and interpersonal involvement between and within organizational levels and, in fact, within any power or authority structure (see the dashed-line pyramid in Fig. 3.4).

One way to relieve some of the dysfunctional elements in setting objectives is to begin the planning process at (or near) the bottom of an organization. The primary effort to begin setting objectives thus might be a question rather than an attempt to impose an answer. The question might be phrased as follows: "What do you (or your group), given your knowledge of your present situation, think you can accomplish by . . .?" The individual or group must then be given time to study the question and formulate a plan or a series of objectives that allows for a wide range of response within the hierarchy. The boss or manager may then respond to this plan with his statement of what is desirable, acceptable, and unacceptable and together the manager and the group may negotiate an acceptable set of objectives.

Type A managers tend to be very uncomfortable with participative approaches to objective setting. This is not just a question of managerial style, however, but a question also of the effective or ineffective utilization of available human energy. It is truly astonishing to find that a great number of proponents of management-by-objectives systems and approaches think that it is possible to start with objectives and completely ignore climate issues, mutual planning, or the assessment of needs, interests, and values. As a result many people in organizations can be observed to have "resigned in place"; that is, they are no longer *involved* in the organization's aims and goals, and are simply doing the minimum required to collect the paycheck because finding another job at that time may be inconvenient, difficult, or impossible. Where does the internalized commitment go? As with all living things, it simply dries up and blows away if it is not cultivated and cared for. The energy in living systems, coming as it does from a different source than machine energy, cannot be turned off and on simply by throwing a switch at the beginning of an eight-hour day or a forty-hour work week. While this seems obvious enough, it's amazing to me how so many managers behave as if organizations and their people were, in fact, machines.

The formation of a pyramidal organization structure and the dividing of responsibility into separate functions and tasks is not enough. The third dimension of interpersonal relations must also be included before an integrated understanding of objectives both within the structure or hierarchy and among those who carry out these functions can be achieved. Many managements have misunderstood the so-called informal organization. They may see it as subversive when in reality it is the normal operation of any social system. When rebellion occurs it is usually because the system has been abused in some way by a management that mistrusts it. The kind of integration required for effective formulation of organizational objectives cannot be achieved in a highly authoritarian environment; what is required is openness and an acceptance of the value of subjective perceptions at all organizational levels. As we have said, we need Type B meetings to ensure effective problem finding before we rush into Type A problem solving.

In forming program or project objectives, it is worthwhile to group them into categories of *general* and *specific*. Thus, short-term objectives must be established in the context of the longer-range goals of the organization. Again we are dealing with the question of appropriateness. "What can be done now?" is always constrained by the issue of "What must be done eventually to meet the needs of the total situation?"

The process of developing organizational integration and an internalized commitment to objectives through consensual decision making will be dealt with at some length in the next chapter. Assuming for a moment that individuals and organizations are capable of deciding *what* they want to do, let us now look at the next step: deciding *how* they will do it.

Designing

"If a man is out of step with his fellows," observed Henry David Thoreau, "perhaps he is marching to the tune of a different drummer." Why is it that when we seek to implement what appears to be a clear objective or set of objectives we so frequently discover a lack of clear understanding of roles, responsibilities, and methods? Is it perversity, deviant behavior, or just plain stupidity? Why do we so often find ourselves asking, "What went wrong?" Typically, when we have a failure, we start to look around for the culprit or a scapegoat. "Who didn't do what he was *supposed* to do?" While evidence of deviant or disloyal behavior may initially appear to be what we are looking for, if we look a bit further we usually find that the real culprit is the lack of, or inadequacy of, a design to implement the agreed-upon objectives or program goals.

The possibilities for program or project failures in complex organizational settings are immense. In addition to the difficulty of communicating details so that everyone knows what part to play and what's expected of them, the typical organizational setting is further complicated by intergroup competition, conflicting ideas about the nature of the problem(s), and possibly also hostility and mistrust among participants required to perform joint problem-finding and problem-solving activities. It is for these reasons that we must take the necessary time to design human organizational activities if we expect productive effort of both high quality and quantity.

Observing the industrial scene, we can see vast sums of money being spent to develop industrial product designs of every description. Yet when we view many management situations, we see managers rushing from objectives to implementation often without pausing to consider even the most elementary of design questions. Why is this so? Are not the human organizational problems often as complicated as or more complicated than those of designing a new automobile model or a new refrigerator for this year's product line?

When we look at the problem of product design we see that the designer's primary task is to evolve a *structure* that will *function*. Appearance and/or style is usually of secondary importance to what the product will do. With management it is different; the organizational structure is already there, and while it may be changed from time to time as a result of the introduction of new persons, projects, or programs, it is usually assumed as a given. In addition, the functions and roles of organization members are defined by job descriptions and positions within an organizational hierarchy. While there may be some role confusion and need for training, most people are placed in jobs that are well defined.

Thus the problem of management design is fundamentally different from that of designing industrial products or commercial structures. The results sought by management are not products or services in the strict sense; they are improved *processes* for producing products or services (that is, greater integration and effectiveness in problem finding and problem solving).

For many years after the industrial revolution, management in both government and industry largely neglected and underestimated the importance of the processes of group and interpersonal relations. Most of the emphasis was placed instead on making the "people machine" run efficiently by setting up the correct organizational structure and providing for the appropriate division of labor into specalized functions and tasks. When the importance of the interpersonal process dimension was finally beginning to be recognized in the 1950s and 1960s, it was misunderstood and dealt with for the most part outside of the problem-finding, problem-solving context of day-to-day management and administrative activity. Thus the interpersonal process dimension has not as yet really taken its rightful place along with structure and function. And as long as I-Thou relationships are ignored we will have organizations that treat people as though they were machine parts.

When first introduced, the *interpersonal process* dimension was seen by many managements as a panacea; soon after that it became a headache and finally it has come to be regarded by many pragmatic souls as a waste of time. What was not well understood was how to handle interpersonal issues in a task-oriented environment, and many individuals who valued human relations seemed to be too process oriented and ineffective. The approach described in this chapter provides a method for melding the process dimension with functional (task) activities within any organizational structure.

Designing, then, involves dealing appropriately with *structures, functions,* and interpersonal *processes.* It involves comprehensive planning for the effective implementation of objectives that arise after an in-depth consideration of the needs. It also involves an effort to win others' acceptance of these objectives. To operate otherwise is to seriously risk failure because, as we have observed earlier, groups change best from within. If there is no effective design for gaining internalized commitment to the objectives you propose, your objectives will probably never be accomplished unless you have a lot of personal and organizational power or clout. Even so, many company presidents find themselves wondering, "Why didn't they carry out my instructions?"

In creating an effective design, it is important to determine how the program or project evaluation is to be conducted before you move to the implementation stage. Also, any design needs should be carefully detailed in writing because later, if and when discrepancies arise, a written document may serve as a valuable resource for discovering emergent problems.

Implementing

When needs have been translated into overall objectives, and a design has been developed for implementing program or project objectives for each specific activity, the moment of truth has been reached. All that has gone before is hypothetical and theoretical, in the sense that until you put your design into the air you don't know how well it will fly.

It is in the implementation stage that any flaws in design will appear, as well as specific levels of competence and achievement. Has anything or anyone been left out or forgotten? Does everyone know what to do and how to do it? Was the design comprehensive enough and adequate to meet the needs of the problem situation at that particular point in time? All of these questions highlight the crucially valuable concept of *learning from the experience of the moment.* If your design was built using the model or process structure that we are describing, you will be inclined to look at climate, mutual planning, need assessment, objective setting, and so forth, as these stages occurred within your actual design and as they unfolded during implementation.

If you are implementing a design with others, there will most likely be a dimension of shared experience that can be most satisfying and enjoyable. Implementing a design that proves successful and appropriate to the needs of the situation yields an immediate payoff in terms of improved climate in both the group implementing the design and the group that is participating with you. This improved climate occurs when expectations are met or exceeded. Furthermore, any lack of success need not necessarily be seen as failure or cause for disappointment but may be used as an input for redesign. Let us now look at the evaluation stage in this model of problem finding and problem solving.

EVALUATING: A NEW STAGE OF PROBLEM FINDING

All that precedes the implementation stage may be thought of as idea or theory. All planning for what is to occur at implementation is, in a sense, wishful thinking, for the best-laid plans often go awry. If implementation is the moment of truth, the realization of theory and assumption, then we have succeeded in crossing another psychological river. The size of the gap between what was planned to occur and what actually did occur is the measure to be used for effective evaluation.

We are used to viewing the evaluation process as a time for judgment. We customarily seek to come up with good/bad, right/wrong assessments. We look, with our Type A orientations, to fix blame and pin responsibility, and we are usually unaware of how much this orientation builds defensive and covering-up kinds of behavior. No one likes to be judged; we all tend to hide from it, yet in the final analysis none of us can.

Let us look at a Type B approach to evaluation as an alternative to Type A. If we consider evaluation not as judgment but rather as a *descriptive reassessment of the needs*, we can identify in the gap between what we wanted and what we got an opportunity for forming new objectives and a new design that will move us another step closer toward our ultimate goal.

Viewing evaluation as a descriptive reassessment of needs enables us to employ it as a *feedback* loop. In this way we can measure the distance between where we were when we first assessed needs, where we are now, and where we need to go from here. This technique has been appropriately called a *goal-referencing* approach; rather than stopping the action by making an absolute judgment of success or failure at a fixed point, we can instead make a relative judgment of how well we have moved along a continuum toward the final solution or eventual result we seek to obtain. No one wishes to rely too heavily on predictions of future events in social or in management relations—there is too great a likelihood of encountering new variables even under tightly controlled conditions. Therefore it becomes both necessary and worthwhile to develop an experimental approach with regard to the future, fostering the emergence of the desired results rather than attempting to force them to occur within a rigid time frame that may have been arbitrarily decided on the basis of very limited facts. When we approach problem finding and problem solving in this way, we are actually involving ourselves in a conservation of human energy. We can avoid disappointment, missed expectations, and mutual fault finding, all of which waste energy and lead toward demotivation.

Feedback is the distinctive feature that separates this seven-step evalua-tion model from all mechanistic decision-making approaches that are linear, absolute, or fixed. The problem-finding/problem-solving circle always leads into evaluation as a new emergent state of problem finding. Thus the switch is always turned to "On" and energy is always released toward continuing development. Each journey around this seven-step circle leads potentially to

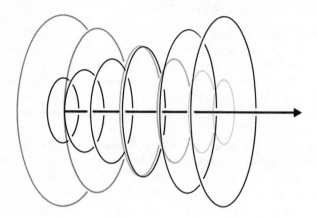

Figure 3.5

Classical Managerial Functions	Stages	Seven-step Model	Modality
Planning Organizing	Problem finding	Climate setting Mutual planning Assessing needs	Type B (subjective)
Motivating (leading) Controlling (evaluating)	Problem solving	Forming objectives Designing Implementing	Type A (objective)
	Problem finding	Evaluating	Type B/A (subjective/objective integration)

Fig. 3.6 A system of management: translating managerial functions to
program/project activity

a widening and deepening grasp of any problem situation and the emergence of the necessary means for arriving at a satisfactory solution. Simultaneously, each movement around the circle also tends to reduce generalities to specifics and enables one to obtain an ever-clearer grasp of the essential features of the problem under study.

Thus, in a sense, movement around the problem-finding/problem-solving circle can be visualized as creating two sets of circles: one expanding as the problem becomes more fully understood; the other simultaneously contracting as the crucial elements of the problem become more clearly identified (see Fig. 3.5).

When we have satisfied the Type B need for inquiry as to the relative degrees of progress and learning that have occurred in the movement from problem finding to problem solving, we can then begin to evaluate where we are in terms of objective numbers, data, factual assessment, and other Type A criterion measures. Thus evaluation may also be regarded as a Type B/A fusion of the results of the prior six steps.

When viewed in its widest possible context, the approach we have described above tentatively qualifies as a general system of management (see Fig. 3.6). It incorporates all four of the classical management functions—planning, organizing, motivating, and controlling—into a dynamic activity. Because it satisfactorily integrates past, present, and future (Where are we now? Where are we going? Where have we been?) and provides instant access to

Input Factors	Output Analysis
Physical/Psychological/Organizational	Working conditions/Tension/Anxiety/Morale/Leadership/Direction/Goal clarity
Key personnel	Involvement/Objectivity
Individual/Organizational/Community	Needs/Interests/Values
Specific/General	Short-term goals/Time limits/Outcomes expected/Long-range goals/Corporate objectives/Department goals
Application/Planning	Clarifying application methods/Clarifying roles and responsibilities
Specific action(s)	Run project(s) while continuing to monitor against general objectives
General outcome(s)	General feedback (for ongoing performance improvement as a reassessment of needs)
Specific outcome(s)	Project feedback (cost/benefit analysis performance review)

each of these three temporal perspectives, this approach provides an excellent vehicle for measuring management activity in terms of progressive output. Most importantly, perhaps, it seeks to obtain a balance between subjectivity and objectivity, recognizing the validity and influence of each and simultaneously avoiding both a lifeless rationalism on the one hand and irrationality or excessive emotionality on the other. This model also provides for a fusion of structure, function, and the interpersonal process dimensions that overcomes the split between the scientific management school of Taylor (1973) and the human relations school of Maslow (1971) and Rogers (1961). Finally, of course, it tends to integrate the human energy system and engage future energy potential for continuing effective action.

When we view organizations with which we are familiar we see many examples of wasted energy. Organizations may lack the ability to diagnose or find problems; task or object (Type A) problems may be identified, for example, while human relationship (Type B) problems are overlooked, or vice versa. Organizations may also lack the ability to solve problems. It is difficult if not impossible to form objectives, design activities, and implement them effectively if we only utilize Type A behavior. Many programs of management by objectives have failed because they have not incorporated or dealt effectively with the Type B world of interpersonal relations, preferring to ignore or suppress subjectivity in favor of so-called rationality or order. Finally, Type A evaluation tends to become fault finding and blame placing when objectives are not achieved; thus instead of renewed interest and energy being stimulated for the next assault on the problem, individuals begin fighting among themselves.

Let us now look at some basic considerations that are necessary for forming effective problem-finding and problem-solving groups.

4 Group Action and Group Consciousness

BASIC CONSIDERATIONS

In Chapters 1 and 2, I presented two energy models, one for the field of action and another for the field of consciousness. These two chapters were developed largely from the standpoint of the individual. In Chapter 3, I presented a process for increasing awareness and moving into effective action. I have come to believe that the dual task of problem finding (discovery) and problem solving (purposeful action) is a tremendously significant effort in human life. It moves us beyond the realm of basic biological functioning that we share with subhuman forms of animal life. It moves us toward ever-higher levels of consciousness and civilized activity, and away from the tendency toward a life of bucolic isolation or of seeking and subduing prey. Fully human life requires us to encounter problem situations and attain mastery over them. In doing so, we grow and develop and expend high levels of energy.

The process of finding and solving problems with others requires us to communicate with language, to use words. But words alone do not enable us to be effective. In fact, words often obfuscate, confuse, mislead, and prevent us from coming to terms with each other and with reality. Words are, after all, abstract symbols, a medium of expression, like paint for a canvas or notes for a musical score. While words have a fixed denotation, like color (red) and musical pitch (E flat), they take on many different connotations or shades of meaning depending on the context or the circumstances of any situation. Even when we are communicating in the same language, we experience further distortion of meaning with accents, dialects, slang, and jargon.

Over and against this ambiguity of words, there are many in any civilized society who strive to bring order out of chaos and to establish language controls. As we well know, language is alive; it changes almost as we use it. Yet it is of great importance to have certainty of meaning. Otherwise human society as we know it, and despite what we think of it at any fixed point in time, could not exist. The so-called universal language of music communicates as effectively as it does precisely because it contacts human emotions and intuition directly. Yet music alone could not meet our needs for transmitting messages. It is too symbolic, too open to personal and emotional interpretation. It is the conscious capacity for speech, for using words, that calls forth our ability to express abstract thought.

The thinking and sensory sides of human consciousness combine to enable us to generalize from experience and to form the universal categories that we call ideas. It is therefore not just words that we seek to share with each other; it is ideas and their meaning, together with the emotions and intuitive insights that ideas and experience engender and flow from. The words or jargon we may use are thus far less important than what lies behind them, and we must go beyond their surface meaning to discover true meaning and authentic relation.

In this chapter I wish to explore the circumstances that prevent meaningful ideas and related feelings from being passed from person to person or being shared openly among persons in a group. To do so, we must look at the contexts or existential circumstances of human groups; we must become aware of the implicit *group situation* and determine the constituents of group effectiveness. As a result we may come to see how human energy flows through the dynamics of group activity.

As the problem-finding/problem-solving process described in Chapter 3 is wholly dependent on group effectiveness, it is perhaps necessary to determine exactly what group effectiveness is and how it may be developed. While one obviously must use words to describe the various dimensions of group life, I seek now to get beyond the words to the actual experience of group life itself; to go beyond the *content* of any specific group activity to the general *process* that can be observed occurring in all human groups regardless of the language spoken or of the business being transacted.

Human groups are *centers of influence.* To begin our exploration of group life, it is necessary to consider the issue of influencing others or being influenced by them.

It is becoming clear from psychiatric studies that humans fear being "engulfed" (Laing, 1969). While this fear can take on morbid or pathological dimensions, in lesser degrees it is quite normal, and its presence in all of us is evidenced by the extreme public interest in such films as *The Exorcist* or *Jaws.* This fear is stronger in some of us than in others, and may give rise to a desire to continually influence others while never being influenced by them; to always lead, but never belong. Healthy social adjustment, of course, requires a give and take between influencing and being influenced, between leading and following. If, however, one has a very fragile or delicate self-concept and is afraid of losing individuality or personal autonomy, of literally being engulfed by another person or a group, it may be better for such a person to try to find an occupational setting of limited stress. If one has an overly strong self-concept, on the other hand, and does not want to be influenced in any way by others, it may be better if that person does not occupy a position of great power and authority; such a person threatens always to engulf others and to deny their autonomy.

Another important concept related to influence that could well be considered before exploring group processes more deeply is that of social distance. Differences in social distance may be observed in different cultures, and as such are manifested differently in different countries (Lewin, 1948). Social distance may be measured by the amount of formality or informality present in a situation and also by the relative appropriateness of touching; of a formal handshake, a pat on the back, or a touch on the arm. Social distance in a highly autocratic or aristocratic setting is carefully maintained as a vehicle or method of protection against outside influence or engulfment by society as a whole. While it protects to a certain extent, it also endangers because it tends to isolate those being protected from reality. As Louis XVI observed, "Aprés moi le déluge." His inability to see the reality of the situation and to take action to meet the existing needs cost him and his spouse Marie Antoinette their heads. The French Revolution of 1789 represented a breaking down of the barriers of social distance that separated one segment of the population, the aristocracy, from another, the bourgeoisie, and the beheading of Louis XVI and Marie Antoinette both symbolized and actualized this process. This distance might well have been bridged or at least reduced with vastly less tragic consequences if the processes of social and cultural change had been known and understood by those who possessed the power and authority at that time. But, of course, knowing and understanding are not enough; there must also be the ability and, above all, the desire to bring about an improved situation.

A third notion that is worth exploring before we look more deeply at the primary dimensions of group action and group consciousness is that of the relationship between expectation and fulfillment.

We all have expectations for one another. Expectations stem naturally from the Type A tendency to organize the world around us to make it meaningful to ourselves. If we do not know another person well, we tend to base our expectations on assumptions. If we do know that person well and have experienced what he or she can and probably will do, our experience tempers or moderates our expectations and makes them more realistic.

Expectation creates a divergence or a discrepancy between an actual situation and an anticipated future situation. If the expectation is fulfilled in the time anticipated, the discrepancy returns to congruence and satisfaction is achieved. This well-known phenomenon is depicted graphically in Fig. 4.1.

If the fulfillment line (curved line) proceeds directly along the line of expectation (straight line) the situation is assumed to be progressing normally. If the fulfillment line drops below the level of expectation (Time 1 to Time 2), anxiety and the fear of failure increase, causing a rise in the level of ambiguity. The increased ambiguity stimulates increased energy flow to meet the target on time. If the fulfillment line exceeds the line of expectation (Time 2

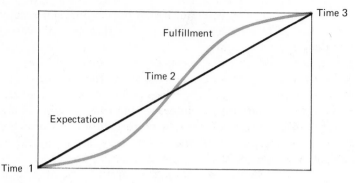

Figure 4.1

to Time 3), a situation of overconfidence or cool superiority may develop out of an assumption of certainty that may be unwarranted. The fable of the tortoise and the hare clearly illustrates this phenomenon. The tortoise, operating with "underslope," tries harder. The hare, operating with "overslope," plays it cool and loses the race. It is important to realize, however, that the tortoise achieved his full potential through steady struggle against the ambiguity of unfair odds. If the hare's expectation line had been set higher, based on an adequate appreciation of his physical characteristics, the hare might have been stimulated to greater effort. But because his expectation line was so low he did not achieve his potential at all. If both the tortoise and the hare were competing against different, but appropriate, lines of expectation for their physical characteristics, the race may have ended in a tie with both achieving full potential. Thus expectations have a great deal to do with human accomplishment or effective performance. Groups also have expectations and experience fulfillment. Expectation and fulfillment form another manifestation of the ambiguity/certainty relation described in Chapter 2.

THREE BEHAVIORAL DIMENSIONS OF GROUP LIFE

With the above basic considerations in mind, let us explore three primary behaviors that determine the characteristic qualities of any human group and tend to define the manner in which it functions. First, however, it may be useful to define the term *group* for our purposes in this chapter. A group is two or more persons joined together for mutual benefit; for the purpose of dealing with a common task or a problem of common concern. While groups may, in an abstract or general sense, consist of thousands (or even millions) of persons, groups in a concrete or specific sense may consist of only a few people, say nine or ten, or twelve at the most. Groups of more than ten or twelve tend to become unstable; that is, their communications or conversational "traffic" tends to become so congested that the group cannot deal with or process all of the information it generates. As a result large groups tend to become hopelessly bogged down when they try to stay together for problem finding and problem solving. Therefore, it is usually helpful to divide groups of fifty or sixty or more into subgroups of eight to ten, and then to negotiate differences from group to group after the problems at hand have been assessed by each. A group, therefore, is any small social unit capable of processing information effectively.

The three key behavioral dimensions of group life are *role*, *choice*, and *transaction*. These dimensions give rise to three primary questions that we all tend to ask ourselves whenever we enter a new situation with a new group of people. The questions are: (1) Who am I in this group and who do I want to be? (2) What do I want to do in this group and how do I want to act here? and (3) How do I wish to handle interpersonal transactions or communicate with others, both inside and outside of this group? Group behavior is greatly affected by member expectations.

Each of these three dimensions may be clouded with ambiguity or clarified with great certainty. The degree or amount of the ambiguity or certainty determines to a great extent what kind of a group it is and how effective it will be. Let us look at each of the three dimensions in turn.

Role—Leadership and Membership

The primary question leading to role clarification in groups is, Who am I in this group and who do I want to be? A corollary question of equal importance is, How do others see me in this group and what do they want me to be? Thus one characteristic of all groups is a potential gap between expectations and realizations (fulfillment) on the part of some or all members. The first question usually arises from unclear or unresolved (ambiguous) issues of leadership and membership. In cases where leadership and membership are clearly defined by previously assigned roles within a specified organizational structure, there is often no room for question. But the primary question of roles must be addressed in both structured and unstructured groups if the group is to become fully effective.

Let us first look at structured membership roles. Some organizational theorists like to believe that jobs or positions are fixed or rigid. Hence they seriously attempt to achieve standardized performance and organizational control by preparing organizational charts, job and position descriptions, and wage and salary classifications for pay purposes. The assumption is that if everyone does exactly what is expected of them the organization or group will function perfectly and will produce an effective output and, therefore, a high return on investment. There would be no role ambiguity. Both common sense and experience, however, tell us that a position description usually serves to clarify only the broad general framework of a position within an organizational structure. No two people ever seem to perform a job in exactly the same way (except in perhaps the most routine jobs) and there can be and usually are wide variations of role response depending on an individual's own sense of that job. This role response varies along a continuum from highly creative, innovative, and self-motivated behavior to an abject and limited tell-me-what-to-do-and-I'll-do-it stance. Thus the job description is not the key to performance effectiveness, as is well known.

Now let us look at structured leadership roles. The organization has appointed a leader and it expects him to plan, organize, motivate, and control the group for which he has been given responsibility. As a result of the appointment and its implicit (and often explicit) conditions for reward and punishment, the new leader sets out to live up to his boss's expectations. In short, he does the planning, the organizing, the motivating, and the controlling that are ascribed to the role of leader. The members of his group have their plans made for them, are organized into task teams for efficient production, are motivated, usually with carrot-and-stick symbols, and are controlled by being required to produce periodic evidence that they are working and producing up to a standard. It is easy to see how tightly structured leadership roles tend to call forth or produce structured membership responses, such as waiting for explicit instructions, doing no more than the job description requires, responding without question to leadership directives, and constantly producing so-called evidence that the job has been accomplished whether or not real progress has been made or cost effectiveness achieved. Obedience to authority is paramount when roles are highly structured and it has been shown that individuals in highly structured situations will go to very extreme lengths to please their boss, even to the extent of physically punishing or hurting others (Milgram, 1974).

Highly structured group situations tend to be very satisfying for individuals who have high needs for certainty or security and a low toleration of ambiguity. But highly structured roles, while producing role clarity and reducing the level of stress present when role ambiguity is allowed, do not tend to produce the most efficient or effective results. This is so because the controls imposed in this kind of group situation tend to reduce innovation, risk taking, and creativity. As there is little opportunity to exercise trust, little if any trust develops. Furthermore, there is little or no payoff for doing more than is expected. Taking on more responsibility is tantamount to threatening the prerogatives, or the supreme decision-making power, of the boss. Thus many people may fail to perform effectively because they are lulled into the false security of thinking they are doing what the boss wants, while the boss is also happy because they seem such loyal and willing workers.

Now let us look at the potential implicit in the *destructuring* of leadership and membership roles. A loosening of role structure opens the door first of all to such questions as, What are we doing and what might we do differently? While there is no arguing with success, it may well be that even greater success is going unrealized because of a lack of reflection on the questions of *what, how,* and *why*. In cases where success is not being experienced there is no choice but to examine these questions critically or continue on a failure path. When individuals are able to question each other's *actions* and *motives,* implicit and unspoken failure strategies may come to the surface. Use of Type B behaviors is critically important here, however, to avoid engendering feelings of failure and negative anxiety.

Destructuring membership roles raises the level of ambiguity for group members. When continued membership in a group is not based simply on meeting the legalistic terms of the employment contract—"a fair day's work for a fair day's pay"—and fulfilling the minimal requirements of a job description, members begin to gain psychological access to the real needs of the group situation. When a climate of openness, honesty, and frank questioning of problem situations and alternative paths to their solution permits them to look also at their own roles and relationships, these members begin to develop a greater sense of identity and purpose. As groups develop increasing competence through the healthy experience of confronting and solving problems, continued group membership tends to be affirmed by a growing willingness to accept responsibility. Group members can be observed attempting to enhance their membership by being helpful, by seeking respect and inclusion, and by supporting the group in its interactions and relationships with other groups or individuals.

Destructuring leadership also raises the level of ambiguity for the leader. Leaders who plan for themselves and consult others about their plans, who organize around the interests, needs, and values of group members as well as around demonstrable competencies, who motivate through participation and involvement, and who foster internalized self-control among group members through periodic goal-setting and group evaluation of progress, are likely to see a dramatic increase in work quality, work quantity, and group creativity. Also likely is an increase in conflict. Conflict, and increased ambiguity for the leaders, occurs when the leaders cannot get exactly what they want when they want it. In reality they usually cannot anyway, but in a highly structured situation everyone tries to create the *impression* that they are getting what they want. Some leaders, in fact, become seduced under these conditions, feeling great satisfaction with their power and control over subordinates and ignoring the demonstrable lack of results in resolving the problems at hand. When leaders, along with members of the group, are able to dig deeply into the conflicts inherent in problem situations, there is usually an observable improvement in results.

In a relatively unstructured group each member must take on a share of the leadership responsibility. It becomes less easy to blame the boss if things go wrong. It also becomes necessary for members to make individual choices and commitment to action, enabling the formal leader to join the group, as it were, and become fully a member of it. This further increases ambiguity for the leader because there is increased risk that he or she may lose leadership status altogether or cease to exercise responsibility for ensuring effective group performance. Neither of these latter results need occur if the leader understands the real nature of leadership and substitutes his or her own competence as the basis for continued leadership instead of maintaining status with formal or legalistic power.

A few years ago, Kenneth Benne and Paul Sheats (1948) identified several behaviors or roles that observably helped groups achieve effective results. These behaviors may be grouped into two sets. One of these sets helps a group to achieve an object or task, the other helps the group maintain effective interpersonal relationships. Both sets are necessary for effective group action when leadership and membership roles have been purposefully destructured. These behaviors may be exercised by *anyone*, not just the formal leader, and it is most helpful if all group members exercise them continuously. They can be summarized as follows:

Leadership behaviors for task effectiveness

1. *Initiating.* Proposing tasks or goals; defining a group problem; suggesting ideas

2. *Seeking information.* Requesting facts; asking for expressions of opinion; seeking suggestions and ideas

3. *Giving information.* Offering facts, information, opinions, and ideas

4. *Clarifying and elaborating.* Interpreting ideas or suggestions; defining terms indicating alternatives

5. *Summarizing.* Pulling together related ideas of others; offering a tentative decision or conclusion for the group to accept or reject

6. *Consensus testing.* Sending up trial balloons to test for or prepare for a possible decision for commitment or action

Leadership behaviors for maintaining effective interpersonal relationships

1. *Harmonizing.* Attempting to reconcile disagreements; reducing tensions

2. *Gatekeeping.* Helping to keep communication channels open; facilitating the participation of others; inviting silent members to share their views

3. *Encouraging.* Being friendly, warm, and responsive to others; offering nonverbal or verbal support to the suggestions or recommendations of others

4. *Compromising.* Admitting error; modifying personal behavior in the interest of building group cohesion or growth

5. *Standard setting and testing.* Testing whether the group is satisfied with its procedures; pointing out explicit or implicit norms that have been set and may need to be changed

6. *Sensing and expressing feelings.* Sensing feeling, mood, relationships within the group; sharing own feelings with other members; soliciting feelings of others

It is clear that no group can function without leadership (and membership), but all group members are able to engage in leadership behaviors when roles are made more flexible. When membership and leadership roles are destructured, groups are much better able to identify problems and work constructively toward real solutions. The respect of group members for the legitimate authority of a leader designated by an organization does not diminish when the formal leader becomes a real member of the group he or she is leading. And respect for the formal leader increases when he or she allows and encourages others to engage in the leadership behaviors described above.

Perhaps it is now clear that raising the level of ambiguity by destructuring leadership and membership roles also tends to increase group and individual energy levels (see Fig. 4.2). If leadership behaviors that increase group effectiveness in task accomplishment and in maintaining interpersonal relationships within the group are exercised, groups will tend to become more alive, more animated, and more satisfying to all.

As a side issue it may be interesting to note the Type A orientation of the leadership task behaviors and the Type B orientation of the leadership maintenance behaviors.

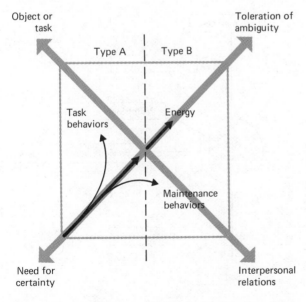

Fig. 4.2 Increasing energy through role destructuring

Some additional notions about role ambiguity and role clarification are worth mentioning here. Ambiguity is not valuable simply for its own sake. It is necessary to increase ambiguity when highly structured roles provide so much rigidity and certainty that human behavior is denied both its spontaneity and authenticity. Often, however, role ambiguity is too high; it then becomes necessary to seek greater role clarification and certainty. Also, role ambiguity and structural certainty sometimes exist together. In such cases role destructuring and role clarification need to be accomplished simultaneously. This point perhaps requires further explanation.

Role incumbents or *role occupiers* constantly receive *role messages* in the form of expectations placed on them by others (see Fig. 4.3). Sometimes these expectations are contradictory, placing the role occupier in an ambiguous or conflict-laden situation. Professor Malcolm Knowles has provided us with a graphic portrayal of this idea. He says:

> The expectations of these different elements in a position-holder's life will be different. For example, the job descriptions specify that he shall carry prescribed responsibilities within defined limits of authority; colleagues expect that he will go outside these restricted boundaries to help them when needed; supervisors often expect him to be tough and efficient while subordinates pressure him to be gentle and caring; his family wants him to make as much money for as little work as possible while the board members want him to do as much work for as little money as possible.

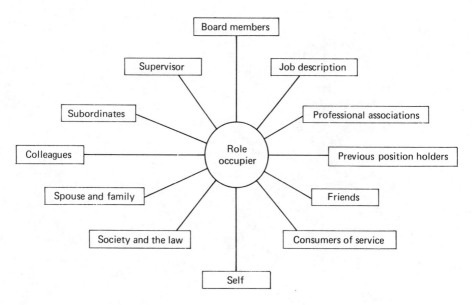

Figure 4.3

The way in which any given role will be understood and performed is determined to the greatest extent by how the role occupier processes and responds to the variety of role messages being communicated by others. These messages come from sources both proximate (the boss, for example) and remote (such as parental influences), and there is a wide variation in how they are received by the role occupier. If the situation in which the role occupier finds himself or herself is confused, or if there are a conflicting variety of expectations and role messages, the occupier must attempt to clarify the situation before he or she can decide upon an appropriate course of action. There is an understandable confusion in many organizational settings, however, between *goals* and *roles*. Much of the difficulty experienced in setting and using organizational goals and objectives and in measuring performance results and output comes from role ambiguity. Unless a reasonable consensus on roles can be obtained and a fairly good level of role clarity achieved, it is safe to predict that the organization's goals and objectives will not be realized. Role clarification is thus a vitally important part of the problem-finding/problem-solving process. In fact it may perhaps best be dealt with during the program or project design stage, after tentative objectives have been set but before they have been finalized. And if the group is not effectively organized or has not worked together before, role problems may need to be dealt with prior to setting objectives.

Malcolm Knowles identifies seven possible options for dealing (or not dealing) with role ambiguity. We quote:

1. He can choose one role-sender to please exclusively (such as the boss) at the risk of alienating all others.
2. He can try to satisfy all role-expectations equally—be all things to all men—at the risk of being seen by all as being two-faced or wishy-washy.
3. He can ignore or deny the existence of conflicting role-sendings at the risk of creating a fantasy world that will collapse under the weight of unsolved problems.
4. He can engage in unending arguments with his role-senders about the unreasonableness of their expectations at the risk of intensifying rather than resolving conflicting expectations.
5. He can find a scapegoat (such as the boss, inadequate subordinates, or the bureaucracy) and blame his difficulties on it, at the risk of making the conflicts all the more unresolvable.
6. He can "pair" with one or more kindred spirits who are not solving their role-conflict problems and conspire to get favored treatment through aggressive action, at the risk of reducing their social system to factional win-lose warfare.
7. He can bring the role-senders from whom he is receiving conflicting signals together in an open, honest problem-solving confrontation, at the risk of having to divert energy from constructive work to organizational problem-solving.

Each position-holder has to decide for himself which type of risk he is ready and willing to take. But in the long run only the last option produces a viable, functional role definition.

Again we can see the potential value of the Type B behaviors for finding and resolving role problems. The spirit of open inquiry, the acceptance and valuing of persons, and the willingness to experiment with alternative solutions, all help to reduce conflict in situtions where the energy level has risen too high and the group is about to break apart. Logic, judgment, and assumption do not generally help to reduce interpersonal stress, but Type A behaviors must be utilized for effective task performance when relationship issues have been resolved.

There are four general categories of role ambiguity and clarity viewed from the standpoint of *person* and *situation*. First, there is personal ambiguity in a clear situation. For many reasons that are personal, private, or unrelated to a particular organizational setting, an individual may find himself internally conflicted. Sometimes the situation is serious enough to require psychotherapy; at other times there may be a temporary crisis situation that will pass by. Under these conditions individual performance is almost certain to be impaired to some extent until the conflict is resolved.

Second, there is personal ambiguity is an ambiguous situation. This is the worst condition of all—one in which nothing seems to work. A group of conflicted individuals in a conflicting situation may generate so much additional conflict among them that hostility may erupt, tending to violence or destruction of the group. This is the familiar pattern of "fight or flight."

Third is the situation where the individual is clear and the situation is ambiguous. In this case, if other individuals are also clear (or unconflicted) they may solve the problem through joint effort. If the situational ambiguity cannot be resolved for whatever reason, the individuals may make personal decisions to carry on and do what appears to be most constructive under the circumstances. Situations of too high a level of ambiguity tend to reduce risk taking and increase an individual's need for security and safety.

The fourth situation is one of combined role clarity and situational clarity. This situation is ideally conducive to a constructive working environment provided that roles are not so tightly structured that the problems raised previously are engendered. When role clarity and situational clarity are combined, conditions are favorable for increased risk taking and increased toleration of ambiguity, which generally leads to more creative and more effective performance.

Robert Kahn *et al.*, in the excellent but quite technical book *Organizational Stress* (1964), present significant research data to support the contention that too much role ambiguity may lead to emotional and physical illness and lowered self-esteem as well as to organizational dysfunction. Thus situational ambiguity may well be a leading cause of personal ambiguity or inner conflict.

A key concept advanced by Kahn *et al.* for reducing the negative effects of role ambiguity is that of the potential effectiveness of information processing. Information itself can have a therapeutic effect. According to Kahn, much role ambiguity is induced as a result of the difference between the information *available* to a person on the job and the information *needed* to perform a job effectively. Thus managers who operate with great confidentiality and secrecy are perhaps unwittingly increasing role ambiguity and reducing organizational effectiveness, while simultaneously increasing personal defensiveness and discomfort. Highly authoritarian organizations usually tend to distort their internal information systems. Thus it appears that the final result of any closed organization (or society) is first stagnation and then self-destruction. Some confidentiality is necessary, of course, for any delicate negotiation, but there is always a question about the amount of confidentiality actually *necessary* versus the amount *felt* to be necessary. Kahn's research indicates that role performance expectations are seldom communicated clearly or adequately enough. Thus we may conclude that members of complex organizations might benefit substantially by periodically taking the time to explore each other's roles and relationships and by seeking ways to work more collaboratively and supportively. Not only is this effort conducive to mental and physical health; it is also directly beneficial to the organizations involved. Again we must stress the value of using Type B behaviors for probing and inquiring into conflict-laden or ambiguous role situations. Much patient understanding is required to undo complex frustrations that build up in highly Type A-oriented organizations.

Choice—Decisions and Norms

The second primary question upon entering a new group situation is, What do I want to do in this group and how do I want to act here? This question comes to terms with the issues of decision making and group norms. How do I decide what choices are going to be most beneficial for myself and for others? Do I go along with the group, even if I don't agree? Do I challenge the group and risk my membership in it? What is the best way to do this? These and other similar questions are the familiar paradoxes and dilemmas that confront all of us who live and work in the world with others. Answers to these questions may be found when we examine group decision-making processes.

It is true that the extent to which persons are involved in making decisions on issues that directly affect them, to that same extent will they be responsible for carrying them out. Having decisions made for one is not a comfortable or agreeable situation for a mature adult. We tend to naturally resist situations in which we are treated like children. We like to make decisions for ourselves and act on them responsibly and if others are making decisions that affect us we like to be involved.

Let's take a look at decision making. There is very little problem with simple decisions: I am thirsty; I pour a glass of water and drink it. There is much more of a problem with complicated decisions. When I myself am facing a difficult situation and have several conflicting choices, I try to get as much information as I can and make a choice on the basis of the facts, my feelings, and my intuitive understanding and perception: I may succeed or fail but the choice is mine. The greatest problems, however, lie with decisions that involve others. Group decision making is usually far more difficult than individual decision making (except possibly in very complicated technical areas). As most organizational decisions are made by individuals working closely with others or by groups, it is important to understand group decision-making processes and how to facilitate them.

Benne and Sheats (n.d.) identified six primary causes of group difficulty in decision making:

1. *Conflicting perception of the situation.* If group members view a problem under discussion in different ways, no effective decision will be made until the differing perceptions are explored and understood by all.

2. *Fear of consequences.* The possible outcomes of an impending decision may overwhelm a group. The ambiguity of fear may have a paralyzing effect on a group's ability to come to a decision, unless the fear is encountered openly and dealt with effectively.

3. *Conflicting loyalties.* Individuals usually have memberships in several groups at a time. Multiple memberships may serve as hidden agendas that create pressure within a decision-making group and need to be identified for free choice to occur.

4. *Interpersonal conflict.* Personal differences, interpersonal conflict, or role ambiguity within a group can provoke defensiveness, antipathy, and biased discussion, preventing full clarification of the issues.

5. *Methodological rigidity.* Groups can be so frozen by a decision-making method (for example, as prescribed in *Robert's Rules of Order*) that free and open discussion of a problem and its various related elements is limited.

6. *Inadequate leadership sharing.* When the group does not *share* leadership functions and relies too heavily on a designated or a self-appointed leader to tell them what to do, a decision may be made that lacks group commitment and acceptance of responsibility for carrying it out.

These six barriers to effective decision making are generally familiar. Inexperience in working with groups or lack of understanding of group decision making can severely limit the freedom of choice for some or all group members. Restriction of choice leads directly to a loss of commitment and reduced energy.

Let us also look at some "counterfeit" forms of decision making, which often cause group members to assume that decisions have been made when in reality they have not.

Decision making by *self-authorization* is experienced when someone makes a statement and then promptly proceeds to act on it without checking to see whether or not it has met with approval or disapproval; for example, "I think we should turn our attention to agenda item number seven next. . . ."

The *handclasp* is a name given to the phenomenon of two or more members joining forces to decide an issue for other group members: "Yes, Virginia, that insight really puts things in perspective. So then, it's decided, tomorrow we will begin."

Baiting is a form of decision making in which pressure is put on other members to either agree or disagree: "No one disagrees, do they?" Or, "Everyone agrees, don't they?"

Authority-rule decision making can come about through the prior existence of a power structure and the implication that no time can be wasted with idle discussion (the idle discussion being about any issue the group in power is opposed to or is not interested in).

Decisions made by majority vote or polling, like decisions made by arbitrary authority, often run into conflict when put into action. Approaches like "Let's take a poll to see where everyone stands" may seem democratic, but they often result in blocking the expression of minority or dissenting opinions that might have been valuable in developing more creative solutions.

Any decision by *unanimous consent* may have been made during a rush of emotional fervor and some important issues may have been neglected that will arise later, causing questions about the authenticity of the unanimous vote.

The negative consequences arising from the above forms of decision making are all associated with exclusion of group members from real involvement in the decision-making process. When this occurs, the inevitable result is the loss of that member's commitment. A way out of this dilemma can be found in the developing of skills required to reach decisions through *consensus.* Consensus allows for the searching out of objectives, with care being taken that conclusions are not reached too rapidly. All members need the opportunity to commit themselves to a decision in their own way and to the extent that their abilities, needs, and interests allow them; this opportunity will ensure commitment. Extra time taken with dissenting members can often produce valuable and unforeseen opportunities for improving a solution or its application. Dissent may signal a rejection not of the whole plan or idea being presented but only of a small part. Careful discussion of opposing views greatly extends the range of creative possibilities when handled with patience and understanding. However, because of the resulting conflict and dissent a group must be able to tolerate a high level of ambiguity if it is to make decisions in these ways. Groups that cannot tolerate ambiguity thus cannot usually make either effective or creative decisions.

I have found that a critical element in helping groups to become effective decision makers is that of support. When one group member starts to build on what another member has said, progress is being made. The kind of supporting behavior I am referring to might take the following form: "Well, I really like what you said, and I think we could also . . ." or "Well, I don't agree with you completely, but when you said . . . I see a possibility for taking that idea and . . ." or again, "Could you say that one more time, because I think I heard something in what you said that gave me an idea. . . ." When supportive behaviors start to develop within a group, members start to listen to each other and the group begins to collaborate in problem-finding and problem-solving activity.

One word of caution must be offered, however, regarding decision making by consensus. There is a danger of developing *groupthink*. Janis (1971) points out the potential of cohesive in-groups to develop a dominant mode of "concurrence seeking" that passes for decision making by consensus (see also the Abilene paradox, Chapter 2). This is actually a counterfeit form of decision making by consensus because all members consciously or unconsciously suppress dissent, thus not reaching true consensus at all. The symptoms of groupthink can be easily recognized, according to Janis, because all of them involve an unwillingness to test assumptions against reality. These symptoms are a Type A phenomena. The issue of groupthink again raises the question about the positive value of constructive conflict. It may be that our concern for maintaining discipline and order in organizations has so discouraged the expression of dissenting opinion that we must finally arrive at a choice between groupthink, open conflict, or passive resistance. Type B behaviors allow us to handle conflict constructively, but if they are not valued in Type A organizations there will not be a tendency to use them. Hopefully, we have learned in the past few years the importance of listening to and considering the implications in dissenting opinion. When dissenting opinion is suppressed because of Type A judgments about the dissenters, disaster is being actively courted should the dissenter turn out to be correct.

Another key aspect of the individual exercise of free choice in groups arises from a consideration of *group norms*. Norms represent the way things are usually done by that group; they are the behavioral expectations that are built into any social situation. Part of the problem we all experience in entering any new group or social situation is a feeling of uncertainty about what the norms or expectations are; we cannot really relax and get comfortable in the situation unless and until these questions become resolved through our participation in the activity of the group. In the early stages, we are very alert to behavioral cues; "When in Rome, do as the Romans do" is an exhortation to follow group norms.

Group norms tend to form very rapidly and often, in the absence of other information, around very insignificant data or facts. I once heard a story (whose authenticity I cannot verify) about a psychological experiment with group norms in which twenty-four people were invited to participate. The participants entered a room with no furniture, no drapes, and no telephone—a completely empty but well-lighted, well-ventilated large room that could comfortably hold three or four hundred people. The participants were told that they must restrict their conversation to small talk: they could talk about anything in the room, but they could not enter into any serious or intellectual conversation about any subject at all. As they entered the room, each participant was given at random either a plain blue card or a plain red card; twelve cards of each color were distributed. The cards were about fourteen inches square and were brightly colored so as to be highly visible. The participants were given no information about the cards, and when all twenty-four people were in the room the psychologists left. The participants had been instructed not to leave the room for any reason until the psychologists returned. When they did return, in about an hour, they found two groups of twelve participants each, formed into two circles: a red group and a blue group. In the absence of other information, a group norm had formed around the color of the card that each person held in his hand. I can imagine some of the conversations that must have occurred during the development of this norm: for example, "Why don't you get over there with those other blue card holders?"

While group norms are important for maintaining social and organizational cohesion, norms that remain sacrosanct or unquestioned may form the basis of a stultifying conformity. While a certain amount of conformity has value and provides stability, too much leads to stagnation and loss of creativity. In fact there will be little growth or forward movement in any group until some of its norms are questioned. Paradoxically, whenever someone questions a group norm, he or she tends to raise the level of ambiguity and may be perceived as threatening or attacking the group's leaders. The one who says "I don't like what's going on here" might receive "We were getting along fine till you opened your big mouth" for a response. The one who chooses to challenge group norms puts his or her group membership on the line. But when a group is bogged down or going around in circles instead of discovering or solving problems, there often can be no forward movement until norm-challenging questions are raised. Challenging norms and raising the level of ambiguity engages and raises group and individual energy. If ambiguity is raised too much, however, the resultant conflict will probably lead to expulsion of the challenger. Challenging norms always involves an exercise of free choice in deciding how much risk to take, and again, the most helpful and nonconflicting way to test norms is to utilize Type B behaviors.

Transaction—Interpersonal and Intergroup

The third primary question for any new group member is, How do I wish to handle interpersonal transactions or communications with others, both inside and outside of this group?

Many individuals are noted for their excellent one-to-one communications in private; their competence in working with groups of three or more persons, however, often leaves much to be desired. Why is the one-to-one relationship so attractive? First, perhaps, because of its intimacy: "Two's company, three's a crowd." Secondly, it seems to be an ideal setting for distributing rewards and punishments. Someone once observed that the definition of confidential information is "something you tell only one person at a time." Giving and receiving information of a confidential nature conveys subtle psychological rewards for both parties involved in the transaction; it increases the sense of interpersonal closeness and belonging (membership), and it also tends to create an obligation. Obviously, this kind of transaction can give communications a subversive dimension that can have a powerfully destructive or divisive influence on other group members. Furthermore, if transactions have a highly Type A orientation, it is likely that an attitude of exclusion toward other group members will develop, further diminishing openness and candor. This is the well-known phenomenon of *clique formation*.

Perhaps the greatest advantage of groups of three rather than two is in the potential for balance and objectivity that any third party provides. This is particularly true when the structure is flexible enough so that any one of the three can play the third-party role at any time. When no third party is present to assess the two-party transactions, there is no opportunity for feedback on the respective roles being played by each of the two parties and on the relative degrees of freedom contained in the choices being made. In the case of supervisor/subordinate relationships, subtle (or not so subtle) pressure can be applied without fear of other eyes judging the potential unfairness in the situation. Constructive results seldom emerge from coercion, but many people place great faith in it and it does raise ambiguity that in turn stimulates energy. We may conclude that while coercion works sometimes, more effective methods are usually available.

Richard Walton of Harvard University has prepared an excellent small volume on third-party consultation and interpersonal peace-making (Walton, 1969). Managers and administrators in all kinds of organizations might do well to foster the development of three-way communications habits in their organizations to overcome some of the pitfalls and disadvantages inherent in the one-to-one relationships so typical of organizations today.

It is often interesting and informative to watch for communications patterns in groups of three or more people. Some people seem to do most of the talking; others apparently don't like to talk at all, but their presence is strongly felt just the same. Some people speak directly to others, looking into their eyes, and others don't look at anyone directly. Still others seem to choose special communication links; that is, they seem to talk to the same few people all the time, either looking to gain approval for their ideas or seeking a closer identification with others.

Patterns of influence and respect can also be observed in the communications processes of groups. High-status group members seem to be allowed to get away with interrupting or cutting off lower-status members, and sometimes members wait for one person to speak on their behalf or on behalf of everyone. Certain sequence patterns can develop as well; for example, Frank speaks after Sam, who follows Susan, who follows Bill, who follows Frank. This pattern may repeat itself several times until a continuous circle develops that prevents others from getting into the conversation at all. If that happens to you, remember that people have to breathe. When someone breathes you can usually get an "edge in wordwise," as they say.

A frequent consequence of an interrupting or blocking type of communication pattern is the assumption that organization or structure is lacking. Power is then sought for a chairman who is able to control the group with strong authority. Edgar Schein (1969) says, "This solution substitutes external discipline for internal control. It misdiagnoses the problem as one of organization rather than recognizing it as a problem of lack of concern of the members for each other, resulting in insufficient listening." Understanding the reasons for communications and listening problems in groups and being able to help alleviate these problems can be an extremely useful skill for any manager or administrator: in fact in organizational life today, it may be vital.

An issue of great importance in interpersonal communication is that of *semantics,* the science of word meanings. As we said, different words mean different things to different people, so it is important to try to pick up on the "language spoken here" if one wants to communicate effectively. For example, you probably would not quote Shakespeare if you were addressing a convention of cost accountants—not that a lot of cost accountants might not like Shakespeare, but there are other subjects and quotations that are likely to have much more impact. In addition, I have found that many people dislike words they describe as jargon. While every field has its technical words and phrases, jargon usually develops as a kind of shorthand notation to simplify speech and to facilitate communication. Often it does the opposite. If one is feeling uncomfortable about not understanding a particular word or phrase it seems best to inquire about its meaning. I have found, however, that the greatest feelings of insecurity arise because not knowing the jargon can indicate that one has only a marginal membership in the group. Communications patterns and processes can create powerful bonds of inclusion and exclusion.

Another important area of interpersonal transaction or communication is that of nonverbal communications. Once I had the opportunity of working with a group of trainers and adult educators in Puerto Rico. I was conducting a one-week management workshop, and much of the time the group preferred to work in Spanish. This was also agreeable to me, because although I cannot speak or understand Spanish, I felt they could get more accomplished in their native language even though they all spoke English quite well. I was thrilled and astonished to learn how much meaning I could pick up from the nonverbal elements of communication—from facial expressions, laughter, gestures, and the general mood or tone of the conversation as it ranged from thoughtful and quiet to animated and expressive. Hall (1959), Birdwhistell

(1961), and others have written excellent books and articles on nonverbal communications. Nonverbal expressions have been shown to have deep cultural origins, to represent a kind of silent language; it may well be that, like music, nonverbal language speaks directly to emotional and intuitive zones of consciousness.

A major breakthrough in understanding interpersonal communication was achieved when the late Eric Berne developed the theory of *transactional analysis* (1964). Berne viewed the *transaction*, the verbal message exchanged between two persons, as the basic unit of social relations. As such, analyzing the kinds and qualities of transactions became the key to understanding much about the relationship between one human being and another; hence the term transactional analysis, or TA, emerged. Berne stated that all of us have three different ego states; that we are in a sense three people in one. These different states Berne labeled Parent, Adult, and Child. Psychiatrists and psychologists have known for some time that we are influenced in adult life by events that occurred in our childhood. They have often not known exactly how prior events affect us, nor have they known to what degree our memory of them is operative. Now, thanks to some excellent neurophysiological research performed by Dr. Wilder Penfield (as reported and used by Eric Berne), there is much greater certainty about these issues. Penfield's (1952) experiments proved conclusively that every event of conscious perception in our entire life is recorded and stored in the brain. These events, when prompted by appropriate stimulation, can be played back into our consciousness like a tape recording. Two of Penfield's findings are most significant. The first is that the brain plays back only sensory data; that is, singular recollections or impressions of actual events. The brain does not play back mixtures of memories and generalizations or abstractions about them. One might say the information comes back *clean* and *straight*, directly as it happened, like a verbatim account. The second, and most exciting, finding is that the singular recollections or impressions of events that are stored and played back are kept and represented not merely as *facts*, but also as *feelings*. In discovering that both the simple idea of a past event and our feeling about it are inextricably locked together, so that one cannot be evoked without the other, Penfield eliminated forever any validity to the notion that facts are more important than feelings or emotions. The counsel one occasionally hears to not become emotional is impossible to observe. Every human being is a thinking, feeling person, and thoughts and feelings impress themselves *simultaneously* upon our consciousness. Thus feelings are also facts, and facts are always interlocked with their associated feelings. Penfield's research also tends to confirm the fusion of both consciousness and action discussed previously.

Let us take a closer look at the ego states of Parent, Adult, and Child. The states of Parent and Child come from our prior life experience and are recorded in our memory, being brought to consciousness by means of appropriate stimulation.

The Parent state is recorded in our memory as a recollection of our own parents (and of other parent figures we encountered as children). Berne pointed out that we are usually influenced by both our father and mother; therefore there is always a potential conflict between the two parties in the Parent state that leads to a weakening or fragmenting of the parental recordings. He divided the Parent state into two categories—the *critical*, or controlling, and the *nurturing*, or accepting. These categories also conform directly with the Type A and Type B behaviors and represent fundamental behavior categories.

Berne describes the Child ego state as adapted and natural. "The adapted child is the one who modifies his behavior under the parental influence" while the natural child is represented by a "spontaneous expression: independence or a searching creativity, for example." In our structural concept, the adapted child conforms to the Type A world imposed by his or her parents, while the natural child uses Type B behaviors.

The Adult state is that of our present (here and now) situation. When we become able to identify the influence of our Parent and Child ego states on our behavior and can recognize which state is operating, we are able to deal more directly and authentically with others. This notion was made clear by Berne when he disclosed the effect of *complementary* or *crossed* transactions. These are diagramed in Fig. 4.4, which shows all of the possible transactions that may occur between each of the three ego states of any two persons.

Complementary transactions are those in which there is a direct correspondence between two ego states. Adult speaks to Adult and receives a direct response. In complementary transactions the response is appropriate and expected. For example, Question: "Where are you going?" Answer: "To the

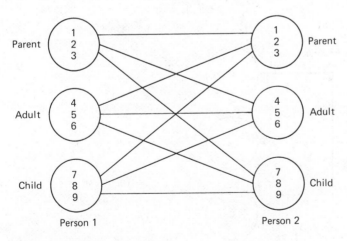

Fig. 4.4 A relationship diagram

store to buy some bread." Another example of a complementary transaction is found where two different ego states are in direct correspondence, for example Parent to Child and Child back to Parent. Parent: "Put on your shoes." Child: "Help me untie the knots."

Crossed transactions, on the other hand, are those wherein there is no direct correspondence between two ego states. For example, Adult speaks to Adult ("Where are my shoes?") and the response, instead of coming directly back from Adult ("I put them in your closet"), comes back either from Parent ("If you put them where they belong, you would be able to find them yourself") or from Child ("I planted flowers in them"). A crossed transaction is diagramed in Fig. 4.5.

Crossed transactions are usually confusing and ambiguous. As such, they increase the energy level or block its flow and thus lead to conflict. Complementary transactions maintain an even balance or flow of energy and provide role clarity and an easy and open exchange of information.

Berne also describes what he calls *ulterior* transactions wherein more than one level of meaning is being employed. An Adult conversation may be taking place, for example, but double meaning introduces a form of play or deception at the psychological level that is characteristic of a transaction between two Child states; that is, a game is being played. Berne describes two forms of ulterior transactions, the angular and the duplex, and shows how these forms of communication lead to breakdowns in interpersonal relationships.

Another important dimension of transactional analysis is that of *life position*. Life positions were described vividly by Thomas A. Harris in his well-known book *I'm OK—You're OK* (1969). According to Harris, a life position is taken by each of us as a result of our experience of ourselves and others and our beliefs about ourselves and others. Harris says, "Very early in life every child concludes 'I'm not OK.' He makes a conclusion about his parents

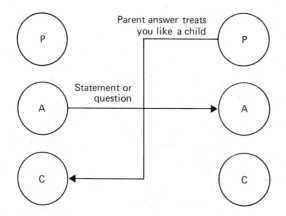

Fig. 4.5 A crossed transaction

also: 'You're OK.' " This decision about ourselves and our parents gets recorded and becomes the foundation of dependency, and it may block the emergence of interdependent or authentic adult relationships in later life. Other possible positions are, "I'm not OK—You're not OK either," which comes about when the child for whatever reason ceases to receive affirmation (or positive strokes), and "I'm OK—You're not OK," which comes about when a child has been brutalized by a parent and as a result has learned to lick his own wounds and to survive without parental love and affection. This latter is what Harris calls the "criminal position" and may well be the origin of criminal behavior. The final position is called "I'm OK—You're OK" and is different from the first three, all of which tend to operate at the unconscious level. This final position comes about as a result of a conscious decision made by the Adult ego state and is a dimension of maturation. While it may be held only some of the time instead of all of the time, it is also the hallmark of the effective integration of Type B (the capacity for acceptance of others) and Type A (willingness to make decisions and take action) behaviors that we see as necessary prerequisites for competent problem-finding and problem-solving activity.

Transactional analysis helps us to unravel some of the mystery and frustration that surrounds much interpersonal and intergroup communication. It is easy to see why many managers and administrators would prefer one-to-one relationships, especially if they are constantly presented with subordinate attitudes that telegraph the hidden meaning, "I'm not OK" or "You're not OK." Managers may themselves feel that they're not OK or that others are not OK and may not realize how their beliefs and feelings about others can engender attitudes of conformity, low risk taking, and dependency among subordinates. Whenever "not OK" rears its ugly head there is a loss of human energy and a blocking of efforts to succeed in problem finding and problem solving. When "not OK" emerges between individuals or in groups, Type B behavior becomes restricted and Type A behavior becomes utilized for blocking, defending, and attacking rather than for facilitating collaborative effort needed for task accomplishment.

The tremendous interest in transactional analysis in recent years gives ample testimony to the fact that a great many people in organizations are aware of the existence of interpersonal conflict and would like to be able to take constructive action against it. Dorothy Jongeward and Muriel James collaborated on an excellent book, entitled *Born to Win* (1971), that combines transactional analysis with insights from Gestalt psychology. They have also prepared a fine book of practical exercises in TA called *Winning with People* (1972). Both volumes help readers significantly in developing an understanding of how organizational conflict develops and how it can be resolved. I have found one additional insight particularly helpful: it is called the Karpman triangle. According to this theory there are three roles that arise in all conflict situations: *victim, persecutor,* and *rescuer.* If you want to figure out what "games" are being played in a conflict situation in which you are involved, try to diagnose who is playing each of the three roles. Then try to find out how the different role recipients see themselves in the situation and what payoffs exist for all three. According to Karpman, there must be a payoff or the game ends for one, two, or all three participants.

In considering the theory of transactional analysis we have so far looked at transactions between individual persons.* We may also consider the processes through which groups transact business or information with each other. We are all familiar with the notion of turf. Geographical boundaries have served as points of conflict for centuries, and there is always an incipient question about what belongs to whom. We have also seen how quickly group norms are formed. Personal identity and a sense of belonging combine to create in-group/out-group boundaries that are just as real and likely to be protected as geographical ones. Showing identification and "purpose of visit" is often just as crucial in entering another group as it is in crossing through Checkpoint Charlie into East Berlin.

What is it in organizational turf or boundary that is significant in terms of human energy potential? What are the skills needed to enter another group effectively and gain membership in it? How can I enjoy membership in more than one group at a time without finding myself in an untenable position? How can I move freely from one group to another? These questions are crucial to management and we shall discuss them more fully in the next chapter; it is nevertheless interesting to consider the potential of transactional analysis in assessing problems that exist from group to group or between groups.

There is, of course, much more to the subject of transactional analysis. A brief overview is presented here only to demonstrate the importance of understanding these issues as one of the key behavioral dimensions of group life.

When we consider the problems inherent in role clarification, participative decision making, and transactional analysis, it is little wonder that we experience the kinds of individual, organizational, and community problems that we see everywhere. Yet we must come to terms with these issues and problems in order to bring about improved situations and greater effectiveness in building authentic personal relationships and in accomplishing necessary tasks. And as life appears to be getting more complicated every day, we need to learn about these issues in order to cope effectively with present realities.

---

* The theory of transactional analysis is derived from the psychoanalytic theory of Sigmund Freud. As such it is based on operational aspects of ego function and is essentially ego psychology. Carl Jung transcended ego psychology by introducing the theory of the unconscious and by joining the ego and the unconscious into a unified theory of the self (psyche). To expand Freudian TA into Jungian TA, change the circles in Figs. 4.4 and 4.5 to action and consciousness matrices and contemplate the potential influence of the personal and collective unconscious on the roles of Parent, Adult, and Child.

GROUP CONSCIOUSNESS

In Chapter 3, I referred briefly to Jung's concept of human consciousness. It is now appropriate to ask if there exists a collective or group consciousness. Are there commonalities of consciousness that can be observed from group to group or among all human groups in general? It appears that human groups possess a group consciousness that is more than the sum of the total consciousness of individual group members. There is a special awareness of what it is like to be a part of this or that group. Some groups seem to enhance the well-being of some or all of their members. Other groups seem to operate in ways that are detrimental to some (or even all) members. By the same token, some individuals seem to enhance group activity, while others inhibit it; some exert positively destructive influences. What accounts for the differences of conscious awareness in groups?

When people meet in a group for a common purpose they bring to that meeting the sum total of their knowledge and experience, their background, traditions, and culture. They bring their personalities and idiosyncrasies, their

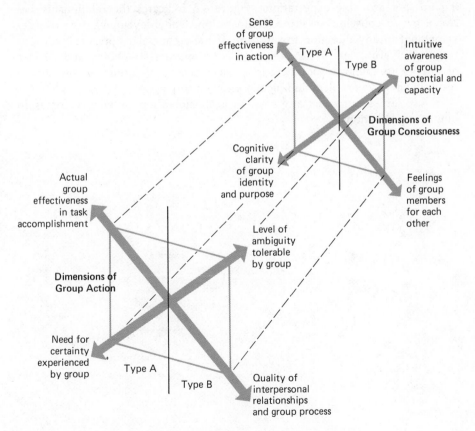

Fig. 4.6 Dimensions of group action and group consciousness

present levels of human energy, and their present levels of awareness of the behavioral dimensions of group life. Thus group apathy, group conflict, group indifference, and group creativity are all directly traceable to the combined individual awareness of group members.

What is at stake here is a very basic and important concept. Issues of influence, social distance, and expectation have a profound effect on how people feel about themselves and others. If people in a group feel that they have little or no influence on the group or on the leader; if they feel a lack of closeness and a lack of informality, coupled with manifestations of social distance; and if their expectations are not being met or fulfilled, there is every reason to believe that individual and group energy will be greatly diminished.

Not only are individual feelings important, but also what individuals think about the group, what they imagine or intuitively understand about it, and what they actually experience by being part of it. Thus all four dimensions of individual consciousness combine to make up group consciousness. Group action is a result of group consciousness, and group consciousness must be raised to improve performance when the group itself is not performing up to reasonable expectations. Figure 4.6 indicates the relationship between group consciousness and group action. Underdevelopment or overdevelopment in any direction toward any of the eight polar opposites will lead to group dysfunction. What is needed is an appropriate ebbing and flowing of energy to integrate both group consciousness and group action and to result in effective problem finding and problem solving.

Now let us turn our attention to a consideration of energy forces in human organizations.

5 Conserving Energy in Human Organizations

In the previous chapters I have endeavored to sketch in some detail the energy fields of human action and human consciousness. I have also expressed the belief that problem finding and problem solving are vitally important human activities and I have shown how energy forces are involved in these activities. In Chapter 4 we saw that our social and work lives require all but a very few of us to interact constantly with others; thus the energy dynamics of group and interpersonal relations are of key concern and we must be consciously aware of them to be effective in our problem-finding and problem-solving efforts with others. Nowhere does this appear to be more true than in large, multigroup organizations. Yet most organizations, be they government entities or segments of private enterprise (and many of our smaller organizations as well), systematically and consciously waste much valuable human energy precisely because they pay little attention to the development of Type B behaviors and Type B consciousness.

Wasted energy is less apparent in directly measurable production jobs. Workers whose output is linked to the operation of machines have little choice other than to keep pace, resign, or be discharged. In these settings the human energy crisis reveals itself with absenteeism, labor disputes, accidents, and even acts of deliberate destructiveness. There are, of course, millions of production workers who continuously produce work of top quality, but a variation of only a few percentage points in production levels is sufficient to produce a problem of crisis proportions.

The major manifestation of human energy waste today is much more prevalent in service occupations, in white-collar and clerical jobs, in administrative positions of every description, and particularly in the ranks of management. Energy waste may be found at its peak wherever output is difficult or impossible to measure and wherever effective performance is dependent upon collaborative interaction between individuals, departments, divisions, or even whole companies. It tends to occur at its very worst in the interpersonal relationships between supervisors and subordinates and among the various levels of the ranks of managers. Today's crisis of human energy causes the loss of billions of dollars annually, a loss that goes largely unrecognized not only because the causative factors are quite difficult to identify or measure but also because many managers and administrators have come to accept this wasteful situation as normal. Some managers try to rationalize its manifestations with Type A labels. We have grown quite accustomed to hearing, for example, such things as, "They can't get along because of personality differences," or "He's a troublemaker." There is also a marked tendency to reward those who stay out of trouble, get along well with everyone, and always look busy. Those who make waves or rock the boat, on the other hand, even though they may possess a high level of energy and have a proven record of outstanding accomplishments, are somehow regarded with suspicion and trepidation. In most organizations in which I have worked, individuals who took risks, especially in the area of interpersonal relations, were often passed over for promotion; they soon grew impatient with the organization and finally resigned to seek greener pastures. In many organizations it is a well-known fact that the best people always leave.

The human energy crisis is a critical problem today not simply because it is enormously costly but also because it has become so integral a part of our culture. Cultural problems are extremely difficult to solve precisely because they tend to operate at an unconscious level and because changes require the disruption or rearrangement of accepted norms and practices. As we saw in Chapter 4, questioning group norms raises conflict; yet without a certain amount of conflict, within bounds, there can be no progress.

How did this tendency to waste human energy become so deeply ingrained in our culture? It may be valuable to sketch a historical picture that will show how we developed two of our most cherished symbols, symbols that are a major cause of our present extraordinary difficulty. These two symbols, which I shall describe momentarily, are imbued with great power precisely because they have been associated with such remarkable success in the past. The difficulty today lies in not recognizing that successful concepts and practices may, when conditions change, become at best useless and at worst dangerous. The critical issue is that of discovering the changed conditions in time to take corrective action. We are in danger today because the net effect of the human energy crisis is a subtle but persistent erosion of our strength as a nation and a lowering of our standard of living; wasted energy is the fundamental cause of the rampant inflation and simultaneous unemployment so characteristic of recent years. Let us examine how we reached this most unenviable position.

The ambiguity of the opportunity facing a young nation with rich natural resources, inexpensive and abundant immigrant labor, and vast tracts of undeveloped land called for entrepreneurs who could provide the structure and control necessary to turn potentially promising situations into financial successes. Enormous fortunes lay waiting in mining, agriculture, manufacturing, transportation, finance, and even entertainment for those highly motivated individuals who would be able to put human and material resources to work. Leaders in business and industry learned very early that it was absolutely necessary to build effective human organizations if they were to successfully manage their ever-growing commercial empires. In the United States large organizations evolved naturally from successful small ventures, and by 1850 a large number of corporations in a variety of fields had come into existence and were flourishing. The nineteenth and early twentieth centuries brought the Industrial Revolution, begun in the eighteenth century, to full flower. So-called Yankee ingenuity, the capacity to devise ways of solving complex mechanical (and also business) problems, brought our nation to the position of being the most economically powerful nation on earth by 1940. Our success in World War II added political and military leadership to our established economic prominence. However this preeminent position was not won without great human cost and sacrifice. The major point to recognize is that the sacrifice was made possible because nearly everyone was committed to the tasks to be accomplished.

American workers left the land and flocked to burgeoning cities, where they were joined by the disenchanted and dispossessed from Europe and elsewhere. They were filled with rising expectations, a great faith in America, and a willingness to work hard to achieve a better quality of life than their parents and grandparents had known. They possessed great energy; the less energetic and the less confident had been left behind. They demonstrated a willingness to take risks and to place trust in an uncertain future. Many were well rewarded, some handsomely, and that great American phenomenon, the middle class, began to emerge.

As purchasing power increased the nation's economy grew and grew. And so did prices and wages. As demand increased, production had to be increased to meet it. Workers found it necessary to organize and bargain collectively for increased purchasing power and management had to find more efficient means of production. As the population grew by leaps and bounds, the consumption of goods and services rose astronomically. It has continued in this manner to the present day.

It must be observed that nearly everything the great entrepreneurs did seemed to work beyond perhaps even their wildest expectations. Men like Andrew Carnegie, Henry Ford, John D. Rockefeller, and dozens like them combined to build the greatest private productive enterprise in history. And this enterprise is still growing on a worldwide scale as United States companies expand into multinational conglomerates and meet their foreign counterparts in an international marketplace. Nothing breeds continued effort as much as success.

It is only natural that the large number of professional managers who have now taken over the reins of the major United States corporations would have a healthy respect for the basic ideas of the early entrepreneurs. These ideas, having worked so well, cannot be discarded lightly. However, though it is perhaps foolhardy to criticize success, today we are finding ourselves in a situation that seems to call for a wholly new strategy. If the past hundred years could be characterized as a period of industrial expansion and colonial consolidation, as a period of profit taking arising from the reduction of colossal ambiguity to certainty, the next hundred years may well be a period of increasing ambiguity coming about as the result of new forces arising to challenge established authorities everywhere. This appears true on the international as well as the domestic scene. Many groups today are raising serious questions about the success of our great industrial enterprise. They say it is not as successful as it appears and has brought with it evils such as pollution and discrimination, to name just two. The use of overt or covert force against the present challenges to the establishment will inevitably meet counterforce and counterresistance. The net effect will be destructive and costly. As an alternative we need to now develop a counterstrategy, aimed simultaneously at increasing our toleration of ambiguity, reducing the sources of conflict, and conserving human energy.

I will now attempt to demonstrate that the two great normative assumptions on which industrial era organizations have been built are hopelessly inadequate for the task that lies ahead. The two familiar symbols that characterize these assumptions are the machine and the pyramid.

THE GREAT MACHINE MODEL

In order to bring about the control necessary for a large organization to function it was necessary to find a suitable model and a symbol of organized efficiency. Nothing could be more suitable or inevitable during the industrial revolution than to seize upon the model that was the primary focus of everyone's attention: the machine. The assumption was that humans could be molded and shaped into organizations that would function with machinelike efficiency. The primary concern was to develop a rigid structure that would operate with repetitive efficiency, generate a minimum of friction (conflict), and have a high degree of task effectiveness or output. It is easy to see the mechanistic influence behind terms such as "unity of direction," "chain of command," and "span of control." No machine could go in several directions at once without destroying itself. Connecting rods of the proper size and strength were used as spans to connect wheels in a locomotive, for example, to provide for simultaneous turning. Chains were also typical of the machine era, and the notion that a chain was only as strong as its weakest link provided sufficient motivation to replace "weak links" (poor performers). Those in the "chain" of command were entitled to proprietary information; others were not. When things weren't going well, managers were told to "tighten things up." A "turn of the screw here" and the "replacement of a part (person) there" were seen as necessary to keep the machine in operation. The top man conceived of himself and was seen by others as the operator of the machine. Other managers were often considered to be simply extensions of (or alter egos of) the top man. In this sense, then, the boss as controller and operator could easily regard himself as the only truly *human* person in the organization. It was his natural function alone to make the rational decisions. Others were there to carry them out. Training programs for managers were developed to improve capacity in rational decision making; training programs for workers were developed to increase skill or to condition them to perform as required. Usually the development of creative or innovative capacity in workers was ignored. First it was thought there was no place to use this capacity; then suggestion plans were developed to catch accidental worker discoveries, or "sparks." The machine was set up; all "they" had to do was run it. There developed a distinction between *heads* and *hands:* heads were the bosses and thinkers; hands were the workers. The idea that hands could also think was considered totally irrelevant.

The bureaucratic machine model ran also on the twin principles of accelerating power and repetition. Those who gained power were stimulated to seek more and greater power. The idea of releasing power to others was unthinkable, for control could never be relinquished or relaxed. If something worked, it was to be repeated again and again indefinitely. If something did not work, it was to be tried again and again until it did work. One underlying assumption was that anything could be made to work if enough effort and energy were expended. Quantity began to be valued over quality. Human energy was channeled and released on a regulated, routine basis. A standard work week and a standard work day became the measure for production. Human power was harnessed, much like water, electric, or steam power. It was turned on and off at the beginning and end of each shift—every day, week after week, year after dreary year. Even school took on the characteristics of industrial machinery. Schools prepared workers to take their place as machine parts. Alvin Toffler (1970) stated it well:

> The whole administrative hierarchy of education, as it grew up, followed the model of industrial bureaucracy. The very organization of knowledge into permanent disciplines was grounded on industrial assumptions. Children marched from place to place and sat in assigned stations. Bells rang to announce changes of time.

> The inner life of the school thus became an anticipatory mirror, a perfect introduction to industrial society. The most criticized features of education today—the regimentation, lack of individualization, the rigid systems of seating, grouping, grading and marking, the authoritarian role of the teacher— are precisely those that made mass public education so effective an instrument of adaptation for its place and time.

Both the attitude and the organizational approaches of machine theory are pervasive and deeply rooted in our society. They are found in all kinds of organizations—including government, churches, universities, and hospitals—as well as in business and industry. Their practices have become a ubiquitous part of our everyday life.

Ironically, because the norms of machine theory are pervasive, lower-level bosses began to imitate the behaviors of the man at the top. When they were treated as parts of the machine, they in turn treated their subordinates in the same fashion. This behavioral mirror may have worked well through the 1940s, but the tremendous increase of organizational complexity and task specialization that has occurred in the past twenty-five years now requires everyone in an organization to assume responsibility for his or her actions and to be actively involved in making the organization work effectively; everyone must be able to *think* as well as *do*. In addition people have come to deeply resent being treated like cogs in the wheel, and in an organizational system that implicitly treats them that way even managers who try to be different will have little success, for they will suffer from guilt by association with the organization machine whenever they try to carry out its mandates. No one can question the machine as a model of order and control, or that its conception was terribly exciting to our eighteenth-century ancestors. It promised to revolutionize the world, and it has. Nor can one question that Frederick Taylor and many generations of industrial and management engineers have made a major contribution to our economy and standard of living by fantastically improving our industrial production through the application of mass-production methods and production standards. What is questionable is not what machine theory can do, but what it can't do.

Also questionable are the effects that machine-theory organizations have on their workers and managers alike. In recent years many people have begun to realize that it may be the way we have organized work itself that is the cause of our greatest social, economic, political, and even physical ills. As life in our time has become increasingly complex, the organizations in which most of us work have appeared to become less and less efficient and satisfying. The "blue-collar blues" and "white-collar woes" reported in the U.S. Department of Health, Education, and Welfare's study entitled *Work in America* (1973) cuts to the heart of an epidemic problem. The special problems of minorities, women, and the aged compound the difficulty and lead one to ask: Does anyone enjoy working in an organization anymore?

As organizational tension and frustration mount, efforts to improve communications, planning, motivation, and control proliferate, but the economic statistics seem to indicate that we are losing ground. When rampant inflation and increasing unemployment occur simultaneously is there not ample evidence that something is seriously amiss? Can it be that the social and technological changes of the twentieth century have placed so much stress on the nineteenth-century bureaucratic model of organizational efficiency that it has now come close to the breaking point?

It would perhaps be unfair to say, or even imply, that all mechanistic organizations are hopeless. In any age of transition it is always necessary to endure the continuing effects of the old order as new circumstances and conditions arise. It is important to recognize the primary limitations inherent in the mechanistic organization, however, and when the signs of these limitations are becoming more evident it may be appropriate to begin to apply some of the corrective strategies outlined further on in this chapter.

The primary signs of the negative impact of machine-theory organizations are, first, worker or manager boredom, alienation, and disinterest. These symptoms generally arise from overcontrol and lack of autonomy. A second sign is that of a highly task-oriented and uncreative organizational environment where reams of statistics, data, and paperwork are generated but where little progress is made in developing variable solutions to problems or in trying out new problem-solving approaches requiring increased collaboration between individuals and groups. Proponents of machine organization do not conceive of interpersonal interaction. Parts of a machine do not interact or change; they carry out their required function in isolation; when they are rubbed together the friction (conflict) must be either removed with "oil" (rational explanation) or "parts" (people) must be removed or replaced. A third sign is when the organization offers little chance for advancement, personal growth, new experience, or career development. The whole concept of human development is alien in machine theory; machines simply do not develop. They wear out or become obsolete, but growth in the sense of development and change is inconceivable. A fourth sign is ineffective handling of conflict. Organizations built on machine-theory conceptions will not tolerate the ambiguity of conflict or even of conflict-laden feedback. The machine never talks back to its operators. The machine never suggests how it might be set up or when and in what manner it might function best. All initiative thus must remain with the operator, who, as we have said, makes all the decisions for turning on and turning off.

Let us now look at the other great symbol of the industrial era, the pyramid.

THE PYRAMIDAL STRUCTURE

The typical organizational model encountered in multigroup bureaucratic organizations, built on machine theory, is that of the pyramid. The hierarchical model appeals to common sense. The familiar boxes of an organizational chart, connected by lines (showing direct supervisor/subordinate relationships) and dotted lines (showing a reporting relationship to another superior who is not your direct boss), provide a logical structure that allows for clarification of roles, relationships, and appropriate behavior. The pyramid also shows all too clearly that the higher the job's level the fewer people there are at that level—thus authority, power, and responsibility all increase as one moves upward.

I have said the model appeals to common sense, to conventional logic. It also strongly appeals to the emotions. The sense of the ascending order of power gives to those at the top a feeling of involvement and essentiality that creates a strong bond between their own sense of self-worth and their sense of responsibility to protect the organization and disperse its favors and patronage to those most deserving. Thus a hierarchical organization creates a strong magnetic attraction toward the top as power becomes more and more concentrated until it finally becomes ultimate in the one who occupies the single position at the pinnacle.

Within the pyramidal structure itself, roles and functions are divided in accordance with the principle of specialization of labor into two general categories—line and staff. Line (direct productive action) and staff (indirect support services) are established to separate supposedly essential from supposedly nonessential (or overhead) functions and activities. It is of course ironic to see how powerful many staff (supposedly nonessential) departments have become, often at the expense of line organizations, and also how confused and blurred the original simplistic line/staff conception has become in recent years. Far from being simply supportive, many staff organizations have now become controlling. Staff departments exercise control through access to generalized information, usually unavailable to smaller components of line organizations. Hence staff people are in the know and have more or less direct access to senior line managers. Rather than trusting their subordinates to give them a realistic appraisal of operating problems, senior line managers have come to rely increasingly on the statistical reports, charts, indexes, profiles, graphs, and records carefully developed and codified by their legions of clerical and middle-management staff personnel. Many senior managers play the numbers game, preferring to deal with numbers instead of people; numbers have become a favorite and fashionable managerial indoor sport.

The term *pyramid*, literally translated, means "fire in the middle." The term is most apt because this form of organization seems to concentrate the greatest heat on the middle-level management position. It is the middle managers who receive the pressure from both the top and the bottom. Energy in a pyramid moves naturally toward the middle.

In an excellent article entitled "General Managers in the Middle," Hugo Uyterhoeven (1972) indicated that handling conflicting role expectations and managing relationships among peers, subordinates, and superiors in a hierarchy require "a strong constitution and a juggler's finesse." It is entirely possible (in fact, probable) that we chew up and destroy some of our very best managerial talent in the corporate hierarchical meat grinder. In fact, one major American corporation privately admits a 25–30 percent failure rate among its ranks of general managers. There must be an easier and less costly way.

C. Northcote Parkinson's whimsical law, "Work multiplies to fill the time and space available," underscores the fact that in a pyramidal hierarchy there is never enough time, never enough space, and always too much work. Being overworked, overcrowded, and understaffed is a common malady shared by nearly all hardy souls who dare to brave the hierarchical stratosphere by taking a job in management. While apathy, boredom, and lack of commitment often run rampant among those who occupy lower rungs on the ladder of success, most general managers seem to cling to the belief that the present system will work if only they work harder—that finally they will succeed in motivating the apathetic by their good example. What else can they do? The higher you rise in an organization the more committed you are to maintaining its norms, the status quo.

Walt Kelly's memorable comic strip of July 11, 1970, which was aimed at solving the pollution problem, applies equally well to perpetuators of hierarchical organizations. In it, Pogo Possum bravely announced, "We have met the enemy and he is us!" Somewhat ruefully, Charles Shultz's *Peanuts* gang might answer in chorus, "How can we lose when we're so sincere?"

In an effort to solve organizational problems, many top executives play with lives and careers as if the organization chart were a giant chessboard. People are shifted from box to box, often without being consulted, and strategic moves are contemplated for their potential positive effects on profits. Managers in many corporations are expected to move, and refusal of a new assignment is often not kindly regarded. When things are not going well, a shake-up is frequently called for and there is a mass exodus of players or "pieces" to make way for a new "team." Reorganization follows disorganization, recentralization follows decentralization, and when all fail it is time to consider mergers or acquisitions. As a result of arbitrary organization changes, managers are often assigned to organizations and to businesses they know nothing about and the hierarchical order tends to prevent them from receiving honest and straightforward information from subordinates until it is too late to prevent financial disasters of major proportions.

Perhaps it's the anxiety of not having a readily available alternative that forces us to press on in the face of mounting obstacles, or perhaps it is simply a reluctance to come to terms with a system that one has negotiated successfully and from which one has received substantial rewards. Nevertheless, the pressure on the bureaucratic style and practice of hierarchical management continues to grow daily, and those in positions of authority and responsibility are now often seen as increasingly incompetent by their superiors, peers, and subordinates alike. In their insightful, funny, and unfunny study of hierarchies, Laurence J. Peter and Raymond Hull (1969) identified rampant incompetency at the upper levels of organizations as a malfunction in the process of promotion. The Peter principle, that in a hierarchy every employee tends to rise to his level of incompetence, points to an observable phenomenon, but there is a far more complex issue here than this principle seems to indicate. While it may appear as though there is a fixed point beyond which a person cannot develop, most of the evidence from educational research indicates that this is simply not true.

It appears rather that pyramidal hierarchies frequently create no-win situations in which the person in charge of a group or a department appears to be incompetent because of a convergence of forces beyond his or her control.

While you are fighting one fire, four others are raging out of control. Incompetence is a handy label that, when applied, avoids calling attention to a larger issue. It now appears that the very foundation of organizational structure, the pyramidal hierarchy, is hopelessly outmoded. As a result, those still trying to use the methods of the past only appear to be incompetent: the real lack may lie in their not yet having discovered a new theory and mastered the practices of a new approach; of not yet having developed a strategy for adapting to a changed environment. Those who are successful today, on the other hand, are probably already using new methods and succeed in spite of the structural limitations imposed on them by the pyramidal form of organization.

Three additional problems, all of which have intensified in recent times, add to the present dysfunction observable in pyramidal forms of organization. First is the friction between generalists and specialists. Often we find a generalist appointed to lead a department consisting of a group of specialists. The specialists tend to disrespect their new leader ("He's not really one of us and he doesn't understand the crucial issues in our field") while the generalists tend to look at the big picture and mistrust a narrow or specialized point of view as being too myopic. The generalists' directions, however, often miss the subtle insights required for effective practice. As the wave of increasing specialization continues, the generalists will not be able to retain leadership positions unless they learn the language and techniques of the highly specialized groups they are leading. One insightful commentator on today's scene claims that what we need is not more generalists or specialists, but more *multispecialists* (men and women who know one field deeply but can cross over into other fields as well) rather than rigid *monospecialists* (Toffler, 1970).

Second, it is difficult for managers within pyramidal hierarchies to determine the exact nature of the problems they face because they operate in situations of limited access, information, and control; this leads as we have seen to more or less constant frustration. Many people feel trapped by the organizations in which they work. They can't solve their problems, but they don't want to quit because they know the same problems exist in other organizations as well. Going through life unsatisfied and uninspired, many people learn to make the best of the situation. As youthful excitement and optimism drains away, people settle down to a routine in which conformity becomes a solidly established norm. It is not surprising, therefore, that managers experience difficulty in motivating others to produce work of high quality and outstanding quantity. Many potentially productive people have long since "resigned in place" and do the minimal work necessary to get by. In order to successfully reengage the energies of these people, leaders must somehow convince them that there is a whole new ball game in which they are invited to play.

Third, we can observe an increasing trend toward pulling individuals from different functional departments and forming them into program or project teams. These teams are transient, but they tend to break down loyalties and to diminish membership in the original base groups or functional departments. The functional department head who loses some of his best people in this manner feels left out of the action. He is requested to stay at his post and leave the exciting battles to the project team. This is a familiar problem experienced in so-called matrix organizations, which are themselves partial attempts to overcome the rigidities and inefficiencies of the pyramidal hierarchy.

Hierarchical Decisions and the Acceptance of Responsibility

Another important contributor to organizational dysfunction in a pyramidal hierarchy is the way in which many management groups choose to deal with problems. One decision-making method that I have seen frequently applied in business and industry can be summarized as follows:

1. A problem situation arises.

2. A meeting or series of meetings is set up to discuss the problem. Facts, more facts, and counterfacts are produced. Rebuttals to the counterfacts are then offered but are usually ignored.

3. A plan for resolution is formulated based on the beliefs of the senior manager presiding at the meeting(s). Other beliefs are generally not discussed.

4. A solution is sought in accordance with the plan dictated.

5. A periodic review of progress is conducted.

6. A decision is eventually made to change people or the organization's structure when the plan fails.

This approach places the senior manager at the greatest possible disadvantage. He has the highest stakes in the game, holds the most cards in his own hands, yet often possesses the least amount of detailed and accurate information about how the game is being played. Usually all others involved have more information about specific parts of the problem than he does. The key question is: Will available information be shared openly? When things are not going well, crucially important information involving organizational or personal conflict frequently does not get out into the open because no one wants to be blamed for not getting along well with others. Under conditions of organizational stress, most people play the game with their cards held close to their vests. Frustration continues to rise proportionately.

Problems that are attacked using the six steps outlined above are seldom fully resolved; instead, other crises arise and the initial problem gets pushed into the background. Sometimes a renewed effort emerges that takes the form of a special project, but eventually problems that can't be solved come to be accepted as the way things are.

Relationships between groups in formal organizational structures tend to follow strict protocol. Conflict patterns typically form in horizontal relationships and are suppressed in vertical or supervisor/subordinate relationships. The solution to conflicts arising between separate structural units (individuals or departments) is generally sought by means of appeals to higher-level authority. Much time is lost in trading and negotiating territorial rights and imperatives and in trying to ascertain the correctness of information so as to determine who is at fault. Examples of this kind are easy to find and are typical of most multigroup bureaucratic organizations. Oddly enough, many people think this situation is normal because they know of no other way. *Snafu* was a term coined in the military bureaucracy to connote that the situation could be expected to be normally fouled up.

There is a most interesting phenomenon that can be observed when one contrasts the organizational pyramid with what I and others have come to recognize as the *information pyramid.*

At the top of any organizational pyramid there tend to be very few people and great density of power. On the bottom, however, the power is widely dispersed among many people, with individuals possessing very little. Power at the top derives from the *possession of information* combined with the prerogatives of ownership or managerial authority. Top executives know more about the overall operation of the organization, and they have a broad conception of how their organization relates to and meshes with other organizations in the general society—suppliers, customers, regulating agencies, and distribution channels. Thus we can confidently say that *information is power.* Organizational decisions are based on information from various functional control centers like marketing, manufacturing, engineering, finance, and personnel. All operating strategies are implemented on the basis of available factual information. Of course there is always a question as to whether the information is reliable or complete (which it usually never is), but the person at the top nevertheless possesses the broadest overall view of what is going on.

Simultaneously, however, the person at the top tends to possess information of limited density or detail. Most executives don't want to be bothered with details at all, even though some details can be crucially important. Detailed *operational* information tends to increase in density as one moves downward through the organization. Descending successively through the pyramidal layers, one finds a decreasing awareness of the overall picture, but much more information about the *specific work situation* or specific organizational problems at that layer. In fact, when it comes to solving problems the people closest to a problem situation often have the best chance of coming up with a creative solution and, although they may be restricted by a limited overall view of what's happening, their viewpoint is needed if management is to avoid operating on the basis of unverified assumptions.

Information tends to flow downward in a hierarchical organization, but it is blocked on the way up by a successive screening out and filtering of negative feedback. Thus the boss at an upper level of an organization almost never receives direct, straight-from-the-shoulder information about problem situations as perceived by the men on the line. Instead, the information is filtered through structured memos, progress reports, statistical analyses, computer printouts, and special studies reports and often becomes lost or distorted in the process. What reaches the manager, therefore, is seldom a reliable basis for sound management decisions.

Much frustration and conflict at the lower levels of organizations occur precisely because information that is possessed there does not flow smoothly upwards. Also, many upper-level decisions coming down are seen as unrealistic and even harmful by those below. No organization can function unless it is guided by those who possess a broad vision of the total situation. The capacity of some to assume leadership has true social and economic value and can benefit all of us. However, leaders cannot function effectively unless they can quickly and accurately obtain (and accept nondefensively) both detailed and perceptual information. What appears to be needed is an effective two-way flow of information to prevent the widespread disaffection and waste of energy that occurs in most pyramidal hierarchies.

From the above description we can see that the information pyramid, which deals with density, detail, perception, and scope of information, is in an inverse position to the structural pyramid, which dispenses authority, responsibility, rewards, and punishments (see Fig. 5.1). Accountability is thus separated from its critical information source. It is no wonder that many of us feel caught in the middle of the conflicts and misperceptions occurring constantly at all organizational levels and all around us.

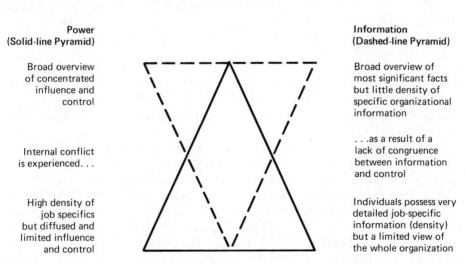

Power (Solid-line Pyramid)		Information (Dashed-line Pyramid)
Broad overview of concentrated influence and control		Broad overview of most significant facts but little density of specific organizational information
Internal conflict is experienced. . .		. . .as a result of a lack of congruence between information and control
High density of job specifics but diffused and limited influence and control		Individuals possess very detailed job-specific information (density) but a limited view of the whole organization

Fig. 5.1 The inverted information pyramid

While pyramidal hierarchies may legitimately be criticized for their tendency to mishandle organizational information and for their ineffectiveness in decision-making processes, by far the most damning indictment stems from the inability of pyramidal leaders to accept responsibility for their actions. When disaster strikes in a pyramidal organization one might expect that the chain of command would work in such a way that the top man would immediately be able to identify the problem situation and its perpetrators, one of whom may be himself. Unfortunately just the opposite occurs; there is a massive tendency to avoid responsibility and to pass the buck. Strong characters at the top will quickly affirm that the buck stops with them but all too often we see the top man in the role of a protected person, one who has not been bothered with getting the full detailed information about a problem situation. Therefore the top man is innocent of the misdeeds perpetrated by his organization and the organization seeks to be excused on the grounds of human fallibility—a victim of subordinates who exceeded their authority.

THE BEGINNINGS OF A LIVING SYSTEM DESIGN

It is apparent from the organizational dysfunction existing everywhere that the ancient and honorable pyramidal form of organization has passed its peak of usefulness. In addition, the widespread belief that organizations are analogous to machines becomes obsolescent when mass production ceases to be the primary need of organizations or of society. In the past decade it has become clear that when the techniques of mass production have been mastered and have proliferated on a wide scale, other problems arise that become critical in turn. We are now becoming well aware that the quantitative approach to both production and consumption produces massive problems when it comes to the question of ensuring such things as clean air, food, and water, quality of products such as automobiles and airplanes, adequate health care for all, satisfying working environments and opportunities, and quality of life for the young and the aged.

Feedback in the form of widespread social protest has begun to make an impact on government policy and on corporate behavior; but we are only at the beginning of a new era for we haven't yet given up the organizational forms and procedures that created many of our present problems in the first place.

There seems to be a growing awareness that great changes are needed, but so far no organizational arrangement has emerged that can effectively rival the powerful influence of the pyramidal form. What then, if anything, can be done to ease the burden our organizations have placed on us? How can we convert the organization machine that tends to use *us* as raw materials into a system of productive collaboration that will free us to become more human and more creative in the best sense of these terms? We must find an answer soon. The twenty-first century will never be able to tolerate nineteenth-century management practices, no matter how effective they were in their own time and place. It has often been said that the night is darkest just before the dawn. It appears that the negative effects of machine thinking as applied to human individuals and organizations have reached (or are about to reach) their peak. We may now look for signs of a new dawn and the signs are in fact clearly present. Marshall McLuhan (1965) expresses the new viewpoint vividly:

> After three thousand years of explosion, by means of fragmentary and mechanical technologies, the Western world is imploding. During the mechanical ages we had extended our bodies in space. Today, after more than a century of electric technology, we have extended our central nervous system itself in a global embrace, abolishing both space and time as far as our planet is concerned. Rapidly, we approach the final phase of the extensions of man—the technological simulation of consciousness, when the creative process of knowing will be collectively and corporately extended to the whole of human society, much as we have already extended our senses and our nerves by the various media.*

McLuhan's insight is at once startling and profoundly simple. The tremendous acceleration of information processing made possible first through the invention of the electronic circuit, which produced radio and then television, combined with the further development of electronic data processing via the computer, has brought us all incredibly closer together and made us vastly more aware of the nature of various situations and events affecting our lives. Now that we are more consciously aware of the problems we face we are experiencing a high degree of frustration because we have not yet developed the organization capability to deal with them. And most frustrating of all is the effort to make organizations more responsive to human needs, for here we run squarely into the culturally rooted machine conception and the pyramidal hierarchy. In the new electronic systems technologies a major guiding principle is feedback. As information is sent forth it intercepts or picks up new information and brings it back to its starting point, producing a changed situation. Thus the feedback loop constantly produces new information, making each sequential step a growing or developing addition to what has occurred before. This is a subtle but radical departure from mechanism, made more so because electronic technology possesses the capacity to fantastically increase the speed with which information is processed. It seems clear that the computer coupled with electronic technology will revolutionize man's conception of himself and will change social and cultural organizations. What has not yet fully emerged is the precise way in which this will occur. However, it is crucial that we find a way to utilize the new technological concepts in a management system that enables man to control his rapidly accelerated environment more effectively.

---

* From *Understanding Media*, by Marshall McLuhan. Copyright © 1965 by McGraw-Hill Book Company. Used with permission of McGraw-Hill Book Company and Routledge and Kegan Paul.

Thus we may well turn to systems science for help in finding a new organizational design. If we begin with a tentative assumption that any organization is a living system (or organism) rather than a machine, we approach a new viewpoint that will enable us to develop sufficiently different operating strategies and tactics to bring about a new situation. One primary characteristic of a living system model of an organization would be its aliveness. This kind of organization would constantly seek to attend to the growth and development needs of its members not by pursuing ancillary training and development activities but by creating conditions where growth and development would arise during and as a result of finding and implementing effective solutions to the primary internal and external problems faced by the organization itself.

A second characteristic of a living system design would be that of a three-dimensional viewpoint replacing the two-dimensional conception of mechanism. In addition to the mechanistic dimensions of rigid organization structure and repetitive function, there would be added the dimension of *process*—an ongoing analysis and assessment of the *way* in which events, problems, and situations are handled. The study of the process dimension has in recent times become a major orientation in such diverse fields as chemistry, physics, medicine, biology, drama, art, music, education, and interpersonal relations. In organizations, the processes looked at would be primarily interpersonal relations. Interpersonal processes would therefore be the *way* through which organizational change and growth would occur, for it is the process dimension that gives life to inert structures and blindly repetitive functions. Process modifies structure and gives it flexibility and adaptability. Process removes the mechanical orientation from function and replaces its repetitiveness with an experimental approach that produces art as well as science.

As we leave the machine age and advance into the age of living systems, we will also tend to develop a new perception of nature. Nature is already beginning to be seen less as an irrational adversary to be harnessed than as the life-supporting system of which we are all a part. The pioneers of the old West constantly battled nature in order to survive. Physical comfort was a great luxury and was seldom experienced. Today's technology has thankfully rendered nature much less harmful and has provided us with great physical comfort. While some feel that technology has now replaced nature as the primary threat to human life, it is technology or science that is helping us to understand what nature and life need for support and maintenance. We are beginning to see with our new ecological consciousness that the problems of individuals (microsystems), human organizations (systems and subsystems), and societies as a whole (macrosystems) are inextricably intertwined. We must conclude, therefore, that effective organizational designs will take these linkages and complex relationships into account. We have reached the point where we can no longer afford to have organizations and societies operating blindly and in isolation. The widely accepted corporate belief in maximizing growth and profits, based on natural laws of supply and demand, will have to be mitigated by a more selective assessment of social needs and more attention to growth and profit *optimization* rather than *maximization*. Also, greater awareness of systems implications is bound eventually to have a profound effect on the strategic planning process that takes place in most large organizations. As organizations (and governments) begin to assess their mission (*what* are we trying to do?), purpose (*why* are we doing it?), and plans (*how* can we best achieve what we are trying to do?) more realistically, it is inevitable that organizational dilemmas will arise. When optimization is sought instead of maximization, machine theory is further forced to give way to system integration, and unbridled competition turns into more orderly forms of collaboration.

Judging from the social needs emerging on a worldwide scale today, it is evident that the primary preoccupation of most individuals in positions of significant power and influence must necessarily be with the maintenance and improvement of the quality of life and of work, for there are no longer vast areas of unexplored territory to colonize. Warfare as a means of gaining political and/or economic advantage is becoming technologically too hazardous to risk, and the increasing accessibility of information (and consequent increase of the numbers of educated people in the world) is forcing world leaders to be responsive to the demands of the living for the support of life itself. It may well be that the key to human survival is in the creation of collaborative organizational structures. This is not to say that competition should be eliminated, but that it cannot be allowed to be the controlling norm as it has been under the mechanistic conception. In living systems competition is organic; it functions like muscular tension, to maintain health and vitality. All component subsystems and organs, like the circulatory system and the heart and lungs, collaborate for the health of the whole body. Could the heart attack the liver or the stomach attack the lungs? If so, no body would survive for long. In fact, when the heart malfunctions it is the whole body as well as the heart that sustains the damage. We may now be well on the way to viewing the whole world as a living organism, a living body composed of various systems (the monetary system, the energy system, the food system) and organs (nations or regional complexes of nations) that must collaborate for the health of the total world body. This view will not, of course, be popular with those who are still mired in mechanistic conceptions of ethnic, racial, or national superiority.

There are three primary needs that must be addressed in order to develop a living system design to replace the present bureaucratic form of organization. First, there is a need to find a new structural form to replace the pyramid. This new form must be capable of being portrayed graphically in chart form. Second, there is a need for a problem-finding, problem-solving process that will effectively overcome We/They polarizations in a majority of instances. Third, there must be a technique for gathering subjective attitudinal information from all organizational members that will be used in management decision making. Once these needs have been met there are two further needs that are required for implementation of the new design. First, an organization must actively seek to make the changeover from bureaucracy, and second, there must be a concerted effort to assist the organization's members and particularly its management in making those changes in behavior and attitudes necessary to support the new structure.

A New Structure and a New Chart

The need for a new structure to replace the pyramidal form is obvious. One requirement for such a structure is that of graphic and visual simplicity; another is that it must have a number of clear advantages over the old. The one symbol that I can find that possesses the above characteristics is a circle, or wheel. The circle is the great symbol of the universe. The sun, stars, and planets find their most natural organization in the emptiness of space to be the circle, or perhaps more properly, the ellipse. The elliptical or circular form enables planetary bodies to rotate in their own respective orbits, yet remain united to the other members of their solar systems or galaxies. The circle has, of course, profound significance for humans as well. The wheel was perhaps our first great technological achievement, and unlike the pyramids it was identified with neither despotism nor slavery. The circle also implies continuous dynamic movement, whereas the pyramid is rooted, static, motionless, and unchanging.

Let us see if the circle, or the ellipse, possesses the necessary characteristics to make it a useful symbol and diagrammatic form for organizational structuring and charting. The first step in using the circular form in an organizational structure is to place the leader at the very center of the chart. This potentially changes both the leader's and the followers' psychological orientations; no longer does the leader have to meet the same expectations as when he or she is considered by self and others to be "on top." When you're on top there is only one place to go—down. You either fall, get pushed, or finally yield to the irresistible pull of gravity on your physical strength and health.

The many psychological and emotional problems connected with the implementation of organizational policies of promotion, demotion, and transfer provide ample evidence of the inadequacy of the vertical arrangement. Problems involving demotion are particularly distressing when they involve those at the top. Some chief executives, in fact, have to be kicked upstairs to an honorary board chairpersonship or directorship as a result of ineptness at the helm. If the chairperson of the board is also the chief executive officer there is no place to go; thus even the very top officer of a corporation must finally encounter failure at the pinnacle of success. Rearranging positions at the center of an organization (or even having two centers for awhile, in a manner analogous to the biological process of cell multiplication and division) would perhaps remove much of the sting or sense of defeat that is experienced when a leader is removed from the top. Demotion, instead of being conceived of in downward terms, could instead be a movement outward, away from the center of the circle.

Placing leadership at the very center of an organization potentially increases responsibility and decreases excessive or arbitrary use of authority. If any one thing led to the decline of the monarchical form of government on a worldwide scale it was the abuse of authority and the failure to exercise responsibility. One connotation of the word *reign*, in fact, is that of supreme authority without responsibility for meeting the needs of the governed. Thus the ancient monarch could sit in resplendent glory, attended by his or her court, and simply bestow favors or penalties upon the petitioners or culprits who appeared begging and pleading before the royal feet. In these situations there was no accountability to the governed. And it was this failure of the monarch to use power and authority responsibly that led directly to the Magna Carta, the Declaration of Independence, and the French and Russian revolutions. In our own day this process of holding the authority figures responsible has continued, but limitations to prevent the abuse of authority have largely been imposed from outside of any organization through law and government regulation or from above the hierarchy through the aegis of boards of directors, trustees, or even stockholders. The notion of a force that holds management or government accountable from within the organization is only now beginning to be appreciated.

While the advent of collective bargaining and the rise of organized labor did begin to limit authority from within an organization, the rise of the large international unions created another political force outside the organization that was often strong enough to gain government support and impose changes from outside. This is a potentially divisive approach, and regardless of its necessity or legitimacy the reactive win/lose struggle between management and labor has been costly and harmful to organizations and workers alike. It is unfortunate that workers were forced by unresponsive managements to struggle so hard to achieve basic economic rights. Paradoxically, organized labor now has so much power in some areas that management rights are being severely limited and organizational profitability is in some cases being greatly restricted.

Gordon Lippitt (1969) addressed the problem of organizational renewal with a most thoughtful and enlightening study of circular forms and processes of integration, differentiation, and conflict resolution from within organizations. Not only is such renewal possible, it is a positive necessity if we are going to achieve levels of productivity and profitability necessary to maintain our present economic system in a state of vibrant health.

Organizations conceived in circular form may be thought of as centers from which products or services (or both) emerge. The process of production may be conceptualized as an internal build-up of energy or capacity that is then released or disseminated outward to purchasers or consumers on the basis of need or demand. The chief executive officer at the very center of an organization would be primarily responsible to all of the organization's members, to its stockholders, and to consumers. If this responsibility were truly and effectively discharged through peripheral circles or layers of managers there would be much less need for government regulation and enforcement. The circular organization would be a self-regulating system, much like the healthy human organism that would be its model. Four external spectator groups—government, labor, stockholders, and special interest groups—would watch over the processes of interaction between and among the peripheral circles, intervening directly with the chief executive (or designated representative) only to cope with aberrations or abnormal situations, hopefully rare. Figure 5.2 illustrates this type of organization.

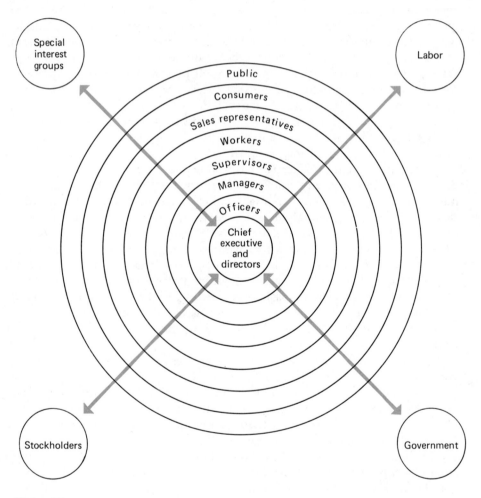

Figure 5.2

Being at the center of an organization makes you primarily responsible for being aware of what's going on around you. If you are at the center you may be much more accessible to those inside the organization than if you are seen to be at the top. You are also less free to enter into negotiations with those in outer circles without first consulting those at the inside. And if you do not live up to your internal commitments the organization may either implode upon you or explode and disintegrate, leaving you alone and devoid of the source of your power. These are powerful stimuli to staying alert. Perhaps, then, we might visualize the president, leader, or chief executive at the very center of the organization serving as "its most responsible person." Fanning out around the center and directly connected to it are those key executives—vice presidents, commissioners, or administrators—who share actively in the leader's responsibility and who are responsible for major functional areas of the total organization. See the diagram in Fig. 5.3 for a visual representation of this relationship.

Now we may further distinguish staff functions (supportive and specialized service organizations) from line functions (direct productive organizations) by using solid and dashed circles and lines (see Fig. 5.4). Each line and staff organization system may be expected to have its own individual subsystems. It is the nature of staff department subsystems to interact with line organizations directly; thus the staff groups tend to provide the organizational cement that holds the entire structure together. This conception changes the image of staff from that of indirect labor or "overhead" (often used in derogatory fashion) to that of providing necessary integrative support in keeping the organizational structure viable and intact. For this conception to take

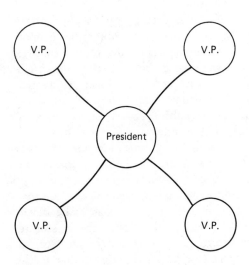

Figure 5.3

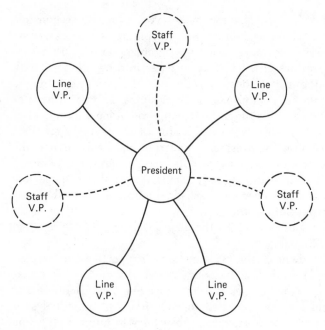

Figure 5.4

hold, staff executives must learn to behave less like policemen or monitors and more like consultants and helpers. The dashed lines connecting staff and line functions in Fig. 5.5 provide a graphic picture of a potential internal communications network within the organization.

When any part of an organization is not nourished by an appropriate supply of information its function will be impaired and it will tend to atrophy and eventually die just like any living organism. The flow of information within an organization can be likened to the flow of blood in the human circulatory system. Information goes out from the center to inform or "aerate" the organization. As it goes, it gathers "impurities" in the form of questions, resistance, misconceptions, and additional (possibly very valuable) insights. As these inputs flow back to the center of the organization they carry with them the organization's psychic contents; and it is of crucial importance that the leader appreciate and recognize these inputs and take them into account in the decision-making process. This kind of two-way information flow or feedback system is vitally necessary for effective management of any complex organization. A second or external feedback system also needs to be developed to obtain information from clients, consumers, citizens, the electorate, or anyone else to whom the organization provides goods and/or services.

The organization structure now begins to take on shapes familiar to the molecular biologist—the cellular structures of living organisms. Larry Witte, an administrator at a large Boston area hospital, suggests that organizations

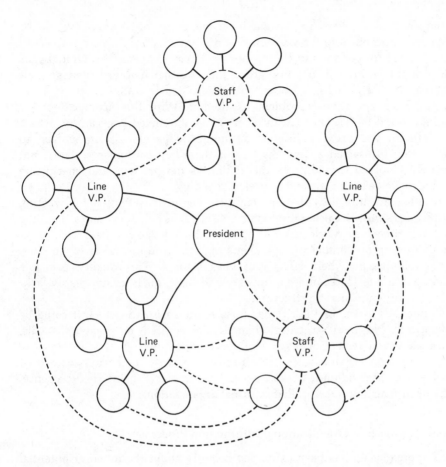

Figure 5.5

may operate like amoebas, expanding and contracting in reaction to pressures and forces from the immediate environment. I like this idea, and when we consider that organizations represent much higher forms of life than amoebas we can see the importance of allowing organizations, as "suprapersons," the opportunity to breathe freely. The ideas expressed above are also analogous to the *ringi* system of management prevalent in Japan. The Japanese are very process oriented due to the deep influence of Confucianism and Buddhism on their culture (Arai, 1971).

There are a number of additional advantages to be gained from circular forms of organization and first among these is the potential for greatly improved communications. Members of both staff and line groups would be expected to be competent in group dynamics (see also Chapter 4) and would have to work through potential or actual interpersonal and intergroup conflicts as a requirement for continued organizational membership. One-to-one meetings would be discouraged and inclusion/exclusion "games" would be considered antithetical to the very concept of organization; thus a norm would be established for conducting all appropriate business openly. Individual staff leaders might be invited to a line group meeting that involved their specialized areas, or individual line leaders may be invited to a staff group meeting if a particular operational problem required it. With this arrangement far less time would be wasted than in meetings of the mixed-bag variety, where those present are often uninterested, unknowledgeable, or uninvolved in what's being transacted among the two or three key participants. Those not intimately involved shouldn't be there; time is too precious and energy too valuable to waste sitting around in useless meetings.

Another advantage of the circular form lies in its potential for creating *dual memberships*. Because individuals would often belong to more than one group at a time they would have to openly acknowledge and deal with problems of intergroup conflict or risk alienating one group in favor of another, thereby diminishing their effectiveness as leaders. This duality principle would do much to foster internal honesty and trust, qualities noticeably lacking in so many bureaucratic structures.

A final advantage of the circular form is the ease with which it could be implemented. No great structural changes are required, no great upheavals, no drastic rearrangement of responsibilities or functions—just a different way of operating, one that uses the interpersonal process dimension instead of ignoring it or pretending it doesn't exist. The circular structure is, in a sense, a way of formalizing the so-called informal organization.

A New Approach to Organizational Information Processing

Much apprehension has been expressed recently about the inherent potential of the computer to push us into the sort of totalitarian form of government described so vividly by the late George Orwell in *Animal Farm* and *1984*. As 1984 is now just around the corner, it is important that we guard against the kind of abuse of information storage and retrieval that serves as an invasion of privacy. However, the computer actually poses a much greater *threat* to autocratic and totalitarian regimes than an advantage, provided that any information system is maintained and operated with openness and honesty.

Most present forms of management information systems (MIS) contain only Type A information: facts, figures, data indexes, and so forth. This information tends to be used by management as a basis for Type A judgments or assumptions regarding operating efficiency or performance. Corrective action is then taken on the basis of these judgments or assumptions, often with no further attempt to find out what's really going on. As a result, most organizational subsystems develop elaborate defensive stratagems for obscuring, coloring, or interpreting information so it can be rendered harmless. The basic idea is not to trust the boss with information that can be used against you. Therefore many management information systems are often loaded with distortions, and even those that are accurate only reveal part of the total picture.

In recent times, great interest has developed in polling. Polling, the statistical assessment of subjective opinion, gets at Type B information—the data of private or personal experience. There are now a variety of interesting methods emerging for getting and using Type B information and comparing it with information of the Type A variety. Some examples of the kind of Type B information that can be measured are those subjective but quantifiable organizational processes that determine morale, leadership effectiveness, levels of creativity, patterns of competition and collaboration, and patterns of growth or stagnation.

Computer-assisted polling can now be used to identify management or organizational problems before they have reached the critical stage. This technique for obtaining rapid feedback promises to be of particular value because situations in today's organizational world tend to change very rapidly, and management needs to adopt a proactive stance if it is to successfully avoid disastrous surprises. The key point to remember is that while subjective perceptions of individuals may be correct or incorrect (valid or invalid), they nevertheless steer or direct behavior. People tend to act in accordance with what they perceive the situation to be. If something is believed to be unfair, people will respond to or react to the perceived unfairness whether there is any real inequity or not (see also Chapter 4).

Computer-assisted polling can be combined with a congruency/discrepancy (or certainty/ambiguity) chart to identify areas of concerns or problems that need attention or correction. The method works in the following way. First, a questionnaire is prepared that conducts an inquiry into the respondents' perceptions with regard to a variety of problems, concerns, or organizational issues (see Fig. 5.6). A response scale, usually from 0 to 5, is used to assess two kinds of responses: (1) how the respondent sees the situation, and (2) how important it is to the respondent that the perceived situation be changed. The questionnaire is designed to reflect not only how any particular group feels about its own performance and the performance of other groups with which it has a significant interaction, but also the group's attitudes toward those critical objective factors that determine the organization's success or profitability.

Second, decisions are made with regard to how the raw data is to be sorted and processed—for example, what groups are to be cross compared. Finally, a congruency/discrepancy chart is prepared to graphically display the findings (see Fig. 5.7). The degree of discrepancy between what two groups perceive or feel is needed represents the degree of organizational ambiguity or tension. Some tension will always exist and is desirable; however, if the levels of ambiguity or discrepancy become too great organizational dysfunction will occur as fight (conflict) or flight (resignation) (see also Chapter 1).

The questionnaire and chart shown in Figs. 5.6 and 5.7 are not particularly outstanding examples but they are presented to demonstrate the tech-

Response Scale

0 = Not applicable	3 = Moderately; sometimes
1 = Practically none; never	4 = Very; often
2 = Not very; rarely	5 = Extremely; always

Write in one number from 0 to 5 in each column for each item.

Degree of importance to change ⟶

How you see it ⟶

1. My immediate manager readily accepts feedback about his/her own performance.

2. Our immediate organization is generally flexible in adjusting to changes that occur.

3. Evaluation of my performance by management is fair.

4. Messages important to my job performance reach me on a timely basis.

5. I get personal satisfaction from the work I do.

6. The performance of our work group has earned it a good reputation.

7. The organization allows me the opportunity to learn and to do the things I want to do.

8. My ideas and feelings are considered when changes are made in this organization.

9. It is important to control personal expense accounts.

10. I am kept informed about the things I need to know to do my job well.

11. People in positions of authority are interested in members' feelings about how the organization is being run—both pro and con.

12. Management attempts to manipulate us.

13. Our wage and salary policy is equitable.

14. Our personnel policy for vacation, holidays, and benefits is fair.

15. The personnel department is effective.

Fig. 5.6 A sample questionnaire

nique for gathering and assessing subjective perceptions of organization members. A careful analysis of data gathered in this manner can point out areas needing improvement, such as staff development, training, communication, policy, or interpersonal relationships. Computers can be used to gather subjective perceptions of employees, clients, or consumers; to assess levels of integration and satisfaction with management policies, procedures, practices, and decisions. They can be designed to probe into very specialized and detailed issues or to gain a general assessment of an organization's climate.

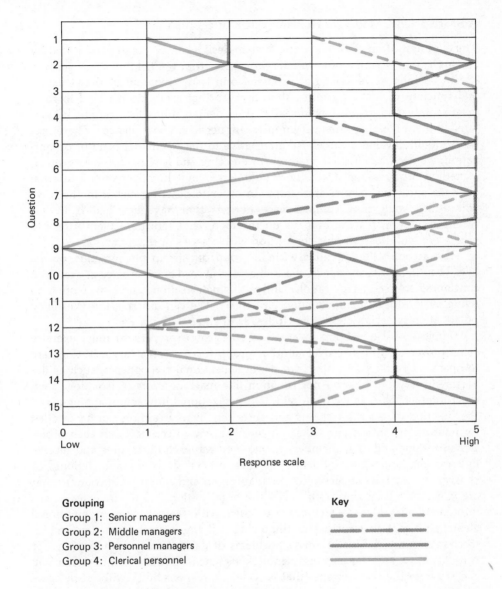

Grouping

Group 1: Senior managers
Group 2: Middle managers
Group 3: Personnel managers
Group 4: Clerical personnel

Key

Fig. 5.7 A sample congruency/discrepancy chart

One critical issue must be addressed when using this technique: management must agree in advance to share the results of the survey with the participants. If they do not, it is very likely that the information sought the next time this technique is used will be distorted. "Government by consent of the governed" is a meaningless axiom unless the "consent" is really present. The degree of consent can be readily established by means of such computer-assisted polling and thus becomes an instrument for increasing both job satisfaction and personal freedom.

A Space-Science Model for Human System Integration

The adoption of an effective living system design can be greatly facilitated by the utilization of some now familiar concepts from the field of space science.

In Chapter 4 we looked at problems and issues inherent in the structure and function of human groups. We observed that group norms tend to form very rapidly and create boundaries or turf demarcations that cannot be violated without creating some very unpleasant negative consequences. Therefore, if we would develop a successful alternative to the pyramidal form of organization, we need an effective method for entering and leaving different groups; a method for breaking down these boundaries and thus overcoming internal conflicts and adversary relationships. In order to describe such a method, we will utilize some now commonplace notions that have emerged from our recent success in placing humans on the moon and returning them safely to earth. We will illustrate this conception with a series of diagrams.

We are only too familiar with in-group/out-group phenomenon or the We/They polarization, which is a fact of our everyday experience as well as a continuing source of frustration. Unless this polarization can be overcome, no living system design can function effectively. We can describe the We/They polarization pictorially with two circles, as in Fig. 5.8.

Typically, also, we are aware that one group (or person) must exercise some power or influence over another group (or person) if organizations are to operate effectively. In other words, organizational components, such as departments or divisions, do not function like machine parts in isolation; they must interact. Nor, as we have said, is organizational interaction analogous to the function of gears, or chains and sprockets, where friction can be avoided by pouring oil on the parts that physically come in contact with each other. Organizations and their members must enter into each other, give and receive information, and exert influence on each others' decisions and actions; in short, they must assist each other in adapting to and coping with changes that are constantly occurring both inside the organization and in the exterior environment. Often these changes are laden with feeling-tones or emotional elements, a fact that further distinguishes a living system from the familiar mechanistic model. Finally, many problems of delegation of authority and/or responsibility, and the seemingly endless arguments about whether or not you can separate the two notions (that is, delegate responsibility without delegat-

Figure 5.8

ing the same or requisite amount of authority), tend to dissolve in the system I am about to describe.

What we observe so often when directives are determined by *We* for *They* to carry out is a reactive resistance pattern: the so-called resistance-to-change phenomenon. When a directive is fired off from the We like a rocket, an explosion is likely to occur at the point where it hits the They, as illustrated in Fig. 5.9. Forces immediately rush to the scene to repel the invader. An analogy can be made to getting a splinter in your finger. Initially you feel the pain, and unless the foreign object is removed at once a small army of white corpuscles is dispatched hastily to the site and proceeds to wall off the area in order to either push the foreign object out or break it down. Many corpuscles are destroyed in the process.

When two groups are equally powerful there is likely to be an effective accommodation or a standoff. But if one group is less powerful than another the directive is often perceived as an imposition or an attack that must be surrendered to. Thus the organizational Theys—subordinate individuals and groups—try valiantly to respond to difficult management requests and directives while simultaneously having to deal with their own internal frustration and anger at being put upon in such a fashion. This is perhaps the greatest source of wasted energy in organizations. As organizational life proceeds in bloody but unbowed fashion occasional victory celebrations are held in the form of summer outings and Christmas parties. Organizational life is thus often lived at a superficial level.

Individuals and organizations that do not internalize their directives—that do not ever commit themselves to or accept responsibility for them—never feel a sense of responsibility for the outcome either; therefore, when the results do not turn out well they refuse to accept blame. Thus the person issuing a directive who doesn't simultaneously take the requisite steps to ensure internalization and commitment is often guilty of creating a self-fulfilling prophecy. He believes his people don't assume much responsibility, and when they refuse to accept responsibility for allowing the failure of his directive he becomes more than ever convinced that he was right all along—he now *knows* they are irresponsible.

A way out of this dilemma can be found by utilizing a familiar concept from space science. If we think of an organization as possessing inner space,

Figure 5.9

and of organizational components as circular systems and subsystems, we can apply the concept of organizational orbiting. Any circular process can utilize the concept of orbit to describe a chronological series of events that link two different spatial objects (or organizational groups) together. Let us use as an example the circular process for problem finding and problem solving that was presented in Chapter 3. We can hypothesize that any organizational group in the position of being They rather than We represents in fact a different dimension or entity in social or organizational space. Thus any We can represent the earth and They can represent the moon. The issue is always one of reducing the organizational and social distance between these two poles by traveling back and forth between them safely and by reflecting on the learning experiences inherent in the journey. The journey is continuous, and is illustrated diagrammatically in Fig. 5.10.

Let us suppose that we wish to visit another organizational group for the purpose of accomplishing an objective arising from a perception of some individual or organizational need. Utilizing a type B problem-finding approach, which we outlined in Chapter 3, we first determine what we are trying to do. We do this by forming ourselves into a reasonably homogeneous We group; in other words, by establishing an effective working climate among ourselves, by planning our effort mutually, and by assessing the needs of the total situation. When the problem-finding process is complete, we are ready to set our objectives; this brings us to the point of making a decision. Utilizing Type A behaviors, we must *tentatively* decide what We wish to accomplish with the They group. Once we have made these tentative decisions we are then ready to design our encounter with them. In this example, setting objectives is analogous to deciding to make a journey to another planet, while the next stage, designing, is analogous to building a space capsule that will get us there, enable us to function in a strange environment, and bring us back safely with mission accomplished.

When we begin to design interventions using the space-science example as our guide, we *must* be concerned with building a design that will get us to where we want to go and help us achieve our objectives. Therefore, we need to consider what the climate is like where we wish to travel. In other words, we must assess the psychological attitudes and physical condition of the group we wish to visit. For example, are They under a lot of stress or tension? Are They ready to receive us? Or do They regard us as a threat?

Figure 5.10

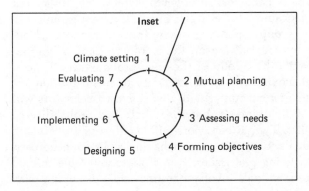

Figure 5.11

In the process of developing a design it is desirable to move again through all seven steps of the problem-finding/problem-solving process described in Chapter 3. Thus in a certain sense we create a wheel within a wheel or, in other words, our design becomes a subsystem within the We/They system framework. Figure 5.11 illustrates this concept.

All seven steps of our design (space capsule) must be phrased in tentative terms. Thus once we decide tentatively *what* we want to do with They we can continue to decide tentatively *how* we will do it. This process takes us around the problem-finding/problem-solving circle again. The questions now become: How do We establish a climate with They and what is the climate like with They now? How do we achieve real mutual planning with They—do They see us as equals, as trying to lay something on them, or what? What are our needs and what are their needs? How can we present our needs and get to hear and understand theirs? and so on.

When we have completed our tentative design and have included our plans for forming objectives with them, designing a joint project, implementing it together, and establishing mutually agreeable criteria for joint evaluation, we are ready to move our space capsule to the launching pad—that is, to go from the design stage to implementation.

Now sometimes, still borrowing from our space-science example, when the climate is really questionable or risky, it is prudent to do a quick orbit of the foreign planet without trying to land just yet. This might take the form of an informal conversation with They of the what-would-it-be-like-if variety. After information of this kind is brought back home, you may then finish your actual design with a lot more certainty of eventual success (see Fig. 5.12).

When you are ready to make the actual journey to implement your design with They, it will be most useful to remember to utilize Type B behaviors in the problem-finding part of your visit and then, when both groups are ready, to change to Type A behaviors in order to arrive at jointly shared objectives. It is difficult to coordinate the energies of two different groups and facilitate the process of two groups operating as one for a temporary period. One must learn to play it by ear, picking up the emotional cues in the behaviors of the members of the other group. If the other group is very Type A oriented and is itchy to get moving it is best not to try to spend too long at problem finding during your first encounter with them. Type B behaviors will be frustrating to a group of this kind. If, however, there is a probability of acrimonious debate or conflict, Type B behaviors will be effective in defusing the situation. Some individuals, of course, resent having a situation defused and see this as a way of avoiding real issues. It is always preferable to deal with real issues unless the individuals involved are incapable of coping with the ambiguity of conflict and seek to avoid it by engaging in overly aggressive attacks or withdrawal into silence or physical departure.

When two groups (or individuals) have engaged in joint problem finding and have achieved a level of shared commitment to jointly developed objectives, they are ready to develop a design for accomplishment (see Fig. 5.13). Whether one or both parties implements the design, a true delegation of authority has occurred because both parties are aware of the issues, problems, and difficulties to be faced and will consequently be ready to assess the results in a spirit of fairness and authenticity.

When the implementation is complete the evaluation stage is reached. Here A and B behaviors may be effectively fused. Did We/They accomplish our objectives? Did our common design work? What new needs do we per-

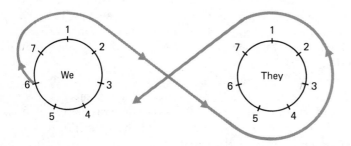

Figure 5.12

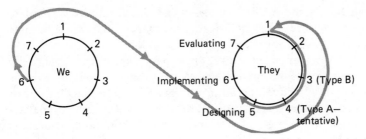

Figure 5.13

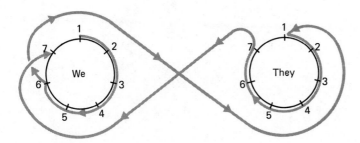

Figure 5.14

ceive now? A shared success in the joint activity, *plus* the freeing of energies and expectations for the next joint effort, usually provide a surge of excitement, optimism, and greatly improved climate. If the experience did not prove successful, everyone knows what needs to be done to solve the remaining problems—and if you have managed to stay *tentative* throughout the process there should be no deep disappointment.

After this shared evaluation has been conducted it is time to return to the privacy of your own group (see Fig. 5.14). You land, of course, at the final stage (evaluating) of your original circle. Against the background of your original problem-finding assessment you can now see the results of your planning, your intervention with the other group, the shared experience, and your combined evaluation. What has been discovered as a result of your journey? Where were you when you started out? What assumptions and perceptions did you have initially? Have they changed as a result of the journey and your intervention?

You have now achieved access to the process of learning from experience and you have also been able to overcome the pitfalls that commonly occur when you operate on the basis of assumptions, judgments, and rational analysis. Only by getting out where the action is and getting involved in the reality of a problem situation do you gain the right to judge that situation or lay claim to personal understanding. If managers and organizations worked in this fashion to overcome We/They polarizations, organizations could become vastly more effective in a very short time.

A living systems model of organizational management can eventually eliminate the negative effects of bureaucracy. When organizational behavior is aimed at achieving both effective operating results and the satisfaction of human needs for participation and involvement, the product of organizational activity will be both profitable productivity and increased conscious awareness of human values and human potential.

6 *Increasing Energy for Learning*

Considering the enormous size and complexity of many organizations today, it is understandable that people who work for or come in contact with them often feel as if they are burrowing in a mammoth anthill or wading up to their knees in a lake of glue. Lost in a nameless, faceless obscurity, they feel that life has lost much of its excitement and meaning. The routine of work goes on day after endless day and the only adventure and excitement that touches many people's lives is experienced vicariously through television and movies. What can be done to restore the sense of personal worth that many seem to have lost? What will it take to move our organizations toward a renewed sense of purpose and an enthusiastic commitment to improving the quality of life and work? Some seem to think we are beyond hope; I do not!

We need success. Small success perhaps, but nevertheless real, significant triumphs that impel us to take greater risks and to discover that we are capable of improving both our own individual competence and the general situation in which we find ourselves. Success brings increased confidence and a clearer vision of future possibilities, but above all it gives us a greater sense of personal worth and a fuller realization of our own identity. It is small wonder that many people today dislike their work intensely; work dominates life rather than serving as a means to personal fulfillment. Work is often seen as a penalty that must be paid for weekend freedom. Perhaps the feeling of powerlessness that permeates so many people's working lives is a result of their inability to see how to change their circumstances; to become, in fact, a new person in a different situation. But change and growth is paradoxical; while it produces increased freedom, it may also create increased insecurity and anxiety.

There are apparently no sure cures for the anxieties of living in a mass society, and there appears to be enough insecurity already. Psychologists tell us that fear of failure, negative fantasies of drastic consequences, and fear of taking risks all result from our having no control over the moment of our birth and no ability to predict the moment of our death. Thus we all have a fundamental anxiety based on the fact that we lead a temporary existence; we therefore must learn to face, and accept, the existential anxiety of human life itself.

There is a pathway, however, that seems to hold great promise both for reducing existential anxiety and for bringing about personal and organizational change and growth. This pathway leads directly to success experiences and enables individuals to decide how much risk they are willing to take and the amount or degree of change they wish to experience or undergo. It is a pathway toward continuing education, but an education very different from that which most of us have experienced during the early years of our childhood.

Most educational theories have been based on the belief that the fundamental purpose of education is the transmission of the totality of human knowledge from one generation to the next. This is probably a workable assumption provided that two conditions are present: (1) the quantity of knowledge is small enough to be collectively managed by the educational system, and (2) the rate of change occurring in the culture or society is slow enough that the knowledge can be packaged and delivered before it changes. Both conditions have disappeared in modern times. We are now living during a period of knowledge explosion in which the rate of cultural change (for example, the introduction of new technology and new social mores, sudden population growth and mobility, changes in basic institutions such as marriage and the family, and so forth) is so rapid that we experience three or four or more different cultural periods in a life span of seventy to eighty years. The diagram in Fig. 6.1, prepared by Dr. Malcolm S. Knowles (1970), presents this picture graphically.

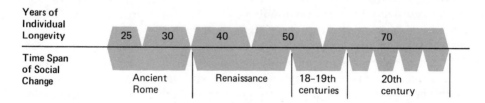

Figure 6.1

Knowles suggests that increase in the rate of change in society leads to doubt concerning the viability of the deeply accepted and traditional transmittal theory of education. Instead of being to transmit all of what is known, perhaps the goal of education could be to stimulate in the *learner* a desire to engage in a lifelong process of discovering what he or she needs to know. If this redefinition is tentatively acceptable, we may consider two consequences that would tend to follow from it. First, education would no longer be primarily or exclusively an activity for children; and second, the responsibility for deciding what is to be taught and learned would tend to shift increasingly away from the teacher and toward the learner. As a result of this new focus it appears necessary to develop a new learning strategy—a strategy for ongoing adult learning.

THE NEED FOR AN ADULT LEARNING STRATEGY

As adults, we can usually find someone who can tell us what we wish to know, but for the most part teachers are not generally available to us as they were when we were children. Those of us who have completed our formal schooling are expected to be capable of performing our various social and organizational roles—if we cannot, the consequences are often personally hurtful as well as detrimental to the organizations for which we work. We may, therefore, experience serious psychological difficulty in admitting that we don't know the answers to any of a number of difficult or perplexing problems, and the tendency of some adults to try to cover up is understandable, even if not acceptable.

The time pressures of daily living may also make it relatively impossible for us to pursue formal educational activities as adults; we therefore need a process for learning how to learn on our own, directly from our experience.

The Chinese philosopher Confucius expressed his belief in the importance of learning from experience when he wrote:

I hear and I forget
I see and I remember
I do and I understand.

Confucius related the acquisition of understanding and knowledge directly to living and experiencing. The process of education, in its broadest sense, can be considered to be ongoing during all conscious and even unconscious human activity. Everything we do potentially involves some kind of learning. Reflecting on the past, acting in the present, planning for the future, all clearly suggest a fundamental approach to learning by doing. Possibly we do not look at all of life as a learning experience or a learning situation. Perhaps our orientation restricts our thinking about education to that taking place only within the narrow confines of a formal classroom. But whether we wish to recognize it or not, the fact remains that we are capable of learning all the time. As we cannot always wait for a teacher, we might well learn how to manage our own continuing learning. If we wish to do so, we could greatly benefit from an educational process that would help us to extract increased knowledge, ability, and meaningful understanding from our total life situation so that all of our activities become part of our education. With a process of this kind, even our mistakes, painful as they are, may become valued learning experiences leading to change and growth rather than causes for alienation, separation, conflict, or denial. Education as a lifelong process of continuing discovery and growth could satisfy our need to relate in a positive and personal way to our own changing experience, and help us to solve our ever new and increasingly complex problems.

And it seems that social problems today are bigger and more serious than ever: crime, poverty, social and racial unrest, and drug addiction are still rampant despite many programs and projects aimed at relieving them. There seems to be a greater need today than ever before for the late Kurt Lewin's prescription for resolving social conflicts through reeducation. Lewin (1948) demonstrated that processes for the acquisition of normal and abnormal social behavior are fundamentally alike. He proved that inadequate visual images (incorrect stereotypes or illusions) are formed in exactly the same way as adequate visual images (reality). The importance of this clarification cannot be overestimated. If we accept the fact that our perception of reality may at any time be correct or incorrect but that it is always visualized by ourselves as correct, and if we also recognize that *it is our perceptions of reality that steer or direct our actions,* we can at last understand the basis of socially divergent behavior and begin to think of ways to develop corrective experiences to resolve the conflicts brought about by the divergence between social illusions and reality.

Furthermore, we are beginning to realize that it is not just the poor, the disadvantaged, and the uneducated that have a monopoly on social illusion and lowered perceptions of reality. All human groups, including those with financial power, political power, or social prestige, will develop distorted perceptions of reality unless they are nourished constantly with a supply of open and honest information no matter how unpleasant or unpopular that information may be. Receiving only the news you want to hear is tantamount to creating a world of illusion. Information is like air; if it is allowed to stagnate, impurities develop rapidly and soon it is unfit to breathe.

Lewin called the method of dealing with divergent perceptions of reality a process of *normative reeducation.* He described normative reeducation as a process that effects not only changes in cognitive structure (facts, concepts, beliefs, and expectations) but also changes in values (attractions, aversions, and feelings of acceptance and status). To be effective, reeducation must go much deeper than the level of verbal expression. It involves a circular transition from old values and ideas to new ones, together with the internalization of new (learned) behavior, which, in turn, reinforces and supports new values.

Lewin specified two conditions as absolute prerequisites for successful reeducation. First, individuals must become actively involved with others in discovering the inadequacies in their present situation and must work together to discover paths leading to improvement; and second, there must be an implicit guarantee of each individual's freedom to accept or reject the new values or cognitive structure. No individual or group can guarantee being correct all the time; therefore, freedom of dissent must be allowed in order to protect the freedom of all.

It is becoming increasingly apparent that our political system is also dependent on the continuing educational involvement of the voting public. In order to ensure that our political system continue to be responsive to the needs of the people, we must have a much greater level of grass-roots involvement in the political process than we have at present. In order for citizens to come together and explore social and political issues thoughtfully and without excessive rancor, grass-roots political life needs to be firmly based in the process of continuing adult education. In the future we may well witness hundreds of citizens' groups, representing a broad spectrum of different interests, studying issues, conducting research and gathering data, weighing the evidence, and presenting their findings. A widespread movement of this kind may go a long way toward freeing politicians from the well-nigh impossible task of developing all the questions (legislative proposals) and providing all the answers (legislative enactments). We probably have many too many laws already and don't really understand the full impact of the legislation that is now on the books. A moratorium on legislation coupled with a period of extensive public inquiry could indeed be most beneficial.

Continuing lifelong education also tends to break down the elitist structures that categorize society into groups of smart—those already "in the know"—and dumb—those who have given up trying to learn. Without this categorization, it may be possible for all of us to be continuing learners, and it could be pointed out that while learning is sometimes difficult for anyone, continuing to strive to learn is an absolute necessity for everyone. Thus all social questions call for answers and no one needs to be told that they just don't understand the situation.

A THEORY OF ADULT LEARNING

Dr. Malcolm Knowles has clarified the differences between adult and child learning in his book, *The Modern Practice of Adult Education* (1970). Knowles does not suggest any fundamental difference between the way adults and children internalize and utilize new information, but he does point to significant differences that stem from the conditions surrounding adult and child learning, and differences that emerge in the learning process as various degrees of maturation emerge. Knowles writes as follows:

> Most of what is known about learning has been derived from studies of learning in children and animals. Most of what is known about teaching has been derived from experience with teaching children under conditions of compulsory attendance. And most theories about the learning/teaching transaction are based on the definition of education as a process of transmitting the culture. From these theories and assumptions there has emerged the technology of "Pedagogy"—a term derived from the Greek stem *paid-* (meaning "child") and *agogos* (meaning "leading"). So "Pedagogy" means, specifically, the art and science of teaching children.

One problem is that somewhere in history, the "children" part of the definition got lost. In many people's minds—and even in the dictionary—"Pedagogy" is defined as the art and science of teaching. Period. Even in books on adult education you can find references to "the Pedagogy of adult education," without any apparent discomfort over the contradiction in terms. Indeed, in my estimation, the main reason why adult education has not achieved the impact on our civilization of which it is capable is that most teachers of adults have only known how to teach adults as if they were children.

Knowles has used the term *andragogy* (the art and science of helping adults learn) to describe the adult learning process and has identified four basic premises, or learning characteristics, around which the differences between the andragogical and pedagogical approaches can be illuminated.

Self-Concept

The self-concept of a child is that of being a dependent person. As children move toward adulthood, they become increasingly aware of being capable of making decisions for themselves, and simultaneously experience a deep need for others to see them as being capable of self-direction. This change from a self-concept of dependency to one of autonomy is what we are referring to when we say a person has achieved psychological maturity or adulthood. Not surprisingly, adults tend to resent being put into situations that violate their self-concept of maturity, such as being treated with a lack of respect, being talked down to, being judged and otherwise treated like children. Because so many of our educational or training environments have been influenced by traditional pedagogical practices, adults tend to come into educational or training programs expecting to be treated like children and prepared to allow the teacher to take responsibility for their learning. When adults discover that they are capable of self-direction in learning, as they are in other activities of their lives, they often experience a remarkable increase in motivation and a strong desire to continue the learning process.

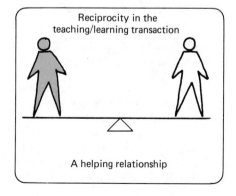

Figure 6.2

Thus the first major difference between andragogy and pedagogy exists in the relationship between teacher and learner and in the learner's concept of himself with regard to his capacity for self-direction (see Fig. 6.2).

Experience

In the course of living, adults accumulate vast quantities of experience of differing kinds. We are, in fact, the products of our experience. Our experience is what we have done; that is, the sum total of our life's impressions and our interaction with other persons and the world. Children, on the other hand, are relatively new to experience; many patterns of experience have simply not occurred frequently enough to have become familiar, safe, or generally predictable. Children are accustomed to depending on experienced adults to give them the basic facts of life and learning that are needed for physical and social survival. As they grow into maturity, however, their experience becomes a rich reservoir of knowledge and a primary resource for learning. Because everyone's experience differs, some more than others, comparing and sharing adult experience becomes a valuable asset in helping adults learn. In addition, if we do not utilize the experience of the adult learner we run a serious risk of rejecting that adult as a person because, as we have observed, we *are* our experience.

In the andragogical approach to education, the experience of adults is valued as a rich resource for learning. In the tradition of pedagogy the tendency has been to regard the experience of children as being of little worth in the educational process because it is to them that the culture must be transmitted. It is probably for this reason that the methodology of pedagogy has been, up to this point at least, largely oriented toward one-way communication techniques: lectures, assigned readings, and audiovisual presentations.

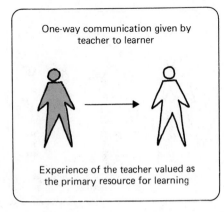

One-way communication given by teacher to learner

Experience of the teacher valued as the primary resource for learning

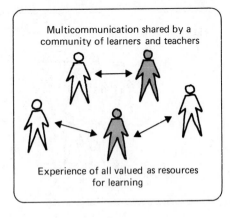

Multicommunication shared by a community of learners and teachers

Experience of all valued as resources for learning

Figure 6.3

Andragogy, on the other hand, abounds with experiential, two-way, and multidirectional techniques such as group discussion, simulation, role playing, buzz groups, team designing, skill practice sessions, and so on. Through such techniques the experiences of all participants can be utilized. When learners begin to function as teachers and teachers simultaneously become learners, the resources of all can be utilized to facilitate the learning process: it is here that the second major difference between andragogy and pedagogy becomes apparent. The distinction is illustrated in Fig. 6.3.

Readiness to Learn

Educators are quite familiar with the concepts of *readiness to learn* and *teachable moment*. It is generally accepted that educational development occurs best through a sequencing of learning activities into developmental tasks so that the learner is presented with opportunities for learning certain topics or activities when he is ready to assimilate them, but not before. It is obvious, for example, that one must learn arithmetic before one can learn trigonometry, or that one must learn the meaning of basic words before proceeding to read history. The main task of pedagogical curriculum development is to sequence and interrelate subjects and skill-building activities to meet the requirements of competency for graduation. Adults, however, have largely completed the requirements of basic education by developing competency in reading, writing, arithmetic, and speech. Their developmental tasks are increasingly related to the social roles that form their immediate concerns: working, living, raising a family, and enjoying art, music, recreational activities, and so on. As adults move from early adulthood through middle age and into later maturity, they experience many different teachable moments, which are called forth by the needs of their social situation. Thus the third difference between

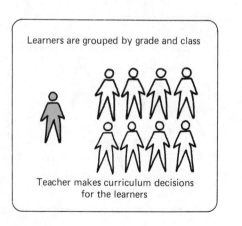

Learners are grouped by grade and class

Teacher makes curriculum decisions for the learners

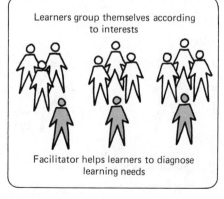

Learners group themselves according to interests

Facilitator helps learners to diagnose learning needs

Figure 6.4

andragogy and pedagogy can be inferred from the process used in choosing the learning content. In traditional pedagogy, the teacher decides the content of what will be learned and also assumes responsibility for how and when the learning will take place. In andragogy, the grouping of learners is brought about in direct relation to individual interests and learning needs identified by the learners themselves. The learners decide what they need to learn based on their own perception of the demands of their social situation and the requirements of the problems they face. See Fig. 6.4 for a visual representation of this difference.

A Changed Time Perspective

Children are used to thinking of education in terms of preparing for the future rather than doing something in the present. They are involved in the process of storing up information for use on some far-off day, following graduation. Consequently, pedagogical practice orients us toward packaged subjects that we may unwrap as needed on our journey through life. Graduation seems to be a sort of ceremonial rite of passage from the learning world into the doing world, and it also seems to carry the strong implication that the learning world is being left behind. But if we agree with Confucius, that all living is learning, we can see that learning is not only preparation for living but the very essence of living itself. When I am actively thinking, doing, reflecting on my experience, discussing it with others, practicing and learning new skills for improvement, and using these skills, I am, in fact, most vitally alive. Learning and living are virtually synonymous.

In the andragogical approach to education, learning is centered on problems rather than subjects. Andragogy is an educational process for problem finding and problem solving in the present; it is oriented to the discovery of

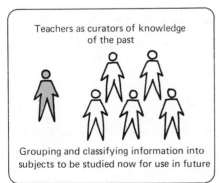

Teachers as curators of knowledge of the past

Grouping and classifying information into subjects to be studied now for use in future

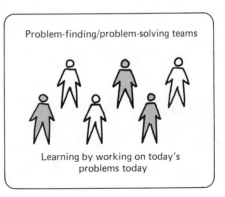

Problem-finding/problem-solving teams

Learning by working on today's problems today

Figure 6.5

an improvable situation, a desired goal, a corrective experience, or a developmental possibility in relation to the reality of the present circumstance. To discover and evaluate where we have been, where we are now, and where we want to go is the heart of the andragogical approach to education, and such an approach enables us to plan for and take positive steps to action within a realistic framework of possibility. Thus the andragogical time perspective is one of immediate application (see Fig. 6.5).

Two things should be made clear at this point with regard to both andragogy and pedagogy. First, many recent educational developments have tended to make child learning more andragogical. For example, the use of experiential learning techniques, the enhancement of collaborative skill development through group methods, and the recognition of cultural and ethnic differences have all been steps toward valuing the learner's experience and recognizing the capacity for self-direction. Secondly, in suggesting that an-

Characteristics of Adult Learners	Implications for Adult Learners
Self-concept: The adult learner sees himself as capable of self-direction and desires others to see him the same way. In fact, one definition of maturity is the capacity to be self-directing.	A climate of openness and respect is helpful in identifying what the learners want and need to learn. Adults enjoy planning and carrying out their own learning exercises. Adults need to be involved in evaluating their own progress toward self-chosen goals.
Experience: Adults bring a lifetime of experience to the learning situation. Youths tend to regard experience as something that has happened to them, while to an adult, his experience is him. The adult defines who he is in terms of his experience.	Less use is made of transmittal techniques; more of experiential techniques. Discovery of how to learn from experience is key to self-actualization. Mistakes are opportunities for learning. To reject adult experience is to reject the adult.
Readiness to learn: Adult developmental tasks increasingly move toward social and occupational role competence and away from the more physical developmental tasks of childhood.	Adults need opportunities to identify the competency requirements of their occupational and social roles. Adult readiness to learn and teachable moments peak at those points where a learning opportunity is coordinated with a recognition of the need to know. Adults can best identify their own readiness to learn and teachable moments.
A problem-centered time perspective: Youth thinks of education as the accumulation of knowledge for use in the future. Adults tend to think of learning as a way to be more effective in problem solving today.	Adult education needs to be problem-centered rather than theoretically oriented. Formal curriculum development is less valuable than finding out what the learners need to learn. Adults need the opportunity to apply new learning quickly.

Fig. 6.6 Implications of andragogical learning theory, as developed by Malcolm S. Knowles

dragogical learning concentrates on the here-and-now situation we do not mean to imply any disdain for the knowledge of the past. What we are suggesting is that adults are likely to be more strongly motivated to investigate a knowledge area in which they are experiencing a present problem than they are to pursue abstract theory for its own sake.

The above characteristics of adult learners have a number of implications for those who would strive to be effective teachers of adults. The first is that an adult educator is not a teacher in the traditional sense of the word. Knowles (1970) makes a penetrating comment in relation to this issue:

> The important implication for adult education practice of the fact that learning is an internal process is that those methods and techniques which involve the individual most deeply in self-directed inquiry will produce the greatest learning. This principle of ego-involvement lies at the heart of the adult educator's art. In fact, the main thrust of modern adult-educational technology

---

Implications for Facilitators or Teachers of Adults

Facilitators recognize adults as self-directing and treat them accordingly.

The facilitator is a learning reference for adult learners rather than a traditional instructor; facilitators are, therefore, encouraged to "tell it like it is" and stress "how I do it" rather than tell participants what they should do.

The facilatator avoids talking down to adult learners, who are usually experienced decision makers and self-starters. The facilitator instead tries to meet the learners' needs.

As the adult is his experience, failure to utilize the experience of the adult learner is equivalent to rejecting him as a person.

Learning occurs through helping adults with the identification of gaps in their knowledge.

No questions are "stupid"; all questions are "opportunities" for learning.

The primary emphasis in adult learning is on learners learning rather than on teachers teaching.

Involvement in such things as problems to be solved, case histories, and critical incidents generally offer greater learning opportunity for adults than "talking to" them or using other one-way transmittal techniques.

is in the direction of inventing techniques for involving adults in ever-deeper processes of self-diagnosis of their own needs for continued learning, in formulating their own objectives for learning, in sharing responsibility for designing and carrying out their learning activities, and in evaluating their progress toward their objectives. The truly artistic teacher of adults perceives the locus of responsibility for learning to be in the learner; he conscientiously suppresses his own compulsion to teach what he knows his students ought to learn in favor of helping his students learn for themselves what they want to learn.

A successful teacher of adults must constantly bear in mind that adults don't like to be talked down to or otherwise made to feel like children. Adult educators tend to be more successful when they level with the learners, when they talk frankly about what works for them and what doesn't work. As mistakes are often an excellent source of learning, adult educators should not be afraid to discuss their own mistakes openly if doing so serves a useful or even a vital purpose. It is not important for teachers of adults to appear as if they have all the answers, but it is helpful if they attempt to respond to all the questions and look to the learners for help in discovering some of the answers that they don't know. In short, the role of the teacher of adults is to openly share knowledge and experience insofar as it relates to the concerns and needs expressed by the learners. In addition, the teacher must never impose his or her ideas and values on others as the only solutions to a problem.

Educators need to provide some structure for the adult learning situation, since total laissez-faire is generally not conducive to effective group activity. They can play a facilitative role, acting as resource persons to help the learners form interest groups and diagnose their learning needs. In doing this they may provide some structure by suggesting different competencies needed to perform various functions or by suggesting several areas of interest into which learners may wish to group themselves to begin the diagnostic process. But the structure needs to be based more on recognition of mutual needs than on authority.

While adult educators try to make much use of experiential learning techniques, transmittal techniques such as lectures, readings, and audiovisual presentations may still be utilized to provide informational content. These techniques are best used, however, to provide a framework or context within which to build a discussion of specific problems or areas of concern identified or recognized as important by the learners.

Recognition of the characteristics of adult learners and the application of conscious effort to take these characteristics into account when designing and conducting adult learning activities will greatly increase the learner's experience of personal success. Success experience in turn increases the availability of energy needed to pursue additional success experience and to take those risks necessary to ensure continuing personal growth and development.

Figure 6.6 will perhaps serve as a handy reference guide for summarizing the ideas presented above.

AN ADULT LEARNING PROCESS

What precisely is an adult learning process? It is nothing more or less than the process of problem finding and problem solving described in Chapter 3, applied with a recognition of the characteristics of adult learners set forth above. In applying the adult learning process it is most useful (but not absolutely necessary) if participants have (or develop) some group dynamics or interpersonal relations skills. In fact, training in interpersonal relations is often an integral part of andragogical education. In addition, as most adults live and work in or have to deal with large organizations, it is also helpful to be aware of the energy forces inherent in the policies, procedures, and practices of large organizations. It may be useful to describe the problem-finding/problem-solving process and its purposes once again with some specific examples of different andragogical applications.

Process steps and purposes	Situational description
Climate setting. To establish an appropriate level of physical, psychological, and organizational comfort and to assist the participants in an active learning situation.	When I encounter a group of learners face to face, it is usually my policy to help them to get into the action as quickly as possible. My first concern is to ensure that the climate is as conducive as possible to learning—that means informality, comfort, and an appropriate amount of tension or excitement among participants. I want to know if people see potential for learning in this situation and to find out what their interests are in being there. I also want to find out what their hopes and expectations are. I like to make sure that everyone knows each other at least a little bit, but that people who know each other very well are separated, as sometimes dependency relationships seriously interfere with learning and growth. As a method for getting myself out of the way I usually invite people to find someone they don't know or would like to know better and to share with that person their expectations for the learning activity that they are presently attending. I like to then invite people to form themselves into groups of seven or eight and to discuss their expectations for about twenty or thirty minutes. I generally ask them to write down their comments on an easel set up before the group so that everyone is able to get a general idea of the issues and concerns.
Mutual planning. To begin to engage participants in the process	I then ask each group to have one person read that group's comments to the rest of the participants. In this way I get a chance to find out what's going on and

Process steps and purposes	Situational description
of forming a learning contract that involves making a personal commitment and a commitment to each other.	I begin to actively consider how I may be most helpful in guiding the interaction of the participants.
Assessment of learning needs. To present a framework or structure for learning that will help learners identify their own needs for learning within a community where the needs of others must be met as well as their own. In this step the processes of climate setting and mutual planning are actively and consciously continued.	When the expectation reports are finished I sometimes by way of explanation present a twenty-minute talk on the seven-step learning process called andragogy. After that I suggest that trying this learning process out may be a way to see if it works and if it is enjoyable. As a way to begin I generally suggest that participants identify from their experiences and beliefs what the ideal competencies might be to enable them to perform the tasks or fulfill the roles they wish to learn about. I might suggest two or three competencies and ask the participants if they can think of others. For example, if they were there to learn about how to conduct an effective organizational development program I would suggest that they would probably need a good deal of knowledge about motivation theory and about various management practices. I would ask them to add to this list, again on an easel that all the group could see. After an hour or two, and maybe a couple of trial cuts, we would together formulate a list of required competencies that would probably come close to hitting the mark (though I would still call this a tentative list of competencies because it would be important to keep it open-ended to allow for development based on emerging experience). After a period of

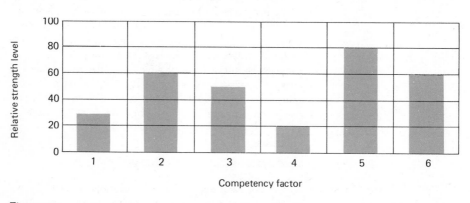

Figure 6.7

Process steps and purposes	Situational description
	refreshment and relaxation I would then ask participants to look carefully at the prepared list and to personally identify their own areas of relative strength. I would not bother with areas of weakness because they are usually indications of the absence of strength. Once people had completed their task of identifying relative strengths in relation to the ideal competencies required, they would have in front of them a personal competency model. This model would indicate gaps of various size (and also, if desired, of varying degrees of importance) and the largest gaps would indicate the areas of greatest developmental need (see Fig. 6.7).
Forming objectives. To enable participants to distill their perceptions of their individual needs for learning into purposeful activities.	From the model shown in Fig. 6.7 it is possible to identify the areas of developmental need and to assign priorities to individual learning objectives. In setting individual objectives it is desirable to help the participants frame statements of objectives in specific and measurable terms. For example, a general goal statement like "I want to become a better organizational development specialist" might be avoided and a more specific objective such as, "I will be able to demonstrate competency in conducting role-play exercises" may be found appropriate, since specific learning objectives need to be carefully distinguished from broad aims and goals.
Designing. To further aid participants in discovering what is needed to translate objectives into realistic programs or projects.	In the design stage the learners must decide what resources they will need in order to accomplish their learning task; what sort of time schedules they should set up; any audiovisual or other media assistance necessary; and how they will monitor or evaluate learning progress in terms of specific accomplishments. If the learners are going to involve others in their learning presentation they will need to consider how they will create a learning climate, do mutual planning with their participants, assess needs of others, and so forth.
Implementing. To provide an opportunity for all participants to experiment with their ideas and plans through a concrete or specific application.	Now comes the actual experience for which all of the above was the preparation or the plan. Any gap between actual experience during implementation and the expectations contained in the plan becomes the basis for identifying new needs.

Process steps and purposes	Situational description

This application may be made within the learning program itself or later. Without implementation there can be no learning from experience.

Evaluating. To help participants extract learning from the perceived gap between their needs, objectives, and design on the one hand and their actual experience emanating from their implementation on the other. To help participants reassess needs and plan new learning experiences.

While evaluation may determine how well we did in relation to our objectives, it is also highly useful as a descriptive reassessment of the needs for continued learning after a period of practical application.

Some of the most delightful and learningful experiences of my life were carried out in the above manner in graduate school courses conducted by Malcolm Knowles at Boston University. The freedom to engage in and direct my own learning enterprise and share with others in the process of learning and discovery was truly a "peak experience," to use Abraham Maslow's phrase. Since beginning to learn in this manner I have noticed a decided acceleration in both my own rate of learning and in my ability to make decisions with regard to appropriateness of direction and purpose.

The andragogical process facilitates learning from experience precisely because it purposefully directs learning toward its application in such a way that actual experience can be compared directly with intention. At that moment all four functions of consciousness—clarity of thought, emotional involvement, intuitive insight, and sensory awareness—may be brought into more or less full view of the learners. In addition, and of critical importance, the relative level of ambiguity in a situation (in terms of degrees of risk, potential psychological danger or threat, levels of interpersonal discomfort, and so forth) can be assessed prior to the application phase and moderated to an acceptable level. Success brings about a state of certainty and a tremendous feeling of release; failure, on the other hand, brings about increased certainty as to the need for an improved design based on additional information gained from the application experiment. This cannot in a true sense be identified as failure, but rather is a necessary part of the learning process that must occur as the normal prelude to eventual success. From my many personal experiences with this process I can report with confidence that the stage of descriptive (nonjudgmental) evaluation frees energy and creates the motivational enthusiasm necessary to forge ahead even in unusually difficult situations. It is this very spirit of enthusiasm and confidence that has been greatly eroded in so many educational settings and is desperately needed to reinstill a sense of personal worth. Evaluation used only as a judgmental tool is much too punitive. Judgmental evaluation attempts to motivate through fear and tends to paralyze the muscles, stultify ideas, and generate feelings of self-doubt and self-deprecation. Such approaches only prevent learning from occurring.

The andragogical approach to continuing education can be seen as grounding theory in practice, planning in action, and actual outcomes in a context of continuing effort. It stimulates increasing confidence in the face of risk and constantly widens horizons of creative potential. This approach also tends to show the implicit lack of value in many "canned" or packaged learning programs. With an andragogical approach each learner inevitably becomes his or her own curriculum designer; in fact, the freedom to select both sources and resources for learning is the continuing guarantee of the development of individuality, uniqueness, and creativity. Each person's values and ideals determine to an increasingly great extent the direction in which he or she will choose to travel. Obviously this is not an educational process for those who prefer to depend always on the teacher or any other authority figure for guidance, direction, and permission to proceed.

Perhaps it is important to make a further comment here about authority and control. Some people exposed to an andragogical educational experience for the first time are uncomfortable with the relative reduction of formal structure and the increase of personal choices. As a result they may mistake the openness of the evaluation method for an invitation to slacken their efforts rather than an opportunity to become more deeply involved in learning and doing. Also, a learner who has grievances or is experiencing some personal conflict with the organization for whom he or she works (or who is in conflict with society as a whole) is likely to project some of these feelings of anger or hostility onto the leader of an andragogical education activity. If such a learner does not project these feelings by showing overt hostility toward the leader figure, he or she may instead act them out by creating conflict with other learners. The reduction of role rigidity and structural authority then serves the additional purpose of bringing hidden conflicts and animosities out into the open, where they can generally be dealt with in constructive and helpful ways. A very tight authoritarian structure, on the other hand, operates in a manner analogous to the behavior of carbonated water in a capped bottle on a warm summer day. When shaken vigorously the bottle gives no external sign of a problem; therefore, it is very easy to assume that no problem exists. When the bottle blows up in your hand, however, it is too late to release any pent-up energy gradually.

Perhaps there is also another reason for some educators to prefer a tight, authoritarian structure over a more relaxed and open learning posture. If those who would be teachers of adults have not yet become comfortable in dealing with their own emotional responses to stressful situations, they may not feel able to handle the emotional responses of others. While there is always an outside risk of losing control of a situation as a result of some unforeseen event or reaction, this risk can be reduced almost to zero through reading the feedback responses of others in relation to the ambiguity/certainty relation described in Chapter 1. If there is too much ambiguity and tension, add more structure and control. If people seem to be feeling too directed and controlled, the indication is that more mutual planning and shared need assessment is called for.

When conflict does arise it is usually best to adopt Type B behaviors and stay with them unless such conflict is occurring because of too much ambiguity or vagueness in the situation or in your own leadership behavior. In these cases it is important to decide quickly what you want to do, state it very clearly and definitely, and act on it if others agree.

ANDRAGOGY AND MANAGEMENT

Because of the growing interest of many industrial corporations and government agencies in the andragogical education process and also the great potential it offers for improving both interpersonal relationships and task effectiveness, Malcolm Knowles has recently turned his attention to the role of the manager as an educator of adults. Knowles (1972)* says:

> The "role of the manager" has been a favorite object of study of the behavioral scientists now for several decades. And their findings have done much to move management theory away from early conceptions of the managerial role as a simple, mechanical, organizer of work to a more complex conception of the multiple roles of the manager. For when the behavioral scientists studied what effective managers really do, they discovered that they perform a variety of roles—planner, organizer, supporter, adjudicator, coordinator, communicator, listener, operator, and teacher, to cite a few—and that each role requires its own unique set of competencies.
>
> A strong thrust in recent developments in management theory has been the increasing emphasis placed on the last-named role, teacher. For, in the long run, the executive who makes the greatest contribution to his corporation is the one who is able to release and develop the potential of the human resources that are his company's principal asset.

* From Malcolm Knowles, "The Manager as Educator," *Journal of Continuing Education and Training*, Vol. 2, No. 2. Copyright Baywood Publishing Company, Inc., 1972.

Thus, according to modern management theory, every manager must be an educator, too.

But the fact is that adults differ in certain crucial ways from youth as learners. This is an insight that has emerged only recently from the growing body of research in adult education.

So it is not enough for managers to be educators. They must be adult educators.

There are many opportunities for the application of andragogical learning principles in business, industrial, and government settings. Andragogy may of course be used for training and development, but it may also be used for action research programs aimed at organizational problem finding and problem solving, for team building, and for performance appraisal. In fact, it may be used whenever a situation calls for recognition of the characteristics of adult learning behavior. A convenient management check list like the following may be useful for self-rating the degree to which your own management style complements that of an effective adult educator. You may wish to have a group of your subordinates rate you on these factors and then look with them at any congruencies or discrepancies that may exist.

Do I create a social climate in which subordinates feel respected?
Low   1   2   3   4   5   6   7   *High*

Do I treat mistakes as opportunities for learning and growth?
Low   1   2   3   4   5   6   7   *High*

Do I help my subordinates discover what they need to learn?
Low   1   2   3   4   5   6   7   *High*

Do I help my staff to extract learning from practical work situations and experiences?
Low   1   2   3   4   5   6   7   *High*

Do my staff members have responsibility for designing and carrying out their own learning experiences?
Low   1   2   3   4   5   6   7   *High*

Do my staff members engage in self-appraisal and personal planning for performance improvement?
Low   1   2   3   4   5   6   7   *High*

Do I permit or encourage innovation and experiments to change the accepted way of doing things if the plan proposed appears possible?
Low   1   2   3   4   5   6   7   *High*

Am I aware of the developmental tasks and readiness-to-learn issues that concern my staff?

Low   1   2   3   4   5   6   7   *High*

Do I try to implement a joint problem-finding and problem-solving strategy to involve my staff in dealing with day-to-day problems and longer-range issues?

Low   1   2   3   4   5   6   7   *High*

Malcolm Knowles (1972) says that managers need to create an educative environment for people to live and work in and intimates that doing so has an important simultaneous benefit: "Isn't it fortunate that an educative environment—one in which each individual is experiencing increasing self-fulfillment —is also a productive environment?"

It is apparent that individuals who are deeply involved in learning more about what they are doing will tend to be much more productive than the apathetic or disinterested.

THREE ANDRAGOGICAL APPLICATIONS

Three different learning approaches to utilizing the andragogical process are described below. They represent widely different examples of the application of this learning process in totally different settings. The first one describes an andragogical approach to teaching a college chemistry class; the second is a plan for an individualized learning program for senior or high-level middle managers; and the third is a program for the technical training of craftspersons in a large public utility.

The College Chemistry Class

In a college chemistry class forty-two students were required to learn a series of highly technical and complicated procedures in a sixteen-week semester. Instead of keeping these students in a win/lose competitive relationship with each other based on the assumption that grades must fit a bell-shaped distribution curve, this professor asked the class if they would like to join him in an adventure in collaborative education. The goal was for everyone in the class to receive an A by being able to demonstrate that they could perform every one of the required operations or procedures correctly by the end of the semester, in addition to having a thorough grasp of the theory presented. In order to achieve this goal they would have to collaborate with each other. After some discussion the class reached a unanimous agreement when they were convinced the professor was not trying to trick them.

The first two weeks were spent identifying what had to be learned and what the specific competency requirements would be for earning an A. Together the class members and the professor decided that twenty-minute input sessions by him as the expert would be sufficient. Therefore the professor lectured for only twenty to thirty minutes on each major section of the course and spent brief periods demonstrating techniques and procedures. The remainder of the class time was devoted to group work. Seven groups of six students each formed into problem-finding/problem-solving teams. After each presentation the professor asked for seven volunteers who felt they could serve as resource persons in helping to facilitate the learning of the material presented in the lecture. These seven, who changed from week to week, became the team leaders of their groups. The professor in turn became a resource person to the team leaders, so that if a group was stuck it could get specialized help. During the semester groups that were unable to get all their members up to the required level of competency during class time agreed to meet after class so that their group did not become less effective than the others. The students enjoyed this type of learning environment and found that they actually learned more themselves when they were helping others learn. At the end of the semester all forty-two of the students received legitimate A grades. The performance on the exam was astonishing compared with the other chemistry classes. The professor was delighted with the results but was afraid he would get the reputation of being an easy marker; he was also apprehensive that he would have some difficulty with the dean because of his departure from the traditional approach to learning based on competitive win/lose norms.

Complex content can be handled much more effectively when a serious attempt is made to find out what is already known by the learners, thereby allowing them to concentrate on learning what they need to know. This approach also makes it easier to determine if the amount of material to be assimilated is appropriate for the time available. It seems much more practical to reduce the content or extend the learning time than it is to create conditions of failure where some of the brightest students feel barely competent and others cannot cope at all.

The Fifth-Level Managers

Promotion to the fifth level of management in most large corporations involves a series of changes that must be coped with effectively if the manager is to continue to grow and move upward to the sixth and seventh levels and beyond. It may be worthwhile to look at these changes in order to design a continuing development program for fifth-level or general managers.

It seems clear that promotion to the fifth level is a significant, if not *the* significant, turning point of a career. It is clearly the doorway leading out of the ranks of middle management into a position of corporate leadership. One question that emerges is how effectively the fifth-level manager rises to meet the leadership challenge. Granting the nature of hierarchical organizations, we could in general observe the fifth level to be more isolated and less involving than the fourth. Second, it is more specialized; the incumbent finds himself in a one-of-a-kind position, where there is less lateral competition. Third, the incumbent has reached a level where the population has thinned out drastically. Will he or she ever get to sixth level or is this the end of the promotional line? If it is, is there not a profoundly seductive tendency to begin preparing for retirement or at least slowing down a little after the dizzying climb? Fourth, the level of compensation at the fifth level begins to satisfy the need for additional income. While individual circumstances vary, increased compensation at the fifth level tends to occur at or near the peak demand for preferential expenses: college educations, vacation homes, travel, and so forth. As life at the fifth level goes on, the potential of increased income as a motivating force tends to become less and less.

The fifth-level assignment by nature requires more dependence on the effectiveness of subordinates in meeting the needs of the business. At the same time it increases frustration because there is no longer (for the most part) direct access to line operating managers on a personal basis; instead, one must work through one's department heads. There is thus a great increase in the need for expertise in developing and fostering a climate of enthusiasm and excitement in others that keeps everyone in the organization moving toward significant goals and stretching for improvement.

Granting the above factors, it would not be surprising to find a good many incumbents in fifth-level assignments tending to play a less-than-venturesome role in any corporation. Maintenance of the status quo tends to become more rewarding than fostering development. Staying on your own turf is encouraged, so it's hard to find out what's going on in the other fellow's yard, even if it can have a profound effect on your own operation. A reactive posture of seeking to eliminate problems and staving off disasters can easily predominate over one of proactivity, which involves risk taking and an emphasis on developing the potential inherent in positive action.

If the above characteristics are at all representative of the fifth-level culture, what are the needs for a continuing development program for those who are already assumed to be developed? Even though we recognize that the need for growth, change, and development never ceases during our lifetime, powerful beliefs operate to prevent us from engaging in such activity when we are presumed to have already achieved success. One is that education ends with the receipt of a degree or a diploma. Another is that education only occurs in a formal or institutional setting. A third is that learning and doing are separate activities; that learning is an activity of the mind involving the acquisition of theoretical concepts in a classroom, while doing is behaving pragmatically in the real world of events—where theory is somehow seen as unrealistic and as a deterrent to swift and practical action.

In light of the above considerations, it was considered worthwhile in one company to undertake an informal continuing education program for the ongoing development of its fifth-level managers. The program was aimed at achieving the following goals:

- To assist each participant in formulating a plan for personally relevant continuing education

- To provide specific inputs of management and organizational theory

- To require each manager to put the concepts discussed into practice in an actual real-life situation in his regular assignment in order to learn both cognitively and through experience

Its objectives were as follows:

- Increased managerial competence, demonstrable both quantitatively and qualitatively in specific program applications

- Greater awareness and involvement by participants in actively supporting the primary goals and objectives of the company; in short, improved teamwork and interaction by participants with others at the fifth level and above

- Increased enthusiasm and interest stemming from understanding and using a new and effective strategy for resolving difficult and persistent management problems

The proposed continuing education program was to be designed by the participants within a general structural framework provided by the program director. A sixteen-day program was planned, spread evenly over a period of six to seven months. With the exception of the first session, which was to be conducted at the company offices and would consist of a one-day preplanning or introductory meeting, each session would consist of a two-and-one-half-day residential meeting at a convenient and comfortable (motel or hotel) location. Six two-and-one-half-day sessions were anticipated, although some program time beyond the fourth session was to be utilized in half-day units for individual participants as required.

Education, management, and organizational issues and concerns emerged naturally as the program unfolded. The program moved from an identification of needs to the formulation of specific individual and organizational objectives. As objectives became firm, participants designed their own projects and/or programs and implemented them in their own way. The results of each participant's activity were evaluated by the other participants and by the program director, leading to a new shared awareness of organizational and individual needs. Thus the program developed a cyclical process that utilized evaluation as feedback for new organizational design. In the course of the program, many individual and organizational needs were met and new ones emerged. It became quite clear during the program that unmet needs form the basis of organizational dysfunction. The strategy here was one that led toward the recognition of needs that seldom, if ever, are identified or met in most organizations; for example, managers became much more keenly aware of the negative impact of the hierarchical organization structure on their own relationships with each other as well as with their superiors and subordinates. Successful implementation of this program resulted in a significant and recognizable improvement in management effectiveness in that company.

Any program of this type works best for those who enter into it willingly. Granting a solid career background of successful performance, there is always concern about continuing to be successful in the future. We believed a group of six to eight fifth-level executives would be the ideal number of participants, and as the program would not involve any of them for more than two working days each month it should not hamper their performance in their regular assignments. In fact, as much of the work in the program was directly related to each participant's regular assignment, two days of concentrated reflection and action each month in itself helped to improve performance materially. This kind of training or education does not wait until after the program ends seven months later for implementation. The participants began using and applying their new knowledge and abilities immediately.

The Craft Development Program

The situation leading to the formulation of a craft development program was as follows. The union had been complaining for a long time that management was doing a poor job of training craftspersons. Management, on the other hand, was spending significant sums of money on expensive specialized courses of instruction conducted in its own training schools. Part of the problem appeared to revolve around the process used to select trainees to fill the training slots available. Someone from the training department would call up and typically say, "I have two slots open for next Monday morning; who can you send?" As often as not the supervisor could not afford to send anyone, as his job was engineered to very tight performance standards; but wishing to be cooperative with the training staff and also trying to satisfy the union's complaint, he would dutifully oblige by sending his least competent performers. When these people returned from training they were seldom given the opportunity to utilize the learning they had received; instead they were put back on routine jobs. They had, after all, received the training, so the management statistics were satisfied and the union complaint could be rebutted. However, there was only minimal observable increase in worker competence in relation to the training dollars spent.

It was decided, after considerable consultation, to develop an on-the-job training need assessment and to use the training school only to meet learning needs that were recognized jointly by the craftspersons and their supervisors. Conducting an effective need assessment involved coping with a fairly complex set of circumstances. First, the craftsperson's job required competence in 130 different tasks of various degrees of technical difficulty. Only two craftspersons out of sixteen in the unit were fully competent in all of the technical tasks, and they naturally held the highest ratings and received the highest income. Management estimated that it took about five years to develop top skills in this job assignment and freely acknowledged that many craftspersons never developed more than moderate skill and that the average craftsperson was only competent in about sixty to eighty of the tasks involved in the job. The department operated fairly effectively because the best craftspersons acted as troubleshooters on the difficult or more complex tasks and the rest performed the simpler or more routine tasks more or less continuously. Furthermore, evidence of boredom existed in the craftsperson ranks, and the union's relations with management were poor. The union felt management was letting the workers down, particularly in training, and management felt the union was doing everything in its power, short of precipitating a walkout, to disrupt the organization. Management acknowledged that it would be ideal to improve the general level of craftsperson competence, but it claimed that the training schools, operated within the company at considerable cost, were doing the best that could be expected. A final problem lay in the fact that because the craft supervisor was responsible for rating the craftspersons' competence and job knowledge, craftspersons were very reluctant to let the supervisor find out their real level of competence lest this knowledge on the part of the supervisor be used against them.

A meeting was held with the union steward, one top- and one middle-level craftsperson, the supervisor, and a consultant trained in andragogical education. The meeting was called for the purpose of dealing with the union's claim that management was failing to train craftspersons. In the course of the meeting, the following plan was unveiled.

A five-page rating form was introduced listing all 130 tasks with two 0–5 rating scales, one to be filled out by the supervisor and one to be filled out by the craftsperson. Each task was printed on the form in the following manner:

Task No. 15 Can you perform transmission raise tests on trunks?

Craftsperson rating	0	1	2	3	4	5
	cannot perform	can perform at low level		can perform at medium level		can perform at high level
Supervisor rating	0	1	2	3	4	5

The key to the proposed training need assessment lay in the process through which it was to be conducted. The process was described at the meeting as follows.

Each craftsperson was to be given a rating form and would be asked to complete it for each of the 130 items. They were to be instructed not to show their own ratings to their supervisor *unless they wished to.* The supervisor would be required to complete the rating form on each of the sixteen craftspersons and to discuss those ratings with each craftsperson privately—although the supervisor would be obliged to admit publicly that such ratings would not and probably could not be correct in every case. The supervisor was instructed to meet with each craftsperson individually and develop a six-month training plan for each craftsperson that would combine formal instruction in the training school with informal training on the job. The plan would be developed wholly on the basis of the supervisor's rating *unless* the craftsperson wished to disclose his or her personal self-ratings to the supervisor. In this case, if the craftsperson's and the supervisor's separate ratings did not agree on any particular item, a process of mutual negotiation was required to analyze the reasons for the discrepancy and to form a mutual plan for removing the discrepancy and increasing competence as well.

A disagreement on any item did not mean that either the supervisor or the craftsperson was right or wrong. It did mean, however, that the craftsperson was required to have an opportunity to prove the supervisor wrong; if the craftsperson was able to do so, the supervisor's rating would have to be changed. In very close cases, both parties would agree not to disagree but to move up or down one rating level in the interests of moving ahead with the planning. In addition, the supervisor agreed to play an active role in making sure that the craftsperson had ample opportunity for both on-the-job and formal training. The meeting ended with the union steward subscribing to the plan, and in a following meeting all the craftspersons agreed to try it as well.

After six months of individualized and personal attention to developing competence, the supervisor and craftsperson ratings were completed again. All craftspersons were willing to compare their ratings with those of their supervisors, and it was observed that extraordinary progress had been made by some and excellent progress by many.

The supervisor prepared a graph (which did not identify craftspersons by name) showing the changes in the department's level of competence in the 130 areas during the six-month period. While it was realized that some competencies take longer to develop than others, it became clear that the members of this department were learning and increasing their skills much more rapidly than members of other departments and that learning development was occurring at a faster rate than had been believed possible. The outstanding feature of the program was that it enabled the craftspersons to take on responsibility for planning their own development with their supervisor, obtaining the necessary support, and proceeding at their own pace. Because the craftspersons were happy with the program, the union was also and labor relations improved significantly.

THE ORIGINS OF ANDRAGOGY

Andragogy is an unfamiliar term to most people. People often ask how andragogy began? Where did the name come from? Has anyone heard of it outside the United States? These questions are typical of those asked by people first exposed to andragogical training or education programs.

The term *andragogy* (or andragology) derives from a combination of the classical Greek verb *agogos* ("leading") and the stem *aner* ("man"). Andragogy is now defined as the art and science of helping adults learn. The word was first used in 1833 by a German grammar-school teacher, Alexander Kapp, to describe Plato's educational theory. Kapp distinguished *andragogy* from *social pedagogy* (basic remedial education for the disadvantaged or handicapped), referring to andragogy as the normal and natural process of continuing education for adults.

The development of andragogy seems to have been much more rapid in Europe than in the United States. In the Netherlands there are at present seven or more major universities granting degrees in andragogy. A similar development has occurred in Germany, Poland, Hungary, and in particular Yugoslavia, where several universities are offering doctoral programs. Andragogy is becoming known in France, England, and in South America. Malcolm Knowles, formerly of Boston University and now Professor of Education at North Carolina State University, introduced andragogy to the United States and is internationally recognized for his creative developmental work in this new field (Van Enckevort, 1971).

While andragogy has been emerging as a new educational process for adults, closely related discoveries that utilize the same basic ideas have been and are being made in the fields of management and organizational development, and also in the fields of counseling, psychotherapy, and social psychology. Andragogy is a unifying educational process that can help adults discover and use the findings from these many specialized fields of study for practical application in situations to stimulate the growth and health of individuals, organizations, and communities. In fact, many European andragogues consider "social case work, counseling, resocialization and reeducative processes, social group work, adult education, personnel management, community organization, and community development, etc." all to be *parts* of applied andragogy (Van Enckevort, 1971). Andragogy is seen in this sense to be the *process* through which the differing contents of specialized fields or activities can be learned and applied in adult settings and situations.

Andragogical learning programs and projects are now beginning to be used extensively throughout the United States, particularly in business and industry and in training programs for social workers. Other applications are being made in community development and in penal institutions. In some cases andragogy has been introduced with considerable success into traditional pedagogical environments, and other applications have found their way into the armed services.

People have also asked how much individuals enjoy andragogical learning experiences. In my own experience reactions have been most positive and favorable, but the other day I received a list of reactions from another program with which I was in no way connected. This list came from a military setting and is printed verbatim without identification of names or places.

A Compilation of Participant Responses

- I feel much more confident as a counselor and problem solver.

- The workshop has provided the tools which would aid my development as a leader.

- I wish I had been exposed to (this workshop) at a much earlier stage, i.e. before commissioning.

- The (workshop) manual left some room for improvement. There's a lot of information in it for a one week workshop—but I will find the manual useful as a resource text in problem solving.

- I feel very privileged to be one of five officers to participate in the workshop.

- I came to the workshop looking primarily for adult education principles and how these principles can be used in my classes at OCS. Additionally, I wanted some skill, knowledge, and information that would assist me personally and professionally. I feel that those objectives were met.

- The workshop's emphasis on active listening and confrontation were especially helpful to me.

- The atmosphere was conducive to participation, and stating our desires at the first made it seem like we were being assisted instead of being taught.

- The two objectives that were covered best were in learning adult education and counseling skills. Impact in both cases was very positive.

- The techniques of counseling . . . . are useful for anyone.

- My only criticism would be the workbook. It is difficult to understand.

- I think the course is very valid.

- This course gave me a whole new way to approach teaching.

- The use of video tape was not warranted by the teaching use it had . . . the time spent watching the TV was not worth the effort.

- The workshop began to have deep meaning when a problem known to us was the topic of the role play.

- The methods used in the seminar could be incorporated into the curriculum.

- I enjoyed the course and will recommend it to others.

- The climate of the seminar was open. . . . many things were shared by the group which in most groups would probably not have been said.

- I enjoyed the. . . . video tape (positive and immediate feedback) and role playing to practice what had been taught.

- This has been one of the more valuable things I have done since coming to OCS.

If the above responses are typical, and I can assure you from my own experience that they are, it is reasonable to expect that adult learning approaches will be utilized more and more extensively by all types of organizations.

If the primary activity of management is problem finding and problem solving, then andragogy is a most useful and effective aid. If the verb *to manage* means only to plan (decide for others), direct (others), motivate (externally manipulate others), and control (force others into rigid and patterned responses), there is no need to consider whether or not managers need to be adult educators. However I have found very few managers to be blatantly authoritarian. What I have found is many managers who are genuinely perplexed by the complexities of maintaining effective interpersonal relationships while trying to accomplish difficult tasks in a limited time frame. Effective performance depends, therefore, on the manager's ability to bring problems to the surface where they can be recognized and dealt with appropriately. This drawing forth, or *educing*, of problems inherent in situations and organizational components is the bedrock task of an effective manager. The most effective systems of management, therefore, are most likely those built upon a solid framework of adult education theory.

7 *Personal Growth*

In the preceding chapter I described an approach to adult learning that places the learner in command of his or her own development and utilizes the teacher as one of a number of potential resources for helping the learner learn. In this chapter I shall attempt to probe more deeply into some of the issues and problems inherent in fostering and guiding one's own personal growth and development. Since ancient times humans have been puzzled and confused by their own nature. Who are these mysterious creatures called humans? And why do they do the things they do? Theologians, philosophers, historians, anthropologists, educators, psychologists, and managers, as well as practically everybody else, in one way or another try to understand human nature and come to terms with it. Saint Paul probably expressed this mystery most succinctly when he wrote "Why is it that I do the things that I would not do and do not do the things that I would do?" The tug and pull of individual inclinations and attractions, manifested as human needs, interests, values, wants, and desires, confront us constantly with the necessity to make choices. While it is the outcomes of these choices that largely determine our unique individuality, it is not clear just why we make the choices we actually make.

Some psychologists have attempted to understand human behavior by analyzing personality traits. One psychologist appears to have identified over 18,000 different traits in various literary sources (Taylor, 1973). If one can assume that there are at least a hundred variations of any trait the conclusion is staggering: differences among humans in regard to personality traits number approximately $18,000^{100}$, well beyond the quadrillion range. Obviously the trait approach toward understanding human personality leads us into a desert where human differences are so many grains of sand. Others, theologians and philosophers, have attempted to build elaborate systems of morality depicting human differences as emerging from an internal and external struggle with the forces of good and evil. Historians have demonstrated human differences in terms of specific events, sometimes moralizing and sometimes not, and cultural anthropologists have shown us that morality is highly culture dependent—that what is perceived as wrong or bad in one culture may be considered acceptable or even good in another. Educators tend to evaluate human differences on the basis of what individuals know. Managers often view individual differences on the basis of what people can do.

Perhaps we can impose some clarity and organization on this confusing array of theories and approaches by constructing a three-dimensional picture of individuality and human differences. If we tentatively entertain the notion that all human individuals differ with regard to knowledge, experience, and the utilization of psychic and physical energy we may have succeeded in identifying three fundamental categories that will serve to vastly simplify the origins of the myriad array of individual differences we observe daily.

I should stress at this point that I do not wish to imply any tendency or desire to make individuals become more alike; on the contrary, it is my deep belief that the ultimate purpose behind centuries of human growth and development is the creation of ever-greater individuality and uniqueness. If we all learn to develop more respect and wonder for the vast potential that as yet lies locked inside of us, we may increasingly come to recognize that mass movements, totalitarian regimes, and other "philosophies of the herd" are collective attempts to avoid and escape the difficulties and anxieties inherent in bravely facing life's demand for growth. Eric Hoffer (1951) expressed this concept with remarkable eloquence:

> A rising mass movement attracts and holds a following not by its doctrine and promises but by the refuge it offers from the anxieties, barrenness and meaninglessness of an individual existence. It cures the poignantly frustrated not by conferring on them an absolute truth or by remedying the difficulties and abuses which made their lives miserable, but by freeing them from their ineffectual selves—and it does this by enfolding and absorbing them into a closely knit and exultant corporate whole.

Most mass movements hold out an attractive but essentially false promise. They cannot successfully lift from us the burden of individual responsibility and in the end they can only succeed in robbing us of our most creative individual capacities.

Let us now proceed to look in depth at the three hallmarks of personal difference—knowledge, experience, and energy. These are the three basic dimensions that determine individual uniqueness. All three of these dimensions change continuously as we move through different stages of development. The wide disparity among individual life histories and career patterns may be largely accounted for by differences in knowledge, experience, and energy. Some people seem to do so much more with their lives than others. And some people appear to be clearly at a disadvantage. If our goal is absolute equality for everyone we will probably never achieve it. If, however, we succeed in creating conditions that allow for optimal individual development for all, most of us will achieve a high level of personal and social satisfaction and will be less likely to want to tear down the social, governmental, and business institutions that are perhaps (with some appropriate changes) our best guarantees of continuing freedom. Inefficient and ineffective as they may sometimes be, these institutions have been built at great cost over many centuries, and human energy may be more efficiently used for their reformation than for revolution.

In the course of looking at personal growth in knowledge, experience, and energy, I will present three growth models, one for each category. In so doing we may cover all of the essential elements involved in personal growth and provide a pathway for further individual exploration. After this task is complete it will perhaps also be useful to consider inner conflicts that inhibit personal growth, including abnormality, which represents the antithesis of personal growth. Finally, we will assess some constraints placed on personal growth in organizational settings.

THE PROCESS OF ACQUIRING KNOWLEDGE

In seeking how individuals differ with regard to knowledge we may initially consider the acquisition of formal education and its assortment of theories and facts. The acquisition of knowledge has, after all, been intimately associated with the process of schooling for a long time. However it is becoming increasingly clear that formal schooling in our society generally aims at creating sameness and not difference. The members of a class, for example, are graded on the basis of how well they each acquire the same information presented in the same way to all. While this process appears necessary in order to produce doctors, engineers, lawyers, teachers, and so forth, it does not necessarily produce individuals who are different. In other words, it produces people who can fill social and work roles, which is obviously important, but it does not tend to produce individuals who can transform society itself. And the reason is obvious. School aims primarily at developing the thinking and sensory functions of consciousness and, by unintentionally neglecting the development of emotion and intuition, tends to produce individuals who are overly developed on the Type A side. One inevitable result is that the arts wind up lagging quite far behind the sciences.

In Chapter 2 we explored Carl Jung's conception of the fourfold nature of human consciousness. In doing so we became aware that each of us typically chooses one preferred functional method of knowing (thought, intuition, emotion, or sensation) plus one additional, supportive function, making a pair (for example, thought supported by sensation, emotion supported by intuition, sensation supported by intuition, and so forth). In the course of his work, Jung became aware of two fundamental tendencies or attitudes in the human personality that also contributed substantially to marked differences in human behavior (Campbell, 1971). The first of these tendencies he labeled *extraversion*. Persons with extraverted attitudes tended to be outgoing and oriented toward action in the world of practical events. The second tendency he termed *introversion*. The introverted attitude was manifested in a tendency toward inner orientation, a preoccupation with ideas, and subjective or even mystical perceptions emanating from an individual's reflection on his or her experience.

As a result of the discovery of extraversion and introversion Jung was able to identify and characterize eight primary psychological types of personalities by combining the four primary ways of knowing with these two fundamental attitudes. Thus in the process of acquiring knowledge we may tend to become an extraverted thinking type, an extraverted intuitive type, and so forth on one side; or an introverted thinking type, an introverted emotional type, and so forth on the other. Jung developed a most interesting and absorbing discussion of all eight personality types and their behavioral characteristics that makes very clear why and how individuals develop personality differences, which lead in turn to interpersonal conflicts. We must bear in mind, however, that Jung also suggested that we all endeavor to come to know the whole range of our capabilities, to develop self-awareness through the resolution of the opposing tendencies within us. This resolution of opposites Jung termed the transcendent function, as we saw in Chapter 2. Therefore, rather than concentrating on personality differences we might instead begin concentrating on personality development: the restoration to balance of our underdeveloped "other sides." In Chapter 2 we also saw that functions of consciousness that were infrequently used (emotion and intuition, for example) tended to lose their energy value and eventually, when there was insufficient energy to maintain them at the threshold of one's consciousness, to disappear, as it were, into the unconscious, only to arise at some inauspicious or untoward moment.

It is because of this, I believe, that at various times and under various conditions individuals are simply unaware or unconscious of what their real needs for additional knowledge are. How can I know what I need to know if I am unconscious both of what I do not know and of my need to know it? The solution to this seeming enigma has also been provided by Jung. It consists of increasing psychic energy sufficiently to bring the unconscious need to the required threshold level of intensity. This insight provides the key to building a personal growth model aimed at raising consciousness and increasing awareness; a model of knowledge acquisition that transforms consciousness. Before we construct this model, however, it is perhaps necessary to consider a vitally important issue.

Receiving and Blocking the Flow of Information

In order to successfully pursue self-directed personal growth and development through the acquisition of knowledge it appears necessary to be aware of the relationship between the four functions of consciousness and our internal responses to external stimulation. We can see in the functions of sensation and intuition an inherent capacity to apprehend the external world directly as existential fact. When I reach out and touch a chair, for example, I immediately sense that I have made contact with an object and intuitively understand the relationship between my hand and the chair. The contact provides a stimulus that is instantly perceived by sensation and intuition (although one or the other perception might be vastly stronger). The other two functions, thought and emotion, act in a kind of secondary fashion; they both involve a response based upon conscious reflection and, here again, either response may dominate the other.

The engaging of two functions of consciousness through stimulus and the other two through response poses an interesting problem, especially when we recognize that thought and sensation may either dominate emotion and intuition or be dominated by them, or that any one function may dominate the other three.

The key process in the acquisition of knowledge is that of allowing information from outside ourselves to be taken inside, processed and digested (internalized), and assimilated in such a fashion that it becomes part of us and we are able to use it in any way we deem appropriate. But knowledge will only be acquired if it is openly received and not blocked at any stage along the way toward internalization and eventual use. The capacity we all have to screen out knowledge we don't want or need is vitally necessary for the preservation of mental health and perhaps for human survival. It is also, however, a source of great frustration for anyone who is trying to get someone to *understand* something he or she is trying to communicate. Let us look more closely at this issue.

In Chapter 1, I introduced two characteristically opposite sets of behavior: Type A, oriented toward closure and certainty; and Type B, oriented toward openness and the acceptance of ambiguity. We further saw in Chapter 2 that the functions of thought and sensation were Type A oriented while emotion and intuition were Type B oriented. Thus there is a fundamental capacity in all of us to be either open or closed and to move back and forth from one state to the other. Now when we are attempting to acquire knowledge or to understand what someone is trying to communicate to us, we must be in a state of openness in order to receive the information coming into us. Often we *believe* we are open when in fact we are not. This situation, as we all know, leads to great frustration in interpersonal relationships. To gain greater appreciation of this phenomenon it may be useful to look at four characteristic situations, only one of which allows real internalization of knowledge to occur. The next time you are experiencing difficulty in understanding someone even after ascertaining that what they are saying generally makes sense, try to determine which of the other three unworkable situations is occurring within you.

Situation 1 (workable). Emotion and intuition function with a modality of openness (Type B). If one is emotionally accepting of another person and open to their experience, the function of thought will move naturally and easily toward closure and certainty. Thus decisions will tend to be reached quickly and will be accompanied by a high level of commitment. Simultaneous openness of the intuitive function will allow a variety of questions to be raised or problems to be identified. Thus the discussion will have a realistic focus and closure will be achieved around appropriate issues, allowing both parties to see (or to sense) how something would actually work in practice. So we can see that emotional and intuitive openness lead naturally toward and facilitate closure of knowledge (this is what is and I accept it) and sensory satisfaction (this is how I envision it will work), resulting in a high degree of cognitive consonance.

Situation 2 (unworkable). If one is emotionally *closed* and not accepting of another person or situation, thought processes will not lead to closure and a state of cognitive uncertainty or dissonance will exist. If one is also closed to intuition and unaware of inherent possibilities in a situation, sensory disorientation may occur and real problems may not be foreseen. Decisions will therefore tend to lack commitment and acceptance of consequences, and tasks may be pursued more or less aimlessly and without a sense of purpose. In addition, arguments will tend to arise that may not have anything directly to do with the issues at hand, thus increasing the level of cognitive dissonance. It should be noted here that fights do not tend to produce problem resolution; they only increase frustration unless they produce a certain emotional satisfaction that then leads to emotional acceptance (reunion and reconciliation).

Situation 3 (unworkable). If thought eclipses emotion, and if thought processes are open and flowing, there will be an abundance of creative ideas and a great deal of sensory satisfaction regarding appropriateness or suitability. But the rational situation will not create emotional warmth or acceptance because it is one of sterility, and the resulting decisions will not generate real commitment to action (see also the Abilene paradox, Chapter 3). As a result, people will do things and wonder why afterward. In addition, if sensation eliminates intuition and blocks it, there is likely to be a blithe ignorance of potential disasters.

Situation 4 (unworkable). If thought processes are *closed* and become dominated by emotion, unthinking or irrational behavior may follow. This behavior is stimulated by the increased feeling of frustration that is caused by blocked energy. If intuition also rises to dominate sensation, unrealistic ideas may not be tempered by a sense of reality; in the resulting state of fantasy or illusion, physical violence may occur.

So we can again see the necessity of balancing the four functions of consciousness appropriately and of remaining emotionally and intuitively open if we are to gain knowledge, clearer understanding, and more satisfying relationships with others.

A Model for Knowledge Acquisition that Transforms Consciousness

In order to optimize the attainment of personal knowledge it appears necessary to engage all four functions of consciousness in the learning process. The result is often a flash of insight, self-discovery, or the emergence of a highly suitable and unexpected solution. To proceed it is necessary to first determine *your* preferred way of knowing. In our culture it is generally, but not always, Type A: thought supported by sensation; the logical or rational approach. In this case, if you concentrate on how you *feel* about a situation and what you can actively *imagine* about it, along with what you *think* about it and how it *looks* to you, you are beginning to engage all four ways of knowing. If you sufficiently pair and balance the opposites of Type A and Type B consciousness you are calling upon the transcendent function of consciousness; if you succeed in increasing psychic energy you will in turn stimulate insight or self-discovery, and recognize a pathway along which to move forward. This result will not be achieved by everyone, nor is it easy to accomplish this task in the beginning because many of us are so steeped in Type A behavior and consciousness that we have great difficulty in encountering our Type B side at all.

A diagram of the self-discovery process may be useful in order to clarify this somewhat difficult notion (see Fig. 7.1). First let us look once again at the field of consciousness and picture the unconscious standing, as it were, behind and above it. As we saw in the section on induction and expression in Chapter 2, it is necessary to breathe deeply or to back up, as it were, before trying

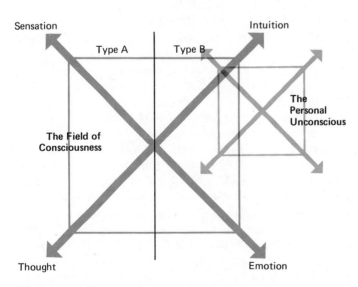

Fig. 7.1 A self-discovery process

to move ahead. So, for example, if you are consciously aware of an object and know what it is and how it appears to your senses, you have to back up into a Type B emotional appreciation, an intuitive awareness, of the object before you can move to a new plateau of conscious awareness and effective action. As you back up into emotion and intuition, psychic energy rises and you approach the transcendent function. If a sufficient energy level is reached, contents in the personal unconscious may reach a level of intensity sufficient to tumble them into consciousness. This is creative insight. When the level of psychic energy is extraordinarily high and sufficient to establish union with the collective unconscious or universal archetypes (see also Chapter 2), the result may be truly artistic expression or a great discovery.

There are a variety of ways in which you can learn to increase your capacity in any of the four functions of consciousness. If you realize that you are underdeveloped in one area it may be desirable to engage in some special exercises or training to build up your underdeveloped capacity and become more centered or balanced. However, many individuals are unable to guide themselves through a systematic process of growth and development because they are unaware of how to go about it. Let us look briefly at why this is so.

It appears that our greatest weaknesses are in those areas that lie in reciprocal relationship to our strengths. I believe that the reason for this can be found in our early childhood experiences, and in this regard I believe that the behaviorists' notion of conditioning is demonstrably effective. It is said that nothing breeds success like success. The experience of success is often so ego satisfying that we are stimulated or motivated to continue to seek more of the same type of success or pleasure enjoyed in the past. As we begin to grow and develop along certain characteristic lines, we determine and continually reinforce our own uniqueness through individual choices made in response to perceived rewards. Choices that are rewarded tend to become self-reinforcing personality traits, while the reciprocal traits remain unutilized and eventually become buried in our subconscious. Thus it would not be unusual to find a person with many years' experience in a career that required a very high capacity for analytical thinking, precise measurement, and detailed accuracy experiencing great difficulty if thrust into a situation that required holistic thinking, open-ended judgments, and the formation of fairly accurate perceptions of human characteristics difficult or impossible to measure. This kind of reciprocal underdevelopment may also be observed among persons whose work is highly task oriented. These people tend also to be task oriented in their recreational activities and potentially underdeveloped and ineffective in areas requiring a great deal of personal empathy and emotional warmth. What is desirable, of course, is to develop capacities appropriate to the varying needs and demands of one's life situation. What so often happens, however, is that those capacities most in need of development remain invisible or undeveloped because attention is fixed on continuing to develop what is already possessed in abundance.

To compensate for overdevelopment in task-oriented behaviors one needs increased capacity for tolerating ambiguity in the field of action, and increased awareness or intuitive understanding in the field of consciousness. This growth, however, must always be built upon a basic foundation of certainty (a reality orientation), because development of a high toleration of ambiguity and high intuitive capacity that is not balanced by a need for certainty and cognitive rationality may lead toward the very passive behavior characteristic of drug users. In other words, if we have overdeveloped our thinking and sensory capacities at the expense of emotion and intuition, the solution would be to develop emotional and intuitive abilities while *retaining* the present level of competence in the areas of thought and sensory awareness.

Let us look now at some tentative approaches for developing thought, sensation, emotion, and intuition.

Thought. Many business executives and leaders of government agencies have found great value in a process described by Charles H. Kepner and Benjamin B. Tregoe (1965). Their book entitled *The Rational Manager* offers a systematic method of problem solving and decision making, and is an excellent approach toward increasing one's understanding of rational decision-making processes. Kepner-Tregoe and Associates of Princeton, New Jersey, also provide courses to help one learn this method and approach to improving rational thinking and problem analysis.

Sensation. Ways of increasing sensory perception (and approaches toward extrasensory perception) have been richly described in the periodical *Psychology Today*. A number of excellent articles provide many insights into how to increase visual acuity, hearing, taste, smell, and awareness of messages that can be received on the surface of the skin. The authors of these articles can almost certainly put one in touch with centers for the development of the described capacities, but perhaps the best-known center for increasing sensory awareness is Esalen Institute in the Big Sur country of Northern California.

Emotion. During the 1950s and 1960s there was a great surge of interest in sensitivity training and encounter groups. Unfortunately, sensitivity training was frequently introduced into organizations with little or no effort to relate its theoretical, emotional lessons to the problems of the practical, day-to-day business and industrial world. In addition, highly task-oriented organizations couldn't seem to understand why extra time and money was needed to deal with the emotional issues inherent in organizational life.

It is now much clearer that emotional maturity and balance is a critical factor in effective task accomplishment. But aside from the business application and the questions raised with T-groups in business settings, many individuals have found sensitivity training to be tremendously helpful to them in their efforts to develop authentic emotional responses and to be more in touch with their real feelings. If interested, you can find out more about this kind of activity from the National Training Laboratories division of the National Education Association in Washington, D.C.

Intuition. Roberto Assagioli, an Italian psychiatrist, developed a technique for developing intuitive capacity called *psychosynthesis.* Training in psychosynthesis is offered at the New England Center for Personal and Organizational Development in Amherst, Massachusetts. Other organizations like Arica and the various Gestalt institutes in major cities of the United States also offer a wide variety of training courses aimed at developing sensory awareness, increased self-understanding, body-mind integration, and increased control of psychic and physical energy. Many of the disciplines used by the above organizations are deeply infused with the practices of the East. There are also great new possibilities opening up as a result of research in biofeedback and in the control of brain waves and body rhythms, and the tremendously widespread interests in transcendental meditation indicates that this practice is helping thousands to gain better control of the functions of consciousness.

While some may find the above suggestions too esoteric, it is important to stress again that personal growth is a matter that must involve free personal choice. Each individual must be free to decide what he or she wishes to do and what will be appropriate for his or her own life situation.

As we have said, to achieve a balance between the reciprocal levels of our consciousness, or the transcendent function, each of us must find his or her own weaknesses. We must then plan our own development strategy so that we may grow in all eight zones of the fields of action and consciousness and move toward achievement of our full potential.

As knowledge, experience, and energy combine in the course of normal

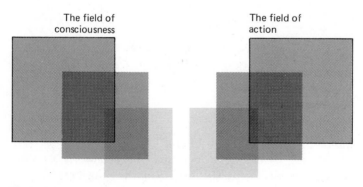

The field of
consciousness

The field of
action

Figure 7.2

human growth and development, the fields of consciousness and action expand. As we emerge from childhood into maturity we generally become capable of vastly greater task accomplishment, deeper emotional and interpersonal involvement, and greater levels of ambiguity tolerance, and our sense of certainty becomes anchored in a broader perception of reality. Thus as we grow and develop, our fields of both action and consciousness grow larger as our capabilities increase (see Fig. 7.2).

Transcendence occurs through achieving integration of the binary combinations of the four functions of the field of action and of the field of consciousness. This breakthrough to transcendence is usually experienced as both increased self-awareness and increased competence and usually results in a reorganization of our self-concept or ego concept in relation to others and to our general life situation.

LEARNING FROM EXPERIENCE

Let us now look at the dimension of human experience. How do I know what I know? If I have credentials from a great institution of learning, it may be assumed that I am very knowledgeable. I may have titles and honorary awards, or I may hold several academic degrees. Yet if the knowledge I have remains locked inside me, if I have become the curator of my own internal museum, there is no demonstrable evidence that my knowledge exists. If I am young, I may show great promise by superior performance on intelligence tests. My IQ may be at the genius level, yet the evidence today suggests that IQ tests do not predict capacity or ability nearly as accurately as is commonly believed. In fact, IQ tests can be demonstrated to reflect the social, ethnic, and educational advantages already enjoyed in very early life by those being tested. Thus they become self-fulfilling prophecies. As a result of this discovery one researcher suggests that we stop testing for intelligence and concentrate instead on testing for actual competence and the rate of competence acquisition over a period of time (McClelland, 1973).

The truth is that knowledge must be able to be demonstrated. No amount of pretence or hiding behind credentials can make up for demonstrable lack of competency or lack of excellence in performance. And the possession of abstract theory without the ability to apply it to real-life situations is useless. In addition, the old pedagogical axiom that if the student hasn't learned, the teacher hasn't taught, is not necessarily true either, for no amount of teaching can guarantee learning. A new axiom may now be substituted—that if the learner has learned, he is aware of his learning and is able to demonstrate it. Demonstrable capacity is the result of internalized learning, regardless of whether the content be music, physics, linguistics, plumbing, or farming. And internalized learning occurs only when a person willingly receives information, integrates the new idea or theory with his or her prior experience, and can apply the information to a concrete or specific situation. Only then, after the experience of *doing,* can I say I *know.* Again we are reminded that many centuries ago Confucius put it succinctly when he said, "I *do* and I *understand.*"

The role of the teacher is to help facilitate learning; learning cannot be forced, the learner must be a willing recipient of knowledge. If real learning is to occur, the teacher must neither block the learner's desire to learn nor must the learner prevent or block the internalization and use of the information presented. Much education today is, unfortunately, a sham; and this is particularly true at the secondary-school and university levels. Fortunately, the rapidly growing trend toward careful evaluation of learning outcomes and demonstrable competencies is evidence that this situation is now beginning to change.

The sham of which I am speaking is well known and costs billions of dollars annually in lost learning opportunity. It operates in the following manner: A course is offered by an institution of learning. The apparent or acceptable transaction at the social level is that the learner pays tuition (or the parents pay taxes) in return for certification by the institution that the course has been satisfactorily completed; that is, *that the learner has learned.* At the ulterior transactional level (Berne, 1964) the learner may adopt the posture of "I'm going to do as little as possible to graduate," while the institution may adopt the posture of equating credits granted with tuition paid. This posture has led many learning institutions to be called "factories" by their students. Educational factories appear to be concerned mostly with quantitative output at minimum cost. Thus the ulterior transaction is a denial of the educational process, and it can lead at its worst to an unspoken but fully recognized complicity between the learner and the learning institution for the buying and selling of credits, which are then presented to a potential employer as "evidence" of education.

This deception needs to be disrupted wherever it exists, for it prevents individual development and personal growth. The attainment of *demonstrable* knowledge is the only valid measure of true learning and in order to demonstrate knowledge one must actively engage in shared experience with others.

Thus another way to assess individual differences is to look at the dimension of experience. In Chapter 6 we observed that we *are* our experience; our life represents the sum total of everything we have been and done. During our every waking moment (and to a lesser extent while we are asleep) information is pouring into us through our five sensory centers. Even if we choose to resist learning we cannot shut off or stop the flow of experiential information that is coming to us constantly. When we engage sensory information with our cognitive capacity and structure it into ideas, we become *informed,* or "formed within." When this cognitive information becomes further enriched with emotion and intuition we tend, as we saw in Chapter 2, to become excited, inspired, and creative. Thus learning occurs constantly and continuously as a result of our daily living experience. Learning is not, as is often believed, only the result of exposure to a formal educational setting or classroom experience; and those who discontinue their formal education may, and usually do, continue to learn at a fairly rapid rate. Their learning, however, ceases to conform to the prescribed pattern of someone else's curriculum design, and becomes more experiential and directly related to their life situation. It is, of course, unfortunate when negative educational experience causes an individual to drop out of school, particularly when the individual comes to believe that learning is a dull and boring activity. But this does not have to happen. It is rumored that Edwin Land, the creative leader of Polaroid Corporation, dropped out of one well-known institution of higher learning on the grounds that it was "interfering with his education." Having never received a bachelor's degree, Land nevertheless went on to achieve great success precisely because he never confused learning with schooling. No one can deny that he has become in his lifetime a "well-educated man," for he holds hundreds of United States patents and personally guided and developed one of America's leading and most creative corporations.

Building Experiential Learning Models

Learning to learn without the benefit of a formal educational program requires personal discipline, a determination to achieve personal growth, and a personal development plan. In Chapter 6, I referred to the process of forming a competency model as an integral part of an effective approach to continuing adult learning. I wish now to delve into this process in greater depth. The key notion, as before, is that the learner take personal responsibility for his or her own learning. This means that the learner decides the pace at which learning will occur and also the degree to which satisfaction with the learning is achieved (in other words, the learner must be self-grading). It is also important to establish how to get feedback or verification from others on one's progress, in order to avoid the risk of self-deception.

The first step in building an experiential development model is to decide what you wish to develop; to decide upon a particular topic, process, or object you wish to know more about. (Usually an adult has been exposed, through interests or through previous education, to some of the more basic elements of any subject he or she might wish to know more about.) Also important is a consideration of the social dimension of the learning we wish to undertake. Seldom do we wish to learn something purely for its own sake. Usually we wish to learn so that we can share our learning in some way, by creating something or by performing, or by doing work for or simply entertaining others. It is therefore important to be able to visualize or imagine ourselves at our future best, doing what we would like to be doing. This conception of goal or self-ideal, as we have said earlier, is important in ensuring sufficient motivation to carry out our plan.

To offer an example of this process of building and implementing an experiential learning model, I personally have been interested in music for many years and recently decided to learn to play the piano. I could picture myself playing for the entertainment of others or simply to relax. As I have had some musical education, I did not have to start at the beginning. I did, however, have to consider the basic competencies involved in playing the piano itself.

In watching and listening to accomplished pianists, one is struck by the tremendous finger dexterity needed to execute complicated musical passages. My first major competency, therefore, was to develop that kind of finger dexterity. Because I am interested in the relaxed, informal type of music written by Cole Porter, Richard Rodgers, Henry Mancini, Burt Bacharach, and similar composers, and because I am also interested in jazz improvisations of these types of melodies, I also realized I would have to develop a working knowledge of chord progressions and a basic understanding of harmony. As I already knew the principles of harmony, the specific competency I needed was to be able to play a melody by ear. Finally, I knew I would have to learn to read piano music. However I decided I would postpone this goal until I had developed keyboard dexterity and harmonic flexibility. I set aside this competency in order to concentrate more effectively on the first two.

In order to implement my simple two-part competency model I acquired some piano music and concentrated on simply reading the melody line and following the guitar chord symbols to identify the correct chord formations. At first it was terrible. I played with great, halting gaps between notes because my head and my fingers refused to coordinate. Gradually, however, I began to make connections more rapidly, to recognize generalized patterns; in other words I began to play without having to think through every step of what I was doing. As habits gradually began to form, what previously required conscious thought became second nature. This reduction of basic operations to automatic response freed my cognitive capacity for other activities, and I could now think about phrasing, melodic and harmonic construction, and eventually the creation of a jazz style and the building of a repertoire of pieces that I could perform competently. Over a period of three years I progressed from total inability to play the piano to a tolerable ability to get about the keyboard and execute fairly simple tunes. I have now sought out a professional jazz pianist to help me develop a more advanced competency model for the next stage of my program.

This same process can be applied to learning practically anything. Decide first what you would like to be able to do or do better. Identify what you can do now and plan how to systematically close the gap between what you are able to do and what you want to be able to do. It is often helpful to separately identify knowledge and skill dimensions of competence. It may also be useful to identify the major roadblocks that you perceive to be standing in the way of successful performance. Your developmental strategy then becomes one of systematically removing roadblocks and developing knowledge and skills in accordance with the requirements you have set.

Therefore the steps in building an individual development model are as follows.

1. Listing knowledge (understanding) and skill (ability to execute) require-ments and preparing a competency chart to identify gaps between present and desired levels of performance (see Fig. 7.3)

2. Developing a plan of action for a specified time period, say three or six months or a year

3. Discussing your plan of action with an objective and friendly observer to obtain assistance in evaluating your performance

4. Implementing your plan of action

5. Demonstrating your new level of competence to your observer at the end of the time period, and preparing a new competency chart based on mu-tually shared perceptions of your progress.

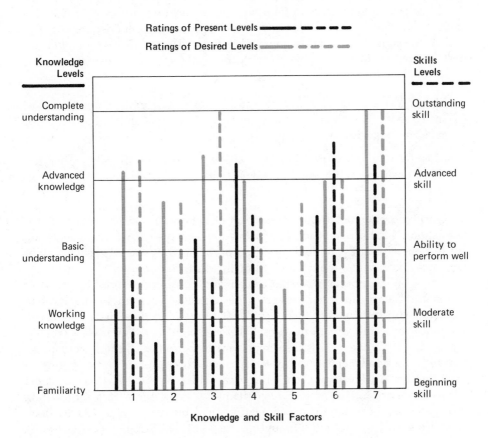

Fig. 7.3 An individual development planning model

While you may have exceeded the desired level of attainment in some basic knowledge or skill factor, it is important to list all critical areas to gain a total picture of the competency you wish to obtain. To formulate your learning objectives it is helpful both to look at the gap between present and desired levels of attainment and to consider the degree of attainment required for effective performance.

It is not necessary to always try to clarify the distinction between skill factors and knowledge factors. Sometimes this distinction is obvious and sometimes the two are inextricably woven together. What is important is to recognize that while some competencies require either a deeper theoretical understanding or the development of greater physical dexterity (or an increase of instantaneous pattern recognition), some competencies require a simultaneous increase of both knowledge and skill.

After you have assessed the gaps between present and desired levels of performance the next step is to design a plan of action to close these gaps. This plan, which should be discussed with an objective observer, may involve reading and discussion to increase your general understanding or knowledge as well as practice exercises to improve your skill in execution. You will also need to determine what evidence you will produce to demonstrate the successful attainment of your learning objectives. These "pieces" of evidence must be written in measurable terms to be really effective. For example:

Must be able to execute all major and minor scales on the piano keyboard (using both hands) by starting very slowly and doubling the tempo or speed of execution twice

Must be able to execute I-IV-II-V-I chord progressions in all keys, varying chord positions and using inversions

Once you have determined your plan of action all that is left is to put it into action. It is important to plan for regular and systematic implementation and to review progress periodically. You may find that you can achieve all of your objectives in one month instead of three. If you do, don't become overconfident. Build another systematic plan and continue to progress at your own natural pace, increasing degrees of difficulty only up to the level of ambiguity you can tolerate. It is important to set objectives that require you to stretch your abilities but not to set them so high that they invoke frustration or disappointment. It is also important to periodically check your progress with your independent observer to make sure you are not engaging in self-deception or developing only those capacities or abilities that you most enjoy. If you are interested in a deeper explanation of the process of learning by experience, I can highly recommend a small but very valuable new book by Malcolm S. Knowles (1975), appropriately entitled *Self-Directed Learning*.

INCREASING PSYCHIC AND PHYSICAL ENERGY

Human energy is *life force.* We recognize that some people seem to move slowly and speak slowly while others tend to be very animated. Some people seem to have a lot of drive, while others seem placid; some work in blinding spurts while others are more evenly paced. Some people seem to have more energy at night than in the morning, and vice versa. There are different gradations of this energy phenomenon among people, and we are generally aware of fluctuations in the levels of energy flowing within us. Sometimes we feel very lethargic and at other times we are full of life and vitality; sometimes we feel down and at other times we are ready to tackle intensely difficult situations. We recognize also that sometimes our energy seems blocked— that there are internal resistances that prevent us from moving into action.

Our energy is the level of psychic and physical force that we have available to bring to bear on accomplishing any task or on developing any relationship we choose. We also know that we have a considerable reserve of energy that is called forth under certain crisis conditions. In emergencies, when we are stimulated by fear, adrenalin flows from the adrenal gland and the level of available energy is greatly increased for a brief period. Unusual physical feats have been performed under conditions of great emergency. Normally, however, our energy level is controlled by our basic metabolism: the rate at which we convert food into body fuel.

Understanding how our energy is blocked or released, stored up or allowed to burst forth, saved or wasted, is crucially important for all of us. Knowing how we react or respond to varying situations of ambiguity or certainty, or to different objects or relationships that attract our interest or attention, is the key to self-understanding. It is also the bedrock underlying various theories of internal or external motivation.

A Model for Releasing Energy

We must at this point look at the linkage between knowledge, experience, and energy. If I am or have become consciously aware of something I need, I may still be unable to determine how to get it. The need may be simply at first an intellectual or cognitive abstraction; for example, needing more money. In order to move into action to get more money, if this really is a need, I must first back up into the emotional and intuitive areas. I must translate the cognitive idea of the need into a want or a desire. I must feel how it would be to have more money and I may intuitively see what I might be able to do if I had, say, a $200-a-month raise. This backing up and engaging of emotion and intuition generates the energy required to propel me into action; it is a primary source of motivation.

The first stage of action is that of ambiguity. Is getting more money too difficult? Perhaps impossible? Are my expectations diminished to the point that I will not attempt to take any steps to improve my situation? Have I set

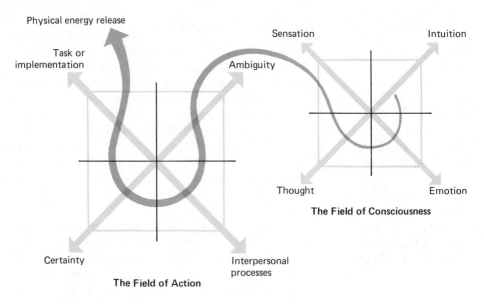

Fig. 7.4 The release of physical energy into task accomplishment

a realistic limit to my want or desire? Two hundred dollars a month may be unrealistic but an extra hundred might be attainable. How much extra work will I have to do to achieve my desire? Am I already overworked? Do I have to change jobs or careers if my needs are very high? Is the risk worth it? If these and other ambiguities are sufficiently resolved, the next action stage is that of interpersonal relations. With whom do I have to work to achieve my desire? From whom do I have to get acceptance? Whom do I have to impress with my worth? Do I have to resolve some interpersonal conflicts first? The next stage of action is that of certainty. This is the decision stage: I must determine what I must actually do to attain my $200 pay increase. The final stage is that of the release of physical energy into task accomplishment. This is the stage of action per se, the stage of implementation. Figure 7.4 depicts this process graphically. Again, as in the induction and expression process described in Chapter 2, blockages may occur that prevent psychic energy from flowing into physical energy.

In order to achieve the fusion of A and B stages of consciousness and action, we may have to learn some new behaviors. Trying out new behaviors may mean experiencing an increase in tension and anxiety. And many of us see anxiety as a harmful thing; we tend to place a higher value on relaxation. The late Frederick Perls (1969) had a great insight about anxiety, however, and his words speak eloquently:

> The stopping block seems to be anxiety. Always anxiety. Of course you are anxious if you have to learn a new way of behavior, and the psychiatrists

usually are afraid of anxiety. They don't know what anxiety *is*. Anxiety is the excitement, the *élan vital* which we carry with us, and which becomes stagnated if we are unsure about the role we have to play. If we don't know if we will get applause or tomatoes, we hesitate, so the heart begins to race and all the excitement can't flow into activity, and we have stage fright.

The excitement Perls referred to is, of course, psychic energy, the *élan vital* or life force that flows within us. When our energy flows spontaneously into constructive activity we are creative and we are free. When we are burdened by expectations implicit in roles and responsibilities we often seek to avoid the ambiguity of facing ourselves. As a result, many of us play games; we make up phony strategies for avoiding reality and for not having to resolve interpersonal problems.

Now let us look at some of the critical factors that inhibit or prevent personal growth from occurring. Increased awareness and realization of how these inhibitors operate is often all that is needed to begin to remove them and continue on a growth-oriented path.

INNER CONFLICTS IN PERSONAL GROWTH

Physical growth requires exercise, involves muscular activity and tension, and, particularly when we are young, results in many painful cuts and bruises. Psychological growth also requires exercise in the form of active involvement with others, and it too sometimes results in conflict and pain.

It is easy to see the process of pain in growth with adolescents as they form and break relationships, and we see it also as they struggle to attain mastery and skill in relation to the use of objects or the accomplishment of tasks. They succeed or give up. They try again and give up in frustration; they try again and succeed, with joy and relief. It is less apparent perhaps that this process continues throughout life—if, that is, we are willing to keep on growing. One way of illuminating the process of tension and release (or ambiguity and certainty) that occurs in the growth process is to look at the dynamics inherent in dependent relationships. Another way is to look at the processes of assertiveness and avoidance, and a third way is to look at self-actualization and self-restriction. Finally we may assess various abnormal adjustments that result from the inability to cope with either developmental or situational conflict.

Dependence and counterdependence. Let us look first at dependence. We may paraphrase a well-known line from *Fiddler on the Roof*: It seems that being dependent, like being poor, is nothing to be ashamed of, but then it is no particular honor, either. We all start off being dependent as children and unfortunately the circumstances of life are such that some of us stay in this stage of development and never move beyond it. We may think of dependency as a stage of rest; it is comfortable to be taken care of and have our needs met by others. If anyone tries to move us out of this stage before we are ready they may raise the level of ambiguity beyond our toleration level; as a result we scream and kick or otherwise engage in temper tantrums. We may be amenable, however, to a gradual process of withdrawal from dependency, although some conflict can usually be expected because it is difficult to balance our own and others' expectations. Such is the state of childhood. At a certain point the maturing or developing person feels that the solicitousness and control exercised by the parental figure is too constraining. Early attempts at having this control relaxed are usually unsuccessful because the controlling party does not usually perceive a need to change the status quo. Tension rises because the dependent person's needs for independence are unmet, pushing him or her into the stage of counterdependence. This stage is very uncomfortable for everyone. It is usually marked by combative and aggressive behavior and can be accompanied by a great deal of projected blame and guilt. As most parents experience this stage of counterdependency with adolescent children, its appearance should surprise no one; it can be like a whirlpool, however, and is very difficult to understand when you are caught up in it as a combative participant. It is at this point that many mistakes are made. Either the parents or the children give up prior to the completion of the developmental process. In the first case parents allow themselves to become overly permissive; in the second case they retain perhaps too great an influence, smothering, as it were, the individual and protecting him or her unduly from the valuable lessons to be learned from difficulties met and overcome.

In the natural maturation process, the third stage of release from dependence is one of new-found freedom or independence. This stage begins as one of release or balance ("I'm free at last") and then usually turns to a new state of unrest, when the formerly dependent person faces the ambiguities of an uncertain and potentially lonely future. Compromise occurs because complete freedom, like the Midas touch, is too much of a good thing. Thus if no one has been irretrievably hurt during the counterdependent period, the independent period generally leads to the fourth stage: a healthy interdependence and mutually collaborative relationship based on a recognition of reciprocal rights and obligations.

Parents and children usually learn to tolerate a great deal of situational ambiguity during this process, and if it follows its natural course the process usually leads to a growth of maturity for both.

Assertiveness and avoidance. Another problem in learning to form relationships and accomplish meaningful work with others is that of *facing the reality of a situation and taking a personal stand with regard to it.* To get at what underlies the tendency to avoid reality, we might find it helpful to look at the need we have for integrating past, present, and future. Dwelling or concentrating too much on the past or on the future is a characteristic way of avoiding the conflict that arises when we have to make active developmental choices in the present. Confronting any present situation or circumstance with the right amount of aggressiveness or assertiveness requires a recognition of the realities of the situation in which we find ourselves and a willingness to make choices for appropriate action.

Accepting the theory from the Gestalt psychologists that only the *now* moment (or present) is accessible to direct experience or action, we can begin to determine the degrees of strength needed for confronting or backing away from the problem of getting what we want. Sometimes very aggressive and forceful action is required, but there is also a risk that we might come on too strong and kill the potential inherent in the situation by dominating it, destroying it, or distorting it in some way. The reciprocal danger is in not coming on strong enough and letting opportunity slip through our grasp because of an inadequate or an overly timid response.

Passivity in our behavior emerges when we believe that the attainment of any goal we might seek is too far off in the future to require any action in the present. In these cases we need to decide which proximate goals are realizeable and let the future (which will usually arrive sooner than we expect it) take care of itself. Passivity also emerges when we believe that the past is controlling the present and the future. Although tradition and cultural adaptation are important and necessary, situations frequently arise that may be handled best by departing from traditional ways or habitual practices. Resting on past laurels or depending on prior experience for all new situations often prevents us from exerting either the activity or restraint necessary to cope with the onrush of human events. It is important, therefore, to take an active and appropriately assertive posture with regard to any situation and try to achieve a sense of balance in our relationships with others.

A model for achieving compromise is presented in Fig. 7.5. This model is derived from the matrix for the field of action previously described in Chapter 1 and elsewhere. It enables you to determine or choose the *relative* degree of strength to place on each of the four poles in order to achieve a workable solution, which always involves some kind of compromise if conflicting parties are to begin to work together effectively.

Self-actualization and self-restriction. Let us now consider a final problem with regard to personal growth and development. When two people meet face to face, either in conflict or in a spirit of collaboration, far from being perfectly matched pairs they are most likely to find themselves at different levels of relative growth or development. This is not so much a factor of chronological age but rather of differences in knowledge, experience, and energy. Thus the foundation of any interpersonal relationship usually rests in inequality.

To achieve interpersonal union both self-actualization and self-restriction are required (see Fig. 7.6). The person who finds himself in a smaller interpersonal square than the other must stretch to try to reach the outer limits of understanding required to communicate with the other person. The person who finds himself in the larger interpersonal square must try to self-restrict so that he or she does not overpower the other person by overreaching that person's limits of ambiguity toleration. This situation is made more difficult because it is often hard to tell at first who occupies the larger square. In addition, changes in one's life situation, such as sudden success or failure, grief and loss, or inheriting or winning a large sum of money can change the dimensions of one's development matrix. It is for this reason that sudden change puts great stress on interpersonal relationships and that periods of great social change are likely to produce high divorce rates, and so forth.

Interpersonal union is achieved when two or more people begin to effectively *inform* each other; that is to say, when knowledge, experience, and energy flow back and forth between two persons, or within a group, so that there is a general recognition that the experience of being together and working together is meaningful, growth enhancing, and worthwhile.

As time flows inexorably onward, change itself is the everpresent constant. And this is desirable because it guarantees that tomorrow always has the potential for continued development and renewal. It is as if the freshness of spring could be experienced with the dawn of each new day. We anticipate our tomorrows and it is this anticipation that gives life much of its joy and meaning.

While we are all in motion, moving inexorably toward fuller actualization of our individual lives, there is always with us imagination about the future,

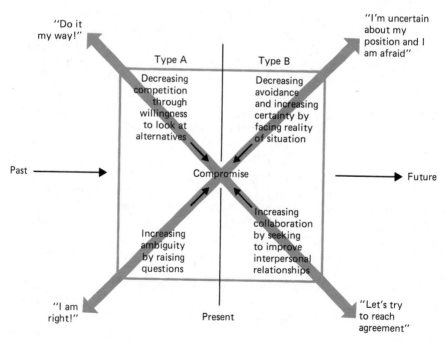

Figure 7.5

Self-actualization

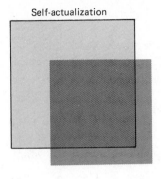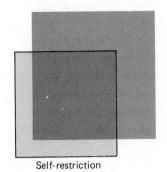

Self-restriction

Figure 7.6

memory of the past, and the reality of the present moment. The lives of others and events in the world around us do not stand still; "Everything," as Heraclitus observed centuries ago, "is in a state of flux." As we grow, energy stimulates our being and fosters our becoming. Our relations with others and the world increase our experience and knowledge, and the ambiguity of new knowledge and experience stimulates us to expend more energy in becoming an always developing person; we literally are charged with the responsibility for creating our own lives.

It is through the open doorway of potential that I meet and experience myself emerging through the process of development in time. If all living is educational experience, a dialogue between the active doing (outer-directed) and reflective thinking (contemplative) aspects of my consciousness is a very personal and unique process that determines my specific identity. It is this conversation with myself that is the basis of an understanding of personal growth. It is this *person* who I am constantly changing, molding, and refining, that I present to others, and it is for this reason that I am never perfectly *myself*. I am always becoming.

Facing the future requires courage and each of our lives unfolds in its own mysterious way. When we are young we tend to be impatient to make things happen. This is both natural and necessary. The impetuosity of youth propels us into discovery of both the meaning and the importance of relations with others. But we soon experience pain because others mirror our own inadequacies. As the experience of our own pain in relation to others simultaneously brings about in us a desire to change and grow, we begin to adopt a more balanced perspective of our own worth and competence. It is here that two opposing dangers must be faced and overcome if growth is to occur at all.

First, there is the tendency to reject a new experience of another and to see ourselves as superior ("I'm right, you're wrong"). Thus we reject the growth potential inherent in a conflict situation. The other danger is to regard ourselves as worth very little and to thus deny our own potential, retarding our own growth for the opposite reason and retiring from the conflict in defeat.

For most of us, it is necessary to go through this *process* many times before we begin to understand the central principle that accepting the pain of interpersonal discomfort is a necessary precondition for internal change and growth. Once we master the principle, however, we are likely to recognize opportunities for its application when interpersonal difficulties arise, and we are thus more able to choose behaviors that are accepting of both others and ourselves—behaviors that make it possible to gain growth and value from the resources and experience of others without denying our own worth or building barriers of conflict and separation.

There are probably occasions in all our lifetimes when all of our past efforts and achievements seem to crumble into worthlessness. Faced by despair and loss of meaning, we do not see at these times a way to go on. These moments are often the signal of a major life change that, negotiated successfully, can lead to the opening of new dimensions of opportunity. It is also at these times, however, that the need for courage reaches its peak. The ability to remain confident in the face of uncertainty, the ability to accept the *value inherent in ourselves and others,* is the very affirmation of our own and others' existence at the deepest human level (Tillich, 1952).

It is interesting to note that *The Wizard of Oz,* the popular children's story that emerged as a motion picture in 1939, the year that Western civilization entered its darkest moment, called for a better brain, increased courage, and more heart to meet and deal with the awesome ambiguity posed by the great wizard who held all the power in the magnificent city. The three heroes of the story found what they were looking for—when accompanied by a little girl and her dog, they discovered that the fearful Wizard of Oz was just a kindly old man manipulating the controls at his disposal to make him appear much more powerful than he really was. If you feel threatened or overawed by someone, or if you are overwhelmed with the sense of your own limitations, it may be helpful to think about a brainless scarecrow, a tin man without a heart, or a timid lion.

Abnormality: The Antithesis of Personal Growth

Unfortunately, some people are unable to face conflict situations in which they find themselves, and reflection on the cruelty and injustice of some of life's situations forces us all to realize that the human capacity to withstand pain and grief has very real limits. Many psychiatrists and psychologists have for a long time intimated that the distinction between normality and abnormality is only a matter of degree. In addition it has become quite clear that abnormal behavior, while manifested with a variety of symptoms, is generally accompanied by drastic changes in the output levels of human energy If abnormality is an exaggeration of normal behavior or an extension of normal behavior into abnormal ranges, we can perhaps gain some insight by looking again at the human energy matrix presented in Chapter 1.

Abnormal behavior appears as a disruption or interruption of the normal flow of human energy. If we look again at the ambiguity/certainty relation and consider how energy accelerates as ambiguity rises and decelerates as structure and certainty are encountered, we find ourselves stumbling on a clue that may lead to an important discovery and provide an avenue for further research in the field of mental health.

Depression. When we view the common psychological malady of depression, we find human beings who feel restricted, constrained, and controlled beyond their ability to cope effectively. Whether internally or externally imposed, the situational rigidity that leads to depression limits people's horizons, their outlook for the future, hope for relief, and expectation of improvement. When this situation of certainty grips a person's psyche strongly the person becomes depressed. When it is very strong we add the term manic; hence, manic-depressive. We observe those persons experiencing this pathological condition to be extremely rigid, tense, and angry. The anger, however, is tightly controlled, and an intense internal struggle is waged as the forces of anger (energy) are blocked and can find no reasonable outlet or release. Suddenly, and often without warning, the manic-depressive may burst forth into a violent and destructive rage. The anger, released at last, floods out and often claims innocent victims in its destructive fury (see Fig. 7.7).

Thus we can visualize a classic exaggeration of tension and release. The movement toward depression draws back energy in much the same way that a catapult is prepared to throw its missile. The release is sudden. The repressed anger snaps back, and destructiveness results. Treatment of the

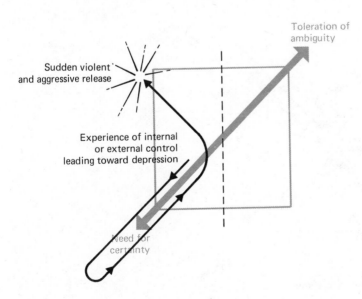

Fig. 7.7 The manic-depressive syndrome

manic-depressive syndrome may well involve helping the victim to release anger gradually and to increase toleration of ambiguity to reasonable limits.

Catatonia. In this very uncertain world the occurrence of a violent or tragic event that shatters a person's life is unfortunately not uncommon. May we make a theoretical assumption that when a psychic shock of this kind occurs at a level greater than the individual victim can tolerate there is a catapulting off the range of the normal into a total state of passivity? Thus we see the catatonic, much like the autistic child: withdrawn, uncommunicative, and isolated. Furthermore, the catatonic seems stripped of his energy resources. There is no energy available; he is psychically disconnected or cut off from his physical energy supply (see Fig. 7.8).

Here again we see a problem of tension and release and this time the phenomenology appears to be the reverse of the manic-depressive syndrome. It is psychic shock that precipitates the victim to a radical passivity in which all energetic tension is gone; the effect is similar to a wire or cable snapping under tension. While careful therapy may restore the tension needed to tolerate certainty and bring about a gradual movement back toward the center of contact with others and the world, sometimes a person suffering from catatonia is lost forever; his psychic life ends with the traumatic event while his physical life goes on—sometimes for many additional years.

Compulsion and obsession. Let us turn our attention to the other poles of the human energy matrix and look at abnormality along the task/process continuum. This continuum, as we saw in Chapter 1, relates to the polarity between directed and reflexive activity (and object and relation) in the field of

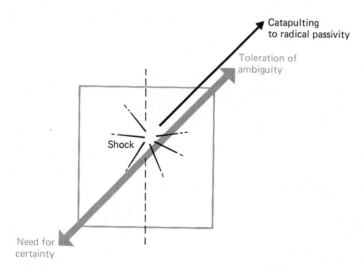

Fig. 7.8 The catatonic syndrome

action. It also relates, as we saw in Chapter 2, to the polarity between sensation and emotion in the field of consciousness.

Many psychiatrists and psychologists have referred to the obsessive/compulsive syndrome as if it were one entity with two manifestations. The human energy matrix tends to show compulsion and obsession as reciprocal opposites. Let's take compulsion first.

Compulsion is totally object or task oriented. It is the I-It relation gone wild to the exclusion of the possibility of healthy interpersonal, or I-Thou, relationships. Basically human activity is healthy when it is directed toward actions freely chosen for good or sufficient reason. Compulsiveness occurs when there is a loss of freedom of choice; when the person is compelled to repeat an activity for the sake of the activity itself. Here we see a typical lack of connection between figure and ground. The activity (the figure) is disconnected from its purpose or from a rational or logical context (the ground).

With compulsion we see continuous, repeated activity without benefit of reflection. Compulsive cleanliness, food grabbing, biting fingernails, all represent the discharge of human energy without conscious direction. And compulsive behavior is directly related to the need for certainty because people suffering from this ailment do not seem to be able to tolerate the least amount of ambiguity; nor are they able to adequately reflect on what they are doing and why.

When we look at obsession we perhaps think of great love affairs or romantic involvements. The notion of obsession implies a fixation; a sense of being caught up by a force from which one cannot escape. It is the I-Thou relation gone wild and separated from objective or task-oriented referents. The very thought of the loved one or loved object paralyzes activity and precipitates a trancelike state of inactivity. The person suffering from this ailment is forever and continuously "processing" the loved object or image of the loved person, and this processing activity prevents the release of energy into directed activity or task accomplishment. Obsession can thus also be seen as operating off the scale of the normal, but in the opposite direction from that taken in situations of extreme compulsion (see Fig. 7.9).

The relationship between obsession and the toleration of ambiguity appears to be important. People who are obsessed are unconvinced and unswayed by logical argument or rational thinking. They are caught up in the ambiguity of the obsession and believe that any minute a chance happening will actually present them with the object of their heart's desire. In short, they believe in miracles and will spend years in passivity waiting for one to occur.

Schizophrenia. The mental illness of schizophrenia has been described as a *split personality.* While psychiatrists have moved a long way from that simplistic notion today, it is perhaps useful to return to it momentarily as a way to describe the phenomenology of the schizoid state. What is it that is split? In the light of recent experiments in neurophysiology it now appears that we

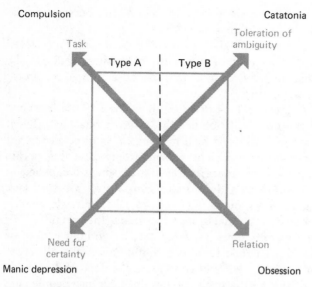

Fig. 7.9 A matrix of abnormality

possess two brains and not one (see also Chapter 2). Because the right and left hemispheres of the brain operate differentially along the lines of the human energy matrix in the zone of action (ambiguity/certainty and task/process) and also along the comparable dimensions in the zone of consciousness (thought/imagination and emotion/sensation), we may hypothesize that what may split is the individual's energy matrix. When, for example, a deep and fundamental contradiction between two important areas of a person's life is experienced and the person is unable to resolve that contradiction, feelings of lowered self-esteem and guilt arise and become doubts as to personal competency and value. When these feelings are projected onto others the resultant feedback may tend to support or emphasize either one side of the person's conflict or the other. But the side that remains unrelieved may continue to have its influence and may also wreak havoc. As an example, let us take someone who grew up under a very rigid and authoritarian family and religious environment and later turned to a loose, free, and immoral way of living. If this person is able to integrate the movement from one lifestyle to the other, satisfying the ambiguities and certainties, the actions and reflections that occurred during the transition, he or she will probably be quite normal. If, however, the person is not able to resolve the contradictions between beliefs and feelings, ideas and imagination, and becomes caught up in a seemingly irreconcilable conflict, two human energy matrices could form like an image out of register. The resultant distortion of the energy field could well result in the appearance of a split personality (see Fig. 7.10).

This situation is likely to be further complicated if the two conflicting situational "constellations" are of differing size, and hence of differing force and influence. Under these conditions it can be extremely difficult for a therapist to gather the relevant and useful information that is needed to design a treatment plan for assisting the patient to bring his or her fields of action and consciousness back together and into focus.

It is not my purpose here to tread too deeply into the domain of abnormal psychology and I wish to assert firmly that the above concepts of the energy forces at work in abnormality are only hypothetical. It is hoped, however, that by looking at the energy implications of abnormality we may gain additional insight into both therapeutic processes and the ways of protecting normal individuals from falling into abnormal manifestations if they should experience an extraordinary period of depression, shock, or intense stress.

It was Kurt Goldstein (1963) who first demonstrated the value of comparing normal and abnormal manifestations for the purpose of constructing reasonable hypotheses leading to further research and increased understanding. The apparent disruption of physical and psychic energy in the mentally ill leads me to believe that research into the dimensions of the human energy matrix and its combinations of opposites and reciprocities may be useful in finding new ways to relieve the pain and suffering of mental illness. And by looking at the abnormal manifestations of human energy we may also gain valuable new insights into normal behavior. Thus we may see in many social and organizational problems tendencies toward depression or toward compulsive or obsessive behavior, and we may also see in normal organizations those tendencies that may be precipitating factors in the formation of mental illness among an organization's members.

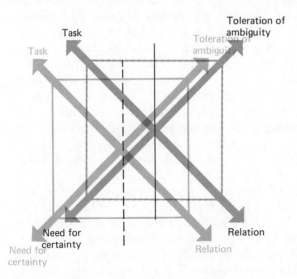

Fig. 7.10 Matrices of a split personality

Let us now look at the issues of personal growth or its retardation from inside the structure of human organizations.

PERSONAL GROWTH IN ORGANIZATIONAL SETTINGS

Personal growth may be enhanced or retarded in the process of working in organizations. It can be enhanced when the potential for increased knowledge and experience offered by the organization enables one to employ one's energies both constructively and fruitfully. It is retarded when others, seeking growth only for themselves, effectively stand in your path or block your way. The failure to recognize the importance of self-restriction and the failure of organizations in general to reward self-restricting behaviors often accounts for the retardation of the growth and development of an organization's members. This process works in a variety of ways. Because the primary issue here is generally one of personal egoism it may be useful to look first at the issue of ego and development and then at ways in which personal egoism works in organizations to prevent growth. A fairly simple scheme for understanding ego function was first described to me by Bert Hayward of the University of Akron when I was attending the American Management Association's Executive Action Course. The notion derives generally from the work of Sigmund Freud and others and has been widely publicized. I shall attempt to summarize Bert's description, which I found particularly helpful.

Ego Development

All of us have a self-concept or self-image. This is basically the way we see ourselves. We also project our idea of ourself into the future and imagine ourselves as we would like to be. This is our self-ideal. Because this self-ideal exists in everyone, most human behavior is goal oriented or purposive. As we go through life and gradually achieve fulfillment of our self-ideal or ego ideal, we tend to gain in self-esteem and are motivated to expend more effort. When we experience failure, the gap between our self-image and self-ideal widens and we experience a loss of self-esteem, resulting in an increase of anger at ourselves (often projected onto others as blame) and feelings of guilt and resentment. Thus nothing breeds success like success, and nothing breeds continuing failure as effectively as the experience of failure. Because we live in the world with others, our progress toward our self-ideal is confirmed or contradicted by the perceptions of others. The way others see us is our public image; thus those whose self-ideals are very high have a great need to maintain their public image and will go to great lengths to receive favorable feedback from others. Actually, the healthiest human condition is that of having a realistic self-concept, a reasonable ego ideal in relation to our abilities, and the capacity to seek and utilize authentic feedback from others as a way of checking on our progress. Our expectations will thus be neither too high nor too low and we will achieve a balance of genuine satisfaction, somewhere well in between euphoria and despair.

At about this stage of Bert's description someone asked, "Does our self-image ever fully catch up with our self-ideal?" Bert replied that he hoped not. When the questioner pursued his point, Bert put his hand inside his shirt and said, "I am Napoleon." He then went on to explain that perfect identity or closure between self-ideal and self-image was a manifestation of psychotic behavior. We must always have a goal or vision of a better future if we would remain psychologically healthy.

Ego development and ego containment are major problems for many. Unrealistic self-images can create havoc. When a person walks through a hallway with V.P. (vice president) written on his forehead, acting as he thinks a V.P. should instead of being naturally himself, he may be unaware that his public image is pushing people away and blocking the flow of both interpersonal and factual information that he needs to perform effectively. It is difficult enough when one holds a high-level job to reduce the harmful effects of people behaving in deferential and subservient ways because of *their* need for you to be a V.I.P. (very important person). If one comes to believe that one is *entitled* to such deference it is just a matter of time before the fall comes, bringing with it the sting and humiliation of personal rejection and defeat. Recently I had the occasion to both observe and speak with the board chairman and chief executive officer of a very large corporation. I was greatly heartened to see him manifest the kind of openness and interpersonal kindness that won instant respect and loyalty. It was good to see this man, who had achieved a very high level of ego development, still maintaining a realistic self-image and still seeking to grow, develop, and achieve his ideals. He was at the top, but he had not yet "arrived." Nor did he plan to; he was going to keep right on "traveling" for as long he lived.

Ego Involvement in Promotion

When the human ego is functioning without the benefit of realistic feedback; when an individual's power and control needs are overly excessive; when success has come too quickly without being earned, there is a danger of an individual's experiencing exaggerated egoism. And nowhere can the manifestation of exaggerated egoism be seen so clearly as in the process of promotion. In hierarchical organizations promotion is usually seen to be the pathway to the achievement of the self-ideal; it is the organizational reward *par excellence*. Promotion has a much more powerful influence on behavior than any other form of recognition, including increases in pay (which, of course, usually accompany promotions). Receiving a promotion is often a highly emotional experience.

It is important to recognize the tendency of many people to select for promotion those that most resemble themselves in behavior and ideals. Perhaps this tendency is an unconscious manifestation of a desire for self-per-petuation; it is, in any event, quite understandable. Life in many organizations is filled with the experience of intergroup rivalry and competition. There is a natural tendency to wish to reduce conflict within a group in order to be better able to deal with the conflict outside. Internal conflict is believed by many to reduce productivity, at least in the short run, and create for outsiders an image of weakness. Strong internal discipline appears to be needed to marshal the resources of the team and provide a sense of sure-footed leadership for all of those whose role it is to follow. In addition, the implicit right of the boss to select whom he or she wants still appears to be deeply entrenched in most organizations as an unquestionable prerogative and a prevailing norm of hierarchical order.

Times are changing rapidly, however, and we have a greater need than ever before to learn to benefit from interpersonal differences and psychological diversity. Selecting protegés who are like oneself can create serious and perhaps unintended barriers to personal as well as organizational growth and development. Oftentimes the complementarity offered by someone very different from oneself provides great opportunity for learning for both parties in any supervisor/subordinate relationship.

Let us briefly examine how the process of promotion can unintentionally feed self-image or ego needs and lead to a reduction of organizational effectiveness. Being selected for promotion usually creates within us a sense of obligation to the one who has chosen us over all others. The period of euphoria or excitement that usually grips us when we learn of a promotion frequently provides us with a pair of rose-colored glasses that prevent us from seeing reality clearly. At such a time it is difficult to create a situation in which one can dispassionately examine, together with one's new boss, the explicit and implicit terms of the psychological contract that both are entering into. In fact, a voicing of one's concerns about the new assignment may even be misinterpreted as a lack of appreciation for the faith and trust bestowed by the act of being chosen. Unfortunately many of us find out after it's too late to negotiate that the job not only does not hold the level of opportunity anticipated, but may contain some great liabilities and hidden pitfalls. The resulting disappointment can severely damage the interpersonal or psychological climate between supervisor and subordinate, and reduce the level of energy needed to achieve outstanding performance.

The feeling of being beholden, however, is perhaps potentially more damaging than the inability to negotiate an interpersonal contract of mutual expectations. If you have been selected on the assumption of your similarity to the boss, it is well to recognize that this assumption is probably based on appearances only. Many of us like to learn by utilizing a role model, and it is both easy and natural to look to the boss as someone worthy of emulation. As imitation is the sincerest form of flattery, and, as some believe cynically, "Flattery will get you everywhere," certain people find it convenient and practical to make a point of emulating the boss. There is great value in using a role model as long as one maintains one's own values. Unfortunately, many bosses have a tendency to project their own values onto their subordinates as expectations. This creates a subtle temptation for subordinates to set their own values aside; first, they do not wish to disappoint their mentor, and second, they may not want to contradict the image of the role they are modeling. It is all too easy to instead pretend to admit one's mistaken impressions to the boss, and to the self, if there is a value conflict. This affectation of humility reaffirms the virtue of the boss as role model and the virtue of the subordinate as patient learner. Conformity, however, like familiarity, breeds contempt.

For the above reasons, it is most important for the boss to reach an understanding with any new subordinate regarding roles and responsibilities. It is also important for the boss to create an open climate that allows for the expression of divergent views and opinions. Here again, Type B behaviors, once learned, can be most useful in developing this climate, which is conducive to problem finding and should ensure the continuing growth and development of supervisor and subordinate alike. Type B behaviors also lead toward ego containment and the reduction of competitive and aggressive impulses. Once the problem-finding processes have been instituted, however, it is vital to also adopt a healthy Type A orientation toward getting the new job accomplished effectively.

If the boss does not initiate a realistic relationship it is left to the subordinate to try to bring it about—through testing, and eventually through confrontation. This is never easy but it is always necessary, and it is in some cases better to bring problems to a head quickly if chances for eventual success seem dim. The beginning of an authentic relationship occurs when you are able to say no to a request and to make your boss understand and accept your point of view, assuming, of course, that you are on solid and defensible ground.

Saying No to the Boss

A great deal of anxiety is experienced by managers and administrators who, faced with a situation in which their integrity depends on their refusing the boss's request, simultaneously find themselves unable to do so. Certainly it is only common sense to recognize that the boss, like the proverbial customer, cannot *always* be right. It may be good business or organizational policy to honor the customer's demands, no matter how unreasonable, but the only rationale for doing so lies in pacification—in maintaining goodwill at any price. For the subordinate to pursue a policy of appeasement works well for neither party, and as the boss usually senses he or she is taking advantage of the subordinate there is an erosion of respect on both sides. Let us look at four possible examples of this problem.

First, with the level and degree of technical expertise that exists in most fields today, unless the boss is an expert in my field I am most likely to know more about my subject than he or she does. If I am advised to take a course of action counter to what I know is either technically correct or feasible from a cost/benefit standpoint, and I do not successfully present my point of view and win consent, I am stuck with an external command contradicted by an internal belief or conviction. If I am then forced to take action under such circumstances, I will devote much less energy to the task because of my internal conflict.

Second, if the boss has as much technical knowledge as I, or if the problem is not technical but organizational, the hierarchical position of the boss places me at a disadvantage. I still must express my point of view, even if it is an unpopular one. To fail to do so is to deny my own conviction and to experience being compromised. I have again lost valuable energy resources needed to get the job done and may also be discovered by others who are aware of my real position or point of view. The discrepancy between my ideals and actions diminishes my self-respect in their eyes, and in turn damages my public image and my self-ideal, resulting in a lowering of my self-esteem and in a further potential loss of energy and enthusiasm.

Third, the boss may be operating from needs that are not directly related to the stated problem. For example, we all have needs for power, for achievement, and for affiliation with others. Because these needs vary in degree and intensity, and because organizations have tended to promote those with the highest power and achievement needs to upper hierarchical levels, the boss may be a person who can make it quite difficult for me to disagree or present divergent views of a problem. In these cases it is even more important for subordinates to say no for the good of the organization. When the boss's ego prevents the proper illumination of a problem situation, Type A behavior will predominate and defensive barriers will arise that lower productivity.

Fourth, creativity and imagination are where you find them. There is no distributive law that increases our creativity and imagination by degrees as we ascend the hierarchical ladder. We are not always just a little dumber than the boss and just a little smarter than our subordinates. It is amazing, therefore, to discover to what degree this belief is entrenched in most organizations. Pecking orders are quite often created around totally unjustified or unrealistic assumptions, and both bosses and subordinates must act to interrupt these pecking orders if they wish to optimize the creative energy potential in their organizations.

Once again we may see the value of the Type B modality. In an organizational climate with a healthy degree of ambiguity toleration, an openness to the experiences and viewpoints of others, an acceptance of persons regardless of rank or station, and a willingness to experiment, it becomes possible to say no with a constructive and helpful orientation that does not incur the Type A labels of insubordination or disloyalty. Being able to say no to the boss guarantees that the organization will hear many points of view up until that time when a final decision has to be made. When all have had a chance to be heard and have their views thoughtfully considered, there is every reason both to expect and to find loyalty, commitment, and enthusiasm in carrying out organizational objectives.

In the next chapter we will look into the issues and problems inherent in organizational development. When the personal growth of individuals is actively aided by processes of organizational development, ideal conditions are fostered for creating the highest possible levels of individual and organizational success.

8 *Organizational Development*

Alice thought she had never seen such a curious croquet-ground in her life: it was all ridges and furrows: the croquet balls were live hedgehogs, and the mallets live flamingoes, and the soldiers had to double themselves up and stand on their hands and feet, to make the arches.

The chief difficulty Alice found at first was in managing her flamingo: she succeeded in getting its body tucked away, comfortably enough, under her arm, with its legs hanging down, but generally, just as she had got its neck nicely straightened out, and was going to give the hedgehog a blow with its head, it *would* twist itself round and look up in her face, with such a puzzled expression that she could not help bursting out laughing; and, when she had got its head down, and was going to begin again, it was very provoking to find that the hedgehog had unrolled itself, and was in the act of crawling away; besides all this, there was generally a ridge or furrow in the way wherever she wanted to send the hedgehog to, and, as the doubled-up soldiers were always getting up and walking off to other parts of the ground, Alice soon came to the conclusion that it was a very difficult game indeed. (Carroll, 1960)

Those who decide to try their hands at organizational development have also chosen a very difficult game indeed. Organizations are alive, wriggling and twisting like Alice's flamingo. When you think you have identified a problem it may well "get up and walk away" before you can solve it. "Ridges" and "furrows" are to be found everywhere to block the path of what seems to be rational progress. And when the flamingo looks you straight in the eye and says, "You too are part of the problem," it is good to be able to laugh and recognize the humor in the situation, for we are all part of the problem.

At this point a definition might be helpful. By *organizational development*, I mean the use of behavioral science knowledge and skills to bring about demonstrably increased organizational effectiveness, higher productivity at lower cost, improved quality of goods and services, and greater human satisfaction and enjoyment in the hours spent at work for all of an organization's members. Much has been written about organizational development in recent years, and many strategies and models have emerged for bringing about organizational changes and for increasing managerial effectiveness. Yet while some approaches have enjoyed considerable acceptance and success, organizational development practitioners and their programs are, for the most part, still functioning as tributaries of support in their organizations. They are not yet part of the mainstream.

There appear to be two basic reasons why this is so. Many executives are not sure that organizational development is at all desirable, and at the same time there is a great deal of controversy and confusion surrounding organizational development practices and methods. While these reasons are significant, they tend to be characteristic of almost any new field of professional practice; a new approach is always questioned by the established order and experimentation predictably produces divergent views and contradictory assumptions. Therefore those who try to play this very difficult game need to be both high risk takers and practical idealists.

It is my contention, based on both personal experience and observation, that most organizations fail to achieve anywhere near their full potential and are in great need of professional help from organizational development practitioners both from inside their organizations and from the ranks of well-qualified outside consultants. There appear to be four main obstacles to greater organizational effectiveness. Two of these obstacles tend to prevent the need for this help from being either properly valued or sought after. Two others prevent this help from being provided in an effective and efficient manner. It may be useful to state these four obstacles from the outset and then look at each one in turn in greater detail. The obstacles are as follows:

- Many, if not most, leaders of organizations question the necessity for organizational development because they fail to see the intimate connection between the developmental process and task effectiveness, between increased job satisfaction and productivity, and between inner organizational growth and economic return. In addition, many leaders are unwilling to experiment with organizational processes and the requirements of their leadership roles make it difficult for them to look at the effects of their behavior on others.

- Most personnel departments and particularly most top personnel executives are still deeply committed in both theory and practice to fostering the machine conception of organization. The theory is compatible with the beliefs of their superiors and its practices are seemingly intelligent, granting the common sense of our present machine-age culture. Practices such as employment, wage and salary administration, training, and so forth are also the specialized functions around which personnel departments are organized. As a result they have calcified into structured roles and have become organizational habits that are difficult to break.

- Organizational development practitioners today are often limited by the fact that they are specialists in the behavioral sciences. While specialized knowledge is important, many practitioners tend to lack the comprehensive knowledge of the organization's basic mission and purposes required to develop a total strategy for organizational improvement. As captives of the personnel department they also experience difficulty in entering into or gaining acceptance in many other areas of an organization (such as marketing, finance, research and development, or engineering, for example), and they are particularly unsuccessful in influencing top management. In addition, behavioral science specialists have not viewed data processing and management engineering as other forms of organizational development and, instead of seeking to join these forces, they often compete with them.

- Executives, personnel officers, and operating managers do not as yet appear to understand the fundamental energy forces at work in human organizations. When their attention is turned toward organizational development issues they are generally interested in various approaches to training or in techniques for improving human relations. The bedrock issues of human energy have not yet become the focal point of discussion in this field and in crisis situations energy implications tend to be totally disregarded.

There are now significant signs that all four of these obstacles are in the process of being removed or materially lessened. As a result we may now be approaching an era in which we will see widespread organizational improvement with a resultant increase in both job satisfaction and productivity. This development, if it does in fact occur, could not come at a better time.

A VISION OF THE WAY

Chief executive officers of corporations and leaders of large government agencies are charged with the responsibility for formulating and directing the implementation of policies aimed at promoting the viability, effectiveness, and successful operation of their organizations. They are expected to provide the vision and the leadership necessary to enable their organizations to move forward surefootedly along the pathway of intelligent progress.

In the daily process of conducting their affairs, however, most are swept along in a maelstrom of internal and external events that allows them little time for philosophical reflection or even for much serious thinking about the deep ramifications of the issues and problems they face. The expectation implicit in the role they play is that they will make timely decisions on issues of critical importance and that the overriding majority of these decisions will be correct, leading to positive and beneficial results. Thus the operational strategies of most firms are highly task oriented and are aimed at securing

highly visible payoffs in a short period (this is also true for those in top government posts because of the high frequency of elections and rapid changes
of senior-level appointments). The resulting operational stance of a typical
top executive is analogous to a wind instrument player who can never take a
deep breath or a baseball pitcher who has to throw continuous strikes without
benefit of a windup.

Most chief executives also tend to be intensely practical individuals who
do not as a rule seem to have much patience with organizational theory or
with experimenting with new methods of management practice or different
managerial behaviors. They tend to repeat the methods of the past and are
passionately devoted to the task of exercising effective control instead of
engaging in the more risky process of developing capacity for increased control
by and within the organization itself. Many top managers visualize themselves, oddly enough, as orchestra leaders. They think it is their job to simply
study the notes and wield the baton. They often see the orchestra as a model
of mechanical efficiency where everyone must execute a prescribed part without
mistakes. Executives who think in these terms, however, often fail to reflect
on the origin of the excellence they observe in musical performance. Musical
art originates with the composer and the arranger and is borne along by the
emotional commitment of the musicians to musical form and the perfection
of its expression. All of the developmental work must be accomplished prior
to the performance. The leader or conductor thus does not "make" music; he
or she simply fosters its emergence at the appropriate time. Similarly, it is
one of the manager's primary responsibilities to foster organizational development instead of simply studying notes and waving a baton. In music it is easy
to see the intimate connection between personal development and task effectiveness, between the musicians' desire for inner satisfaction and their great
energy. In organizations, however, many individuals are robbed of satisfaction because organizations often fail to create conditions where individual
interests and talents are utilized. Most organizations tell people what to do:
they do not tend to ask "Given these circumstances and your talents, what
would you do?" While there is admittedly increased latitude for independent
action as one moves up in a hierarchy, many policies, procedures, and organizational norms stultify both initiative and creativity and organizations often
tend to grow heavier and more cumbersome with increasing size and age. It
is not at all uncommon to see middle-level executives spending great amounts
of time debating minute points of procedure in order to avoid offending or
displeasing the boss in any way. The boss, on the other hand, often does
little to dispel interpersonal discomfort and to create a situation of comfortable informality that would make it easier to face and cope with uncertainties.

Furthermore, the behavior of the typical chief executive does not tend to
be oriented toward developmental processes. Instead of relying heavily on
group dynamics and competency in interpersonal relations to secure deep
levels of understanding and commitment, many chief executives prefer a directive and authoritarian stance. As a result they are able to avoid looking

at their own behavior or its effects on others and, because they remain impervious to interpersonal feedback, they have no data on which to build self-corrective or self-development plans. When executives do approve of group dynamics at all it is quite frequently on the basis that it is fine for somebody else in the organization but it is not needed by them.

While most chief executives acknowledge the desirability of having efficient, smoothly running organizations with high productivity and intense loyalty on the part of employees, they find it extraordinarily difficult to recognize that their own behavior and that of other top corporate officers may actually cause much of the organizational dysfunction they find so lamentable and so costly. In one large corporation an ambitious overseas acquisition resulted in a loss of $50 million a month until this unprofitable venture could be dissolved. What is more appalling is that the executives involved in this caper found themselves unable to clearly explain how it happened. It is, I believe, the deep-rooted desire for success that prevents many executives from really listening to helpful feedback. Closely akin to this is an attitude of self-reliance that prevents them from being open to emotional experience (see also Chapter 7). Many of their subordinates can see the pitfalls of which these executives are largely unconscious and would probably be able to offer very helpful advice if they were only asked in a spirit of real candor and open-mindedness.

Many organizational leaders question the need for organizational development because they truly don't see the connection between internal growth and development and economic return. Corporations tend to be oriented toward marketing, engineering, or manufacturing, for example, rather than toward learning and internal growth. Organizations that have engaged in experimental programs aimed at applying the problem-finding, problem-solving process described in Chapter 3 and in programs that utilize adult learning theory (see Chapter 6) have discovered that a resolution of interpersonal issues and an improvement of the learning climate can produce dramatic improvements in functional departments such as marketing or engineering and even greater improvement in interdepartmental collaboration. In one major utility these methods were applied over a two-year period, and although top managers were astonished at the results that showed up in performance statistics they have not seized the opportunity to apply these techniques in other areas or to acquaint themselves with what really took place. In some cases these programs proved quite conclusively that top management actions during prior years had caused the very problems that the organizational development practitioners were called on to solve. For some top executives the realization that it is one's own management style that is obstructing the organization is simply too threatening a notion to entertain even if there is a high promise of dramatic organizational improvement. Thus the greatest of the four obstacles to organizational development is the overcoming of inertia at the top. This inertia will be too great unless it is overcome by the top executives themselves. And the combination of economic events (worldwide shifts in financial power) and social events (dramatically increased awareness and influence of minorities, special interest groups, and political parties) we are witnessing today makes it imperative that they do.

We must in all fairness observe that American management has been and continues to be tremendously open to innovation and very successful in bringing it about wherever needs for improvement have been obvious. Now that it is becoming increasingly apparent that management *itself* needs a drastic overhaul, we may optimistically look for growing management support for the needed changes. When top management pays attention to a need and gives it its full support, changes do in fact come about. The crucial issue here is one of time. When top management begins a realistic reassessment of its own role, of the nature of its responsibility to the organization and its members, and of the effect of management behavior on organizational results, it will begin to formulate a new vision of the way toward a more satisfying future. Most organizational members will be ready at such a time to lend enthusiastic support and commitment to this new vision.

FROM TRADITIONAL PERSONNEL MANAGEMENT TO HUMAN RESOURCE DEVELOPMENT

The second obstacle to organizational development is that personnel departments and personnel officers are still deeply committed to the norms and practices typical of machine theory. As the machine approach, once so effective, has now become obsolete it is vital that personnel executives develop a wholly new approach. The deep-rooted cultural changes of the fifties and sixties have had a profound effect on present-day organizations. The cultural revolution that has found its expression in a call for increased recognition of individuality, more participation in democratic processes, and greater equality of opportunity has placed those responsible for managing personnel departments in an extraordinarily difficult position. Faced with rising confrontations and conflicts inside organizations, the threat of prosecution or other sanctions from outside, and the perceived necessity, as always, to get the job done, today's personnel manager is put under an almost unbearable strain. It appears, however, that as a result of this trial by fire, the personnel management function is now coming of age. The old name, *personnel*, is being replaced with *human resources*, and accompanying this change of name are significant changes in both identity and practice.

A quick look at the history of the personnel management function will provide some basis for assessing its present problems and for predicting its future potential. By the end of World War II labor unions had grown significantly in strength and power, and the cessation of armed hostilities brought an end to the collaboration between labor and management that had existed for the purpose of winning the war. As one result, a new type of manager was required, one who understood the rapidly growing body of labor legislation and who could handle labor relations problems, which were multiplying quickly. At the same time, postwar industrial expansion was creating a need for more skilled and specialized workers, and organizations looked to their fledgling personnel departments to develop the expertise needed to locate and hire the "best people" in a fiercely competitive labor market. Salary and supplementary benefits became necessary in order to attract highly skilled professionals, and the need for such measures, coupled with pressure from labor for increased wages and benefits and greater equity of compensation, led to the hiring of wage and salary specialists who also took up residence in the personnel department. Finally, most managements recognized the need for training or continuing education to upgrade the performance effectiveness of employees, so training specialists also began to arrive in increasing numbers. By this time the personnel "shop" was becoming crowded.

In the 1960s, in response to growing dissatisfaction expressed by minorities, training of the disadvantaged and upgrading of the underemployed became a major concern of many if not most organizations. Again, personnel was looked upon to meet this need and many personnel managers began to learn the complexities of developing both contacts and contracts with community action agencies and the government. Also in the 1960s, great breakthroughs in organizational and management development emerged, and many personnel managers found themselves becoming knowledgeable in organizational psychology and group dynamics. As the 1970s arrived personnel managers found themselves shouldering added burdens as a result of increased government regulation in the areas of equal employment opportunity (EEO) and safety and health (OSHA). Now, with significant shortages of natural resources becoming a real problem, we may be at the beginning of an extended period of economic instability, a period that may severely limit the potential for continued organizational growth and expansion. As a result, increasing social and psychological pressures may soon build up to the bursting point unless new ways are found to meet the human needs of the foreseeable future. Personnel management thus enters a time of crisis—an entirely appropriate time for a change in name and identity and also for a reexamination of programs and purposes.

Traditional Personnel Management

Many personnel people entered their field because of a genuine preference for working with people-oriented rather than thing-oriented problems. They soon found, however, that people could provide the biggest and most discomfiting problems of all. Some potential personnel people retreated under fire, and found comfortable niches out of the way of conflict; but others pressed on, always seeming to seek out the action and get involved in the thick of it. Increasing toleration of ambiguity seems to be the pathway toward increasing competence in the field of personnel management and today many personnel managers have become highly respected and fully accepted members of management in their organizations.

Personnel managers, perhaps more than other managers, have come to understand the necessity of integrating the needs of individuals, the organization, and the community. However the personnel department is often seen as operating in a way that is antithetical to human needs. In fact this is probably so, because in the face of the great cultural changes personnel departments have not been able to "destructure" fast enough and have not had either sufficient insight, skill, or organizational acceptance to develop effective living system organizations. Hence many of the criticisms leveled at bureaucracy were aimed straight at personnel managers, who were often unrecognized as those leading the effort to correct the situation. In addition, many personnel managers lacked effective methods for getting the information needed to plan corrective action before problems emerged. Thus many personnel departments adopted reactive strategies, and because they were usually immersed in more daily crises than they could handle, it became all too attractive to wade ahead without doing too much thinking. If you could see that you were accomplishing some effective programs near term, it was somehow less important to worry about where you were going. I am speaking, of course, from personal experience.

Today, when many natural resources are growing scarcer and the costs of obtaining new capital (when it is available) for plant and equipment are becoming increasingly prohibitive, the greatest potential new source of wealth may be found in our human resources. In the process of our wild growth and expansion as a nation during the past 100 years, we seem to have developed some incredibly bad habits: habits of wastefulness and exploitation; habits of planned obsolescence as a substitute for real and readily obtainable quality. In the brashness of our youth, we also seem to have adopted the practice of living for today and not worrying about tomorrow, and nowhere is this practice more evident than in our apparent inability to recognize the full value of our human resources and to give to human resource development the attention it deserves.

Unfortunately many of the policies, practices, and procedures of personnel departments do not lead to effective human resource development; so perhaps it is time to rethink and reassess present personnel practices and policies in order to formulate a new approach. Let's look at four traditional personnel functions—employment, compensation, training and development, and labor relations—to specifically demonstrate this assertion.

Employment. Employment usually begins with a requisition. Most requisitions carry a brief description of the job, the salary level, educational requirements, the reporting relationship, and the necessary approvals to add to staff or replace existing vacancies. Once the requisition is received the search effort begins. There are several questions that arise when this approach is taken: To what extent does the employment specialist really know the working environment into which this new employee will enter? To what extent are the really critical factors that spell eventual success or failure ever made explicit at the point of hire? To what extent does the employment department obtain feedback on hiring success or failure and to what extent does this information get utilized to improve employment performance?

The second stage of the employment process is that of advertising the job. This is often done by posting the opening within the organization and then by contacting employment agencies and placing advertisements in various media. Word of mouth is also a frequent method of obtaining qualified applicants. As the influx of resumés and curriculum vitae begins, the employment specialist screens to find the outstanding applicants. Their resumés are passed on to the interviewing department in order to receive an approval to set up personal interviews. Several further questions now arise: To what extent does the person best suited for the job actually get invited for interviews? To what extent is there a real match between the career development needs of the individual and the opportunity provided by the job opening? Do we frequently hire underqualified or overqualified individuals and do we ever know what or whom we are really getting on the day the new employee begins work?

The third stage of the employment process is the personnel interview or a series of interviews that proceed until the final one or two candidates have been identified. And here we must ask: To what extent do the needs of the organization to get someone hired, and the needs of the individual to find a job, get in the way of a realistic assessment of both the candidate's capability and the opportunity inherent in the job? To what extent are we able to select the best candidate when we have had no opportunity to see any of the candidates in action? To what extent are unrealistic expectations built up on both sides during the interview sequence?

The fourth stage of the employment process is verification. This is the stage of checking references and credentials and possibly conducting psychological tests and measurements of the applicant's capacity and ability. While credential checking is always advisable (and occasionally it turns out that someone or other didn't really graduate from Fairbright U. at all), there is serious doubt as to whether the credential(s) prove the existence of the knowledge, competency, or ability that is presumed to be present. Intellectual attainment is one dimension but a college degree is no equivalent for a proven record of success in practical application. And verification of this sort of success is extremely difficult to obtain. Most personnel representatives are quite reluctant (and appropriately so, especially today) to give out any negative information on a prior employee, and in many cases the person being asked doesn't really know the facts anyway. Often only the most vague and generalized information can be obtained in this manner.

Psychological testing and assessment has developed in the past several years into a fairly reliable predictive science. However many feel that psychological testing is a serious invasion of privacy. Furthermore, there is some question about the extent to which psychological test or assessment information is used effectively by the employer and whether it is ever used for the benefit of the person assessed or tested. How often are the results shared with that person? Is a developmental plan ever outlined for the applicant to overcome recognizable deficiencies? Are the factors the tests measure truly calibrated with identifiable criteria for success on the job? Finally, as tests measure an individual in isolation, to what extent do they measure effectiveness in collaboration with others in a real live job situation, over an extended period of time?

Perhaps we go through all of the above gyrations not only because personnel managers are so anxious to assure the hiring department of their competence at picking winners, but also because we have all been reluctant to admit that the only way we can really assess an individual's effectiveness in action is to see him or her in action.

Compensation. In the past twenty to thirty years a fairly sophisticated but highly questionable system of compensation has been developed in most large- and medium-sized organizations. This system has attained widespread popularity and requires an elaborate set of policies, procedures, and mechanisms in order to function; thus it vastly increases bureaucratic paper work. The system involves paying the job and not the person, and is based on the notion of providing a scale of rates and ranges distributed within a pyramidal structure. The initial purpose of this scheme was to guarantee that no organization would pay more or less than other organizations for the same work and also that within an organization there would be an equity of payment for work performed. While the scheme has worked fairly well with regard to these initially stated problems, it appears to have had a generally negative impact on both productivity and performance. Let's see why.

The underlying structure of this system, the job description, is probably its weakest component. In light of the prevailing conception of the organization as a machine, it is only natural that the job description concentrates primarily on describing the *functional* duties that the incumbent must perform. In addition, the job description presumes a rigid and inflexible organizational *structure*. There are four major problems with most job descriptions I have seen. First, they assume that every incumbent will or should perform a job in exactly the same way (and indeed in the machine conception this kind of standardization is highly desirable). Experience, however, shows us that different individuals with the same job description perform the job in very different ways with different qualities of output.

Second, present-day job descriptions tend to be static rather than dynamic. They do not provide for, nor reflect, the reality of the constantly changing situation. In fact, many of the preparers of job descriptions, especially if they are educated into the machine conception, may not really want dynamic changes to occur in the work setting. They seem to prefer a rigidity of structure and standardization in which functional differentiation is clearly defined and permanently fixed. Now this is a great pity, because if organizations are viewed as living entities there is a real need for a process of structural adaptation to environmental conditions. If someone is overqualified for a position initially it is both desirable and natural that he or she seek and be encouraged to find additional duties and responsibilities so that he or she may perform at his or her own level of competence. But often the taking on of additional work is frowned upon. Either the department head feels his or her toes are being stepped on or other peers feel themselves outclassed or outperformed, which stimulates peer pressure to reduce productivity. On the other hand, a manager who asks someone to take on more responsibility is just as likely to be told, "It's not in my job description." Thus the present form of job description tends to limit organizational growth and development.

Third, in describing only functional elements and formal structural relationships, job descriptions do not fully describe the job for purposes of compensation. By leaving out the entire interpersonal process dimension (see Chapters 3 and 4) or requirements for competency in interpersonal relations, job descriptions present a distorted view of work organization and performance effectiveness. If everyone did exactly what was in his or her job description, nothing more, nothing less, I would venture to guess that the level of performance and the climate of interpersonal relations in that organization would leave much to be desired. Therefore we must ask: To what extent are job descriptions useful and how might they be changed to provide a more realistic foundation for compensation practice? Can they be revised to include career path opportunities and educational and training requirements for promotion? And can they be made more flexible so that individuals can expand their own jobs without waiting for a title change or a promotion?

Another problem in current compensation practice lies with job analysis and evaluation. There are a variety of methodologies for comparing jobs and for assigning weighted values to them in order to derive general compensation levels. For the most part, however, this practice is based on a combination of slavish conformity to an existing situation and pure hunch or guesswork. Easy-to-rate benchmark jobs are evaluated first and hard-to-rate, one-of-a-kind (or unusual) jobs are slotted into levels on the basis of goodness of fit. When this methodology is combined with survey data to ascertain what is being paid for similar jobs in the community (or in the industry), the compensation plan is ready for use. However, to what extent can it be determined that one is in fact getting what one is paying for? To what extent is any attempt made to determine the differential value of any particular job or set of jobs in *this* organization at *this* period of time? How reliable is the survey information one obtains in a period of high inflation and would it be more equitable and reliable to tie all compensation plans to the Bureau of Labor Statistics cost-of-living index? If the general level of prices came down (granted, an absurd notion) would it not be appropriate for wages to come down also? Would there not be less of a competitive struggle between wages and prices if they were tied together automatically? And what is equitable compensation anyway?

The final problem with present compensation practice occurs with performance appraisal. There is probably no other practice in personnel management that is so poorly handled and so universally misunderstood. Again, following the machine conception, many organizations impose performance goals from the top down. These goals are usually output measures that in a way are analogous to revolutions per minute, miles per hour, or feet per second. The higher-level managers set performance goals for lower-level managers and don't really wish to hear about the details of any problems or unique situations requiring special considerations nor do they want to consider differential capabilities of people assigned to a job. What is then appraised is the relative degree of success (or lack of it) of the manager or administrator in getting results. So finally we must ask: To what extent does management performance ever get appraised fairly or realistically? Does performance appraisal result in an equitable distribution of salary funds? Does performance appraisal motivate organizationally constructive behavior? Do the present methods of performance appraisal really identify the best performers?

Training and development. Most large and medium-sized organizations have training and education departments. The existence of a multibillion-dollar training effort among United States organizations is ample testimony to the recognition of the need for continuing education and of the fact that constantly changing situations call for an ongoing process of learning and personal development.

Although training varies among different organizations, there seem to be two general classifications: vocational or skills training, and management and supervisory training and development. In addition to the effort expended on training and development within, organizations also allocate considerable financial resources to programs or workshops given outside the work setting and often outside of the organization itself.

For the most part training is delivered in packaged courses. Educational practices follow the traditional pedagogical assumptions about learning and teaching (see Chapter 6 for a different set of assumptions), and students are graded and evaluated with regard to their performance *in the courses* but not on their resultant ability to perform better *on the job*. In fact, in vocational training in many organizations there is often no possibility for the learner to apply the skills acquired in the course he or she attended. This is so for a variety of reasons. Those attending courses are often selected on the basis of availability—the foreman or supervisor lets go those he can afford to lose for a short period and these people often do not want to go. Those returning from courses, on the other hand, are often assigned to crash programs and have no opportunity to utilize newly acquired skills for three or four months or longer (see also Chapter 6).

In management training there is also an observable split between theory and practice, and the ideas presented in many training courses are difficult to apply on the job. Students are advised to generalize from the theory and make whatever applications they can. But there is seldom any serious attempt to provide ongoing management training support and technical assistance *after* newly trained managers have returned to their field assignments. As a result, management training professionals often have no clear idea of whether or not their training or educational programs have actually improved on-the-job performance. This brings us to the following questions: Can classroom training meet the needs for continuing organizational education? If there is not a clear linkage between the theory and skills taught and application, does the organization realize an appropriate return on its educational investment? Are cost/benefit analyses of training effectiveness needed and, if so, how can they be obtained if there is continued organizational acceptance of a discontinuity between learning in the classroom and application of that learning on the job?

Labor relations. Early in the 1950s, two types of personnel administrators began to emerge: those who were interested in the human factor in organizations and were committed to improving organizations' human effectiveness, and those who were more interested in the legal aspects of employment—the labor contract. Of course many personnel managers were deeply interested in both aspects, but there was a tendency to specialize and many saw organized labor as the organizational adversary and chose to spend their careers doing battle on the labor-management front.

Labor relations became the favorite arena of those who were looking for excitement and who were crisis oriented. Nowhere did the spirit of competition thrive more effectively. It was difficult to see or confront one's adversary in the market place. Business rivals were often located in a different city. But the labor adversary came to work every day at your own plant and each day it was stimulating (and sometimes exhausting) to engage in competitive win/lose games with union officers and shop stewards. Management rewarded their labor relations experts for developing and implementing effective strategies, and third-party referees or arbitrators were frequently brought in by both sides to help win disputes. But arbitrators often failed to discover solutions to organizational problems through improved interpersonal relations because they were more interested in finding legalistic solutions, adding to the ever-growing body of labor cases and legal precedents. In fact, labor law has grown so extensively that today it is a major field of specialization in the legal profession.

Labor's representatives were by no means reluctant to join this game. Many union officers gained popularity and advancement on the strength of their ability to confront management and emerge victorious. While many of these victories led to increased benefits and improved working conditions for labor, the working man was often the real casualty of the labor-management wars. And, as big labor became big business, there was a marked tendency to see the same bureaucratic and pyramidal hierarchies develop in labor organizations. Today, some labor unions are even threatened by strikes within their own unions, as disgruntled union employees seek to organize internal unions to combat the union employer who is now seen to be oppressing the worker.

As a result of the history of labor-management relations one might ask the following questions: In the heat of the battle, have we perhaps lost sight of the search for better and more effective ways to resolve labor-management problems? Does labor-management strife really help anyone? Do labor-management struggles contain hidden psychological and economic benefits for the management, labor, and legal professionals who are the actual protagonists? Can we continue to afford the past practices of labor-management relations now that quality and cost competition is a major factor in world economics?

It may be inferred from the above questions that personnel and personnel practices are in many ways responsible for the feeling of many that "personnel departments are not responsive to people's needs; personnel is not really people oriented." This is true, I believe, and unfortunate, because many personnel people really want very much to humanize the work environments of the organizations they serve. Personnel is often both victim and perpetrator of the conditions observed. It is victim because the perceptions commonly held by many employees that "those people in personnel don't really care about us" diminishes greatly the effectiveness of the personnel function. It is perpetrator because it, too, fosters and promotes the same mechanistic procedures and methods that characterize so much of today's managerial and administrative practice. Thus personnel, the one department that offers the greatest hope for leading organizations into living system design and away from mechanistic bureaucracy, has itself been subtly co-opted during its infancy and youthful development by the very mentality it must succeed in changing if it is to realize its own ideals and goals.

As a result of this co-optation personnel departments find themselves in a somewhat schizoid condition. While they are professing concern for human values, they are operating in a manner aimed at keeping the organization operating with machinelike efficiency. Instead of setting an example by organizing themselves into a "life support system" for their human resources, they contrive to handle human needs on a fragmented and piecemeal basis. There is little wonder that so many people report dissatisfaction with their work and their organizations (U.S. Department of Health, Education, and Welfare, 1973).

Human Resource Development

It seems reasonable to assert that creative human resource developers need to adopt a new approach in light of the present conditions of organizational life. Instead of personnel being oriented toward functional areas of specialization like compensation, employment, or training, it now seems more useful to have human resource teams assigned to each major component of an organization. These teams would be charged with the responsibility for meeting all of the human resource needs of the group or organization being served. Their primary objective would be to increase productivity through improving the quality of work and working life.

While there has been a marked tendency in many large organizations to divide human resource services according to functional specialization and to centralize technical specialists in a corporate headquarters location, nothing, in my opinion, is less useful in human resource management than moving services away from people who need access to them. What is needed is the deployment of thoroughly informed human resource generalists throughout an organization, with field support being provided by a small technical assistance, research, and evaluation group at the headquarters level. Ideally all personnel generalists would be well trained in group dynamics and interpersonal relations and would be fully equipped to facilitate organizational problem finding and problem solving (see Chapter 3). As such they would play a key role in management by seeking to improve employee relations while helping groups improve their task effectiveness. Thus the human resource manager would become in effect a management trainer in the field, conducting action research projects and programs to improve group performance and interpersonal relations simultaneously. Each human resource professional would be assigned to an organizational component for a period of approximately one to two years and rotated to avoid losing the independent perspective necessary to provide ongoing organizational help.

In order to overcome the disadvantages inherent in the present mechanistic approach to human resource management, the different personnel functions of employment, training, compensation, labor relations, and so forth, need to be organically integrated so that each member of an organization is treated as a unique individual and can be assisted in meeting his or her own needs for continuing growth and development while in turn helping the organization meet its needs. When an approach of this kind is effectively designed and implemented, the human resource department will have gone a long way toward overcoming the isolation and depersonalization reported by so many who are dissatisfied with organizational life today. This approach implies, of course, that the human resource executive is willing to change the primary strategy of his or her department from a control orientation to a growth orientation.

Another advantage to this approach to human resource management is its structural flexibility and adaptability. Well-trained generalists (or multispecialists, to use Toffler's term) are able to move easily from one organizational component to another; thus an organization served by human resource multispecialists will have a highly mobile service delivery team. Multispecialists are also much better able to adapt to changing needs and conditions and are able to bring problem-solving skills to bear on a variety of problems from a combination of perspectives. In addition to the structural consideration it is simply more satisfying for most human resource staff members to work with a variety of tasks than to spend years as a job analyst or an employment interviewer, for example. While there must be provisions for entry-level, intermediate, and advanced assignments, the multispecialist approach allows for greater flexibility and personal choice in meeting individual career development needs. Above all, when the human resource service delivery system is moved close to the people, human needs can be met in a more personal, caring, and effective manner. Finally, with this approach it would not be surprising to find more human resource managers working their way into the ranks of general management, a feat that is seldom achieved nowadays.

In order to adopt a more creative and proactive approach to human resource development, human resource professionals would need to acquire competencies in the following areas:

Adult education

Group dynamics and interpersonal relations

Program and project evaluation

Problem finding and problem solving

Conflict management and change strategy

Consulting and consulting skills

Management in general and human resource management in particular

In addition, the human resource multispecialist would be expected to acquire a good knowledge of the specific operating problems and issues facing the organization of which he or she is a part.

Human resource professionals also need to recognize the liabilities inherent in the staff role. Staff organizations seem constantly to fall into monitoring or "police" roles. Nothing can be less useful to an organization wishing to foster development and growth than to allow itself to adopt such a judgmental stance. If the human resource department is going to achieve its full potential it must learn to help line organizations develop both the criteria and models for self-evaluation rather than setting itself up in judgment with regard to line performance in human resource management.

Edgar Schein (1969) has popularized the term *process consultation* and has clearly defined the roles and behaviors that lead toward effective organizational intervention and change. I suggest that human resource professionals also take leave of their traditional staff roles and instead take on the roles and behaviors of process consultants, making their primary stance that of evolving a living systems mentality within an organization in place of the present mechanistic one (see also Chapter 5). If this step could be formally recognized by the entire organization all human resource professionals could behave as legitimate change agents and "process facilitators."

The process consulting approach has been identified as a valuable organizational development technique in a recent study conducted by the Institute for Social Research of the University of Michigan (Bowers, 1971). The principal research investigator comments on the process consultant's role as follows:

> A great deal of effort and emphasis is placed upon his catalyzing a process of surfacing data in areas customarily not plumbed in work organizations (attitudes, feelings, individual needs, reasons for conflict, informal processes, etc.). In behavioral specifics, the change agent employs the posing of questions to group members, process-analysis periods, feedback of observations or feelings, agenda-setting, review, and appropriateness-testing procedures, and occasional conceptual inputs on interpersonal topics. Work is occasionally undertaken with members singly, but more often in natural work groupings. An assumption seems generally to be made that human, rather than technical, processes have primacy for organizational effectiveness.

He comments further on the specific application of the process consulting role in a task-oriented environment:

> The change agent who adhered to this pattern typically begins by analyzing a client unit's work-task situation privately, following extensive interviews, in terms of their objectives, their potential resources, and the organizational forces blocking their progress. He consults privately at frequent intervals with the supervisor, both to establish rapport and to obtain that supervisor's commitment to objectives and desired future courses of action. He sets the stage for client group discussions by introducing select bits of data, or by having another person do so. He encourages group discussion, serves as a process observer, but also uses role playing, some substantive inputs at timely points, as well as nondirective counseling techniques, to guide the discussion toward commitment toward desired courses of action.

The behaviors and roles referred to above are congruent with the requirements for meeting people needs in human organizations. The human resource professional needs to be encouraged, therefore, to move away from the Type A modality that supports mechanistic control and toward a fused Type A/B modality that is more effective for problem finding and problem solving (see also Chapter 3).

The effective human resource manager also needs to be a highly competent organizational consultant who is able to diagnose human problems in organizations and take creative and imaginative steps to both free and conserve human energy.

Improving the quality of working life. The past three or four years has seen the growth of a major nationwide effort (with counterparts in several European countries as well) to improve the quality of work; and indirectly of working life itself. A major assumption behind this effort is that improvements in productivity and work quality will flow directly from the successful implementation of changes in the working environment. Such changes must be made in order for workers to devote their full energy and creative talents to high-quality productive effort. Harking back to the studies at Western Electric's Hawthorne plant in Chicago, conducted years ago by Elton Mayo (1945), many individuals and organizations are at last beginning to take seriously those bellwether research findings. It is finally being recognized that it is worker *involvement* that is required to improve the quality of working life. And real worker involvement usually requires basic changes in management thinking and practice, of much broader scope than simply efforts to reduce boredom through job rotation or job redesign or efforts to help workers have better attitudes through the application of human relations techniques. To be truly productive, changes must aim at improving everything in the working environment that is presently diminishing or reducing worker energies or diverting them to nonproductive or even counterproductive activities.

No one is potentially better equipped to lead the effort to improve the quality of working life than the human resource professional. In fact, this effort appears to be the human resource developer's primary goal. Ted Mills (1975) points out that we have now begun to experience a tremendous surge of interest and involvement in *human resource development* (HRD), or *improvement in the quality of working life.* Managements of a significant number of both public and private organizations, as well as of some large international labor unions, have begun or are about to begin measured experiments in improving the human situation in the work setting. Mills says this present surge is very different from the "fleeting fascination with the 'human relations' movement a decade ago; this one has every appearance of coming from a significant change in management philosophy that is expressing itself in permanent alterations in corporate structure." Could it be that machine theory's tight grip is loosening?

Mills mentions significant HRD or quality-of-working-life projects now going on all over the United States and cites four reasons that have been advanced to explain why this movement is now so strong: (1) widespread alienation, boredom, and job dissatisfaction; (2) decreasing motivation and increasing counterproductive behavior; (3) rising expectations and declining institutions; and (4) dying mechanism and changing ideas.

Mills points out the difficulties in building a conclusive case for any of these four reasons and also explains why all four may be partially accurate. He then advances a positive and practical notion that he says emerged "primarily from my research. . . . much of it done in late 1974, after the recession became evident." Mills's own hypothesis is that HRD is now gaining acceptance from those corporate and organizational leaders who contend that HRD provides a high potential rate of return on a relatively low-cost, low-risk investment of resources. The *return on investment* (ROI) hypothesis suggests that the "source of the HRD phenomenon is in business, which itself has discovered—perhaps to its astonishment—that HRD efforts work. It is simply sound management." In short, there is nothing so strong as an idea whose time has come. A further quote from Ted Mills will illustrate this point.

Although most of this school's proponents, mainly the managers and practitioners active in the field, do not wholly disallow some validity to each of the four preceding hypotheses, they lay stress on results. They suggest that senior officers of U.S. businesses are turning more and more to HRD, not so much for remedial action against various troubling socioeconomic disorders, but rather for action toward better management of a conspicuously underdeveloped business resource: its people. They see HRD's emergence in the past few years as a creation of U.S. managers, who have themselves begun to perceive positive bottom-line results from HRD activities—results such as significantly diminished accident, absenteeism, and error rates, and significantly increased morale, quality of product or service, and their important by-product, productivity.

Quality-of-work programs and information on such programs are currently being fostered and disseminated by the National Commission on Productivity and also by the National Quality of Work Center, an affiliate of the Institute for Social Research of the University of Michigan. Both of these organizations are located in the Washington, D.C. area. In addition, as mentioned above, managements of several large organizations in both the public and private sectors, together with labor and government leaders, have begun to collaborate on designing and implementing quality-of-work projects in a variety of different settings. At this writing there are active quality-of-work centers in Ohio and Massachusetts and a growing number of programs in other states.

It is important at the outset to make clear that neither labor, management, nor government can justifiably be blamed for the decline of productivity in the United States or for low-quality goods and services. American workers are certainly among the very best in the world. The labor movement in the United States has on the whole provided great impetus to raising the standard of living for everyone. Management is and has been extraordinarily creative and innovative, and the United States government has actively and vigorously pursued a course truly aimed at providing freedom and justice for all. While there may be much healthy debate about ends and means it cannot be said that we are lacking either in national purpose or in our desire to pull together as a nation. What appears to be lacking is more a result of problems of *interaction* among the representatives of management, government, and labor. Thus it may truly be said that management, government, and labor all share equally the responsibility for improving the quality of their interactive *processes*.

Nowhere is the quality of interaction more in need of improvement than in areas where we have typically encountered adversary relationships. Thus effective programs to improve the quality of work depend heavily on the active involvement of those who have the competence, and confidence, necessary to cope effectively with adversary relationships and to help the combatants harmonize their energies and channel them into mutually beneficial and constructive efforts. Again, it is human resource professionals who can and must fill this role.

Quality-of-work programs also need neutral third-party interventionists to help those in traditional adversary relationships to discover and build on middle ground. In other words, what is needed is not the collapse of adversary relationships; there is a normal and healthy tension that must continue to exist between management and labor, for example. Likewise, effective coping does not mean building strategies for collusion, or for the weakening of one side to the advantage of the other. What it does mean is helping each side understand and appreciate the other's point of view, concerns, feelings, beliefs, and values.

Herrick and Maccoby (1972) recently enunciated four basic principles to serve as foundational premises for defining improvement in the quality of work. These principles are security, equity, democracy, and individuation. They have since demonstrated that these four principles may be elaborated to serve as a basis for the design of a questionnaire to measure the quality of work in any organizational setting and, with acknowledged assistance from the Institute for Social Research at the University of Michigan, they developed a most valuable research instrument entitled The Ohio Quality of Work Questionnaire (Herrick, 1975).

In addition, Herrick and Maccoby have identified ten counterproductive activities (CPAs) that may serve as the basis for measuring the costs of lost or lowered productivity stemming from environments in which the conditions of work are of poor quality (Herrick, 1975). These ten CPAs are:

Absenteeism	Grievances
Accidents	Inventory shrinkage
Tardiness	Machine repair
Turnover	Quality below standard
Strike days lost	Production under standard

While further clarification is needed in order to use these CPA indexes effectively in a particular situation, they do serve as an appropriate basis for allocating and determining the costs connected with poor or inadequate utilization of human resources. Typical accounting systems do not measure the human resource contribution in such ways and, in fact, changes in basic accounting practice may well be required if we are ever to know what our human resources are worth in economic terms. Early efforts and studies in the newly emerging field of human resource accounting appear now to be leading us to a much greater realization of the value of human resources than ever before. Traditional accounting presently takes the human factor for granted and treats labor only as a cost instead of as both a cost and an asset.

It is now clear that efforts to improve the quality of work pay off in both human and economic terms. Highly successful projects at Harmon International Industries in Bolivar, Tennessee, in the City of Jamestown, New York, and elsewhere (*Three Productive Years*, 1974) have demonstrated that adversary relationships can be replaced by collaborative relationships that benefit everyone to the detriment of no one. More of these projects may now be attempted with confidence, using methodologies already known to be successful.

DEVELOPING ORGANIZATIONAL DEVELOPMENT PRACTITIONERS

The third obstacle to effective organizational development is the lack of sufficiently comprehensive strategies to bring about effective organizational change and growth. This situation exists because most organizational development practitioners lack both the breadth of knowledge and the access to top management necessary for effective strategy development and implementation. Being for the most part specialists in behavioral science applications, these practitioners find themselves in large organizations as staff members within the personnel department. From this position they have considerable difficulty in gaining sufficient credibility to be utilized effectively by either highly technical departments such as research and development or engineering or the business-oriented departments such as finance or marketing. The biggest stumbling block, however, is that their expertise (which is often considerable) is not made generally available to the organization as a whole because these practitioners are seldom, if ever, present in the councils of top management. Thus they are not represented at the crucial policy-making level and their ideas are not often considered.

An Expanded View

Perhaps what will bring about changes in this area more than anything else is what Fred Foulkes (1975) refers to as the demands for an expanded role for the personnel department. The great increase in government effort in the areas of equal employment opportunity has placed demands on organizations not simply to change their employment and promotion practices but to change their culture as well. The only members of organizations that are currently able through training and experience to take on cultural change efforts are the organizational development specialists. Unless their skills are utilized effectively we may expect to see a continuing increase in adversary relations and in the number of lawsuits, boycotts, and other interruptions to life and work within the organizational community.

One solution to the problem of limited access to top management is to greatly increase the emphasis on behavioral science theory and practical application in the nation's leading business schools. Initial attempts to utilize sensitivity training as part of the business school curriculum were not too successful, but it is now possible to introduce the interpersonal process dimension into the business schools through the application of adult learning theory (see also Chapter 6) and also through the use of the problem-finding/problem-solving approach (see also Chapter 3) in conjunction with the well-established case study method. If the nation's future business leaders received as favorable an introduction to the interpersonal side of business as they do to the task-effectiveness side, our future top managers might tend to be less task oriented and more balanced in their viewpoints. In other words, they might become organizational development practitioners in their own right.

A potential solution to the problem of overspecialized viewpoint is that of rotating personnel department staff members with organizational development skills into lower and eventually middle-management assignments in finance, marketing, and engineering, for example. When personnel specialists become more integrated into the mainstream of management we can expect them to develop a broader viewpoint and also to send their very best representatives into the ranks of general management as do the other disciplines.

The skilled organizational development practitioner must recognize that historically there are three main approaches to organizational development; only one is based primarily on behavioral science theory. The other two, management engineering and data processing, have a totally different theoretical orientation. What is now required is that the practitioners of all three of these disciplines begin to actively join forces and work together to create improved organizations in the future. The behavioral science specialist must lead this integrative effort because the management engineers and computer specialists are often unconscious of the human consequences of their technological applications and are unaware of the need for behavioral science help. Let us look at this issue more closely.

Three developmental disciplines. Three major assumptions have served as a basis for conducting organizational development programs and projects over the past fifty or so years. These three assumptions are as follows:

1. The productive efficiency and cost effectiveness of organizations can be improved if the methods of mechanical and industrial engineering are applied directly to the work setting.

2. The information needs of organizations have exploded beyond the processing capacity of humans, calling for a solution that can best be provided by computer scientists and data processing technology.

3. Observable problems of human and organizational behavior can be corrected and both productivity and human satisfaction can be improved through the application of behavioral science methods.

These assumptions create a problematical situation. They are all valid, but they lead to three different types of developmental application or strategy, they utilize three different technologies, and they generate much understandable competition among the specialists who purvey goods and services in each of the three areas and who tend to act as if they possess *the* answer to most organizational problems. Furthermore, as programs in all three areas tend to monopolize major amounts of time and money, it is perhaps wise to consider more carefully what we are doing, how we are doing it, and why.

It may be useful to generalize briefly about the three major approaches that organizational development has taken. The oldest and most accepted organizational development practice is that of management engineering. Management engineers seek to improve productivity and to lower costs by improving or changing equipment, work flow, or factory layout; by assigning time limits and staffing loads to productive processes; by exercising control over inventories and materials; and by instituting programs of quality assurance and quality control. While these practices have long been utilized in factories and manufacturing plants, they have recently begun to be applied to a variety of nonmanufacturing situations; notably, for example, in many state departments of public welfare and in hospitals. The negative effects of these engineering approaches are experienced by many people in increased depersonalization and mechanization of their work, leading to increased boredom, job dissatisfaction, and alienation. These approaches do, however, usually increase productive efficiency.

The second most accepted method of developing organizational effectiveness and increasing output has been that of data processing or computer technology. The growth of the computer industry has been phenomenal in recent years and data processing applications have been found practically everywhere. While rapid information collection, storage, retrieval, and processing capability is highly desirable, negative effects of data processing approaches have been experienced. Information overload, a lack of connection between information available and information needed, the distortion of perception that occurs when quantitative data outstrips the capacity for qualitative assessment, have all limited the computer's usefulness. But the computer has also greatly increased productivity.

The third and perhaps least accepted method for developing organizational effectiveness is that of engaging the human element directly and increasing human productivity *and* satisfaction through the use of behavioral science methods. Negative effects have occurred in the past with these methods when they have been applied in ways that have not led to increased organizational effectiveness. For example, human relations training often did not result in improved human relations or in improved productivity. As a result of some of these early approaches and failures, the behavioral science approach in many ways became suspect.

It appears now, however, that interdisciplinary approaches may be most helpful. Behavioral science practitioners are finding data processing increasingly useful and data processing and business systems planners are increasingly turning to the behavioral scientists for assistance in both designing and implementing new systems where resistance to change can be expected to cause problems. In areas where management engineering is being newly applied, such as in government or in hospitals, it may also be helpful to involve behavioral science practitioners in actively designing and implementing required changes in order to avoid the previously mentioned problems that engineering approaches have caused in organizational settings.

A comprehensive strategy. It has been about three decades since the behavioral sciences entered the management environment with a style and excitement that somewhat resembled the arrival in the dust of Main Street of a gaily decorated horse-drawn wagon, whose proprietor was selling snake-bite medicine and other assorted tonics for old age and rheumatism. Now we all know that if you drink too much of that stuff you start acting a little strange. Now that the dust has settled a bit, perhaps we can take stock of the situation and possibly get a new look at where we are and where we can go from here with the behavioral sciences.

One thing is certain. The patent-medicine approach is not the answer. If the behavioral sciences are going to provide a source of real long-term help to organizations, programs that come in fancy packages will prove to be of limited value. This is not to say that there are no worthwhile packaged programs available, but only that it is essential to have someone in an organization who can effectively translate the complex body of behavioral science knowledge that is now available. These translators must be able to deliver this information, and use it inside their organization, in a manner that leads to positive and beneficial results. If an observable increase in human satisfaction, an increased ability on the part of managers, supervisors, and workers alike to utilize their energies constructively and creatively, and a distinct possibility of long-term growth and development are not in evidence early on in any behavioral science oriented program, then the program needs a thorough reevaluation.

Let's look at some evaluative criteria. First, the best programs are those oriented toward long-term development. This is not to say that courses, workshops, or individual training sessions are not valuable, for many of them are, but only to emphasize that all organizations need an overall strategy for development and growth. Managers often recognize special needs and develop courses or programs to meet them, only to discover later that several other needs existed that could also have been met with slight additions to the original format or basic design. If you have an overall strategy it is much easier, and more cost effective, to plan and organize supportive courses and training activities that tie in to the basic program plan.

Second, behavioral science oriented programs must be geared to the level of general educational development in the organization. In other words, the behavioral science concepts must be presented in clear and nonesoteric language, as free as possible from jargon and technical terms. What's more, these concepts must be *usable;* they must demonstrably help organization members to work more effectively together and to enjoy greater work satisfaction. Anything learned and not put into practice will soon be forgotten.

Third, top-level organizational support must be obtained for behavioral science oriented programs and all programs must be directly aimed at increasing productivity and improving job satisfaction simultaneously. If either aim is neglected the program is likely to founder in the long run precisely because some needs will be met and others neglected.

Fourth, I am personally opposed to programs that seek to change human behavior from outside. I prefer, for ethical reasons, programs that seek to help people change from within *if they want to change.* For example, in any free environment I can choose my own behavior. What I choose to do will have some effect on what others choose in responding to me. If I am a very autocratic boss, I am probably this way because over the years this behavior has worked well for me. If I decide freely to change this behavior to a more democratic approach, then *I create conditions of support* in the organizational environment for more democratic behavior, and to that extent I have changed the environment. However I will not change unless I feel that my new approach will be at least as successful as my former approach. Most people want to see a payoff, or a high potential payoff, before they will be willing to risk changing something that already works.

A comprehensive strategy for creating organizational effectiveness must aim at balancing the energies of an organization's members in ways that facilitate the successful accomplishment of tasks at reasonable cost, the development of satisfying and rewarding interpersonal relationships, the maintenance of effective systems of management control, and the fostering of high levels of creativity and innovation. This requires a careful ordering of the reciprocal balances between tasks and interpersonal relations on the one hand and the need for certainty and the toleration of ambiguity on the other. An organization does not need to be overcontrolled, nor can individuals tolerate too high a level of ambiguity.

There are five basic prerequisites to long-term organizational effectiveness. The first two are:

1. A process of ongoing continuing education for all organizational members so that work itself is a continuing source of learning, self-discovery, and personal growth

2. Methods and procedures in the area of human resource management that truly recognize and value the human side of enterprise and create conditions of collaboration, trust, and openness rather than fostering win/lose competition and conformity/dependence relationships

Effective measures taken to meet these two needs will go a long way toward meeting the third, which is:

3. Continuous improvement in the quality of working life to foster the free release of enthusiastic and creative energy rather than lethargic, apathetic, or destructive reactions

These first three needs cannot be met unless the last two are identified and dealt with appropriately. They are:

4. Provision for the continuous and ongoing development of managers and administrators in all eight areas of the fields of action and consciousness, leading toward increased clarity of thought, emotional maturity, intuitive understanding, and sensory awareness. The right to lead must be based on proven personal competency in developing human resources. No longer can organizations afford to allow managers and administrators to behave in organizationally destructive ways under the guise of achieving greater efficiency or tighter control. Both the Type A and Type B behaviors must be developed simultaneously.

5. Both subjective and objective evaluation of the work of an organization's members to guarantee that organizational competence and productivity are rewarded equitably and that physical, psychological, and organizational problems are brought to the surface and resolved in a constructive and humane manner

In creating a long-range strategy for organizational development, one must remember that organizational development is the prerogative and responsibility of the organization's top leader or general manager. But it is not an exclusive prerogative because the general manager has the responsibility to engage others in this effort. If the general manager does not assume responsibility for organizational development the organization will not be as effective as it could otherwise be. Unfortunately, as we have said, many general managers do not see themselves as responsible for developing their organizations. Some see their role as merely controlling; others see it as fostering quantitative growth through the development of new products, new markets, mergers, and acquisitions; others see it as merely making more money or a greater return on investment, ignoring organizational development as a means to achieve this end. Some would like to actively pursue organizational development activity, but they simply don't know how or are afraid of some unplanned or unforeseen consequences. Many general managers may also feel that they are at the mercy of technological specialists whose mysterious "black boxes" contain more woes than the mythical Pandora ever dreamed of.

There are many alternative approaches to organizational development. What is always required, of course, is some informed decision making to determine what is needed, what approaches and methods will be utilized, what consequences or outcomes are to be expected, what purposes are to be achieved, and finally how increased effectiveness will be measured or demonstrated. In trying to answer these questions, the general manager must strive to achieve a delicate balance between the idealistic and pragmatic; to be willing to take risks but not to risk too much. And he or she must rely on the professional expertise of the organizational development professional.

Organizational development professionals must be much more than good behavioral scientists or psychologists. First, they must have a good understanding of the organization they would seek to help. They must know its strengths and weaknesses. They must know its capabilities and how it relates to other organizations with which it does business. Second, they must have a clear idea of what the organization's mission or purpose is, and following from that they must fully understand the organization's operating strategy or business plan. Third, they must come to know the members of the organization and have a good idea what their developmental needs are, and fourth, they must be sure that they know how the organization exercises its financial and operating controls in order to meet its economic or performance objectives. These four points seem logical and reasonable enough, yet I suspect it would be surprising to learn how many organizational development practitioners do not fully comprehend the above issues.

A Divergent Approach

Before we turn to the fourth obstacle to organizational development it is perhaps important to look briefly at a divergent approach to organizational and individual development.

There has been considerable confusion (among those not intimately acquainted with the behavioral sciences) between organizational development practitioners who are essentially humanists and those who hold a philosophical (and psychological) viewpoint that is essentially mechanistic. The latter group are usually referred to as *behaviorists*, and their viewpoint has been most energetically advanced by B. F. Skinner. The humanist group draws its primary support from a much wider variety of sources, notably from Freud and Jung, from Gestalt psychology, and from Kurt Lewin in particular. The behaviorist view diverges from that of the humanists and is indeed much narrower in its outlook and methodological approach. I will attempt to show how this is so. In his book *Beyond Freedom and Dignity*, B. F. Skinner (1972) suggests that there is increasing evidence to support the belief that humans cannot successfully guide their own destiny through conscious effort and the exercise of self-control; therefore, decision-making power should be taken away from them and placed in the environment. Skinner proposes to eliminate questions of human dignity or personal worth by freeing humans from any sense of responsibility; from any praise or blame. This can be done, Skinner claims, by creating conditions of positive and negative reinforcement in human organizations so that people will do what they are supposed to do, because all of us seek pleasure and avoid pain. This eliminates the need for individual or group competency in decision making and places responsibility for control in the hands of anyone who has the power to manipulate the environment. Skinner says it this way:

> By questioning the control exercised by autonomous man and demonstrating the control exercised by the environment, a science of behavior also seems to question dignity or worth. A person is responsible for his behavior, not only in the sense that he may be justly blamed or punished when he behaves badly, but also in the sense that he is to be given credit and admired for his achievements. A scientific analysis shifts the credit as well as the blame to the environment, and traditional practices can then no longer be justified. These are sweeping changes, and those who are committed to traditional theories and practices naturally resist them.

This view has been perpetuated historically ever since John Locke formulated his now famous dictum, "Everything that is in the intellect must come through the senses." Locke saw man as simply the *passive receiver* of external information. Locke's view, which is basically correct but incomplete (see also Chapter 2), has been interpreted in rather extreme fashion by the behaviorists (Watson, Skinner, and others), who arrived at the conclusion that because humans were simply passive receivers of externally generated information, their behavior could be totally molded or shaped by changing conditions of reinforcement in the external environment. These conditions might be positive reinforcers (pleasurable circumstances or events) or negative reinforcers (painful circumstances or events). The further assumption that man, like other animals, would always seek pleasure and avoid pain implied that man could be controlled (always for his own good, of course) by the manipulation of pleasurable events as well as painful events. Positive reinforcers (rewards) in the behaviorist system are seen as being more potent than negative reinforcers (punishments), but both have been demonstrated to be effective in controlling behavior through a technique called *operant conditioning*.

There is a serious question remaining, however. Shortly after Locke's famous statement was made, another great philosopher, Leibniz, in effect countered it with the assertion that "there is nothing in the intellect that is not first in the senses, *except the intellect itself*." Leibniz claimed that while man did receive information from outside himself through the senses, the activity of man's intellect was such that he was not simply pushed or pulled from outside but was capable of internally organizing his experience, leading to purposive self-actualizing behavior (Allport, 1955).

Presently some managers are intrigued by the possibility of increasing productivity through the utilization of Skinnerian techniques of operant conditioning and behavior reinforcement. While these techniques are perhaps effective for certain limited or specific applications, they pose a threat to overall organizational development and to human growth and development as well. The key issue is still the same now as it has always been. "Under some conditions and for certain ends man will undergo pain and avoid pleasure to achieve something of higher value." We must learn to work with one another and to collaborate in a giving and sharing manner; this often involves pain and the forgoing of pleasure. The manipulation and control of others may increase pleasure and reduce pain, but it also results in an erosion of their energy potential and a reduction of their freedom and autonomy as individuals.

By paraphrasing the above Skinner quotation we may show the fallacy of his argument, for it is equally logical when it is turned inside out and recast as follows into humanist terms:

By demonstrating the control exercised by autonomous man and by *questioning* the control exercised by the environment, a science of behavior tends to confirm the dignity or worth of the person. A responsible person doesn't have to be blamed or punished when he behaves badly. He is all too painfully aware of the separation, anxiety, and guilt that this behavior brings about. On the other hand, we possess an inalienable right to be proud of and to receive *joy* from our creative accomplishments, but we do not have the right to brag about or claim any essential superiority over others. A scientific analysis suggests the necessity for both modulating credit and muting blame in situations arising from the relationship between man and his environment, thus justifying traditional practices but urging that they continually be made more humane. The sweeping charge of man's history away from the barbaric stimulates us to greater efforts in the defense of traditional theories of democracy and freedom, toward constantly improving our situation and resisting both those who would suggest that surrender to our environment is the answer to our problems and those who would seek to control us even for our own good.

The principal problems inherent in the Skinnerian view of man and behavior lie in the weakness of its underlying philosophical assumptions, its mechanistic approach toward human life, and its radical abandonment of the active subjective and interior control capacity in man in favor of an exclusive dependence on the pleasure/pain principle and on external control factors that can be manipulated in the environment. In a recent article in *Ramparts* magazine, Edgar Z. Friedenberg (1975) cut to the heart of the problem with behavior modification and showed how it tends to diminish human values. Friedenberg put it succinctly: "You can train a pigeon to execute a complicated dance perfectly by pure application of behavior modification; indeed, there is probably no other way to do it. But such a pigeon cannot be said to have developed an interest in ballet." A similar manipulation of human beings tends to rob them of the opportunity to achieve a deeper conscious awareness of what they are doing and why they are doing it; thus behavior modification aims toward extinguishing higher moral values by reducing all behavior to the pleasure/pain principle, which can have the effect of devaluing human life itself. Let us turn now to a consideration of the fourth obstacle.

INCREASING AWARENESS OF HUMAN ENERGY FORCES

The fourth obstacle to organizational development is the general lack of understanding of the significance of human energy forces. In individuals, organizations, and communities, human energy is the fundamental force underlying all theories of motivation, training, and interpersonal relations. This force needs to be recognized and studied more deeply. Organizational planners need to consider human energy issues and their consequences more thoroughly. Managers might well utilize human energy theory as a guiding principle for management decision making, and organizational development practitioners might well shift their approach from one of motivational issues to one that concentrates on the deeper issues of energy in human consciousness and action. One result of this shift of emphasis would be to provide a new foundation for the discussion of organizational development theory and a new approach to management practice.

There has been a good deal of discussion recently about the nature of change and its effects on human individuals and organizations. It is clear that simply maintaining organizational status quo is tantamount to slipping backward if there are dynamic changes occurring in the general environment. On the other hand, too much change too quickly will produce a paralyzing effect, as was so well described in *Future Shock* (Toffler, 1970). Much has also been written on the phenomenon of *resistance to change* and how it can be effectively overcome in organizations. In fact, many consultants in a variety of organizations have come to consider themselves as facilitators or agents of organizational change. However, it has become well recognized that change simply for the sake of change is harmful. All change efforts need to be grounded in a conscious sense of purpose, and both the actual and potential costs and benefits involved must be considered. What was a bit perplexing about the great emphasis on change in the 1960s was the underemphasis on the necessity of maintaining stability. Subsequently the pendulum has swung back, and many of the forces of change in our society seem to have weakened dramatically.

Likewise, resistance to change has often, I believe, been viewed as a negative force, and resistors have often been perceived as negative influences by those who seek to bring about changes. We can perhaps create a more constructive attitude if we drop such labels as "reactionary" or "radical" and recognize instead that some persons prefer being in the role of changers and others see themselves as stabilizers. What has now become clear, however, is that beneath the issues of change and stability there is a fundamental shift of energy forces. Let us now see how this works.

The Energy Forces beneath Change and Stability

It was Kurt Lewin (1948) who first compared the processes of social and organizational change to the behavior of charged particles in a magnetic field. Lewin depicted *driving* and *restraining* forces as exercising power on each other and suggested that these forces be first identified and then analyzed by a process he called *force-field analysis.*

A typical force-field diagram would look like the one in Fig. 8.1. Each factor driving toward or restraining a change effort would be assigned a weight or a degree of force. Change would occur, Lewin asserted, when the power of the driving forces was increased and the power of the restraining forces lessened. If both sets of forces were equal in strength, the situational status quo would be maintained.

Factors could be identified in terms of tasks, interpersonal relations, or both. For example, let us say that factor 1 in Fig. 8.1 represented the difficulty of acquiring a particular skill to implement a new training program successfully. The acquisition of this skill requires perhaps only moderate effort; therefore we could arbitrarily assign a weight of 3 on the driving side. As there would probably be no resistance to acquiring this skill other than the usual problems of finding the time, exerting the effort, and so forth, we could assign to the restraining side a weight of 1.

Now let us say that factor 3 represents a power struggle between two department heads of equal rank, one of whom stands to lose considerable power and prestige if a particular change is brought about while the other will lose in like fashion if it is not. In this situation both driving and restraining forces can be assigned a weight of 5.

Lewin's model has been used by many groups and organizations seeking to effect planned change programs. It has been a helpful analytical device for sorting out priorities and for designing alternative strategies or courses of action to try out in the face of resistance to change. There is, however, an additional dimension to consider in an analysis of driving and restraining forces. Understanding the dynamic quality of the ambiguity/certainty relation sheds new light on how human energy is brought to bear on either resolving or blocking the resolution of problems in both the task and interpersonal domains.

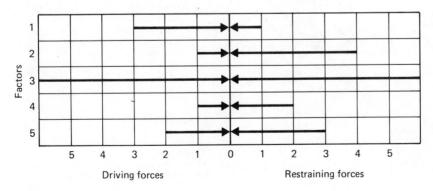

Fig. 8.1 A force-field diagram

Whenever change is introduced into any situation there is an increase in the level of ambiguity, *for change is in and of itself ambiguous.* Conversely, whenever stability, structure, or order is introduced into a situation, there is a movement away from ambiguity and toward certainty. Thus stabilizing forces appeal to individual, organizational, and social needs for certainty. Stability decreases ambiguity and *is certainty producing in and of itself.* But when there is too much control, too rigid a structure, or too much stability, an increase in ambiguity or the introduction of change is required for both individual and organizational health and vitality. The planning of change requires, therefore, an assessment of the forces operating for and against stability and the forces operating for and against change; these forces determine the level and intensity of human energy.

If we consider Lewin's force field in light of the ambiguity/certainty relation (see also Chapter 3), we can clearly see that those who would bring about change in a typical Type A organization are in fact fighting an uphill battle because increasing toleration of ambiguity takes more effort than moving downward to certainty. Therefore the restraining forces usually have the advantage because of the natural tendency of Type A organizations to try to reduce everything to certainty (see Fig. 8.2).

It is particularly useful to view the ambiguity/certainty continuum as an energy accelerator. I came to realize this phenomenon quite clearly while conducting a series of workshops for the U.S. Department of Health, Education, and Welfare during 1972 and 1973. These workshops were to introduce wel-

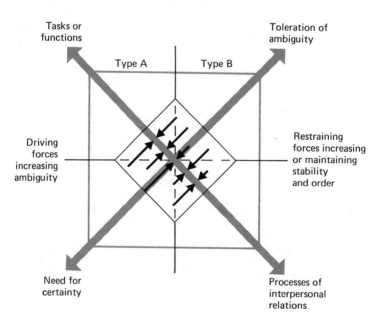

Figure 8.2

fare department trainees to adult learning theory (andragogy) and they were the source of many valuable learning experiences for those conducting the workshops as well as for those participating. Introducing ambiguity into the andragogy workshop setting by gradually reducing the authority role of the workshop director and by involving participants in problem identification activity in small groups, we observed first a dramatic increase in physical animation: laughter, movement, free flow of ideas, more rapid communication, and so forth. This increase in physical and psychological activity was observed to be accompanied by generally increasing psychological tension. At a certain point when the tension level became too high, or when the groups were allowed to continue for too long a period without receiving any directions, a "shock" point appeared to be reached. Expressions such as, "We don't know what's expected of us," "You leaders aren't doing your job," or "There's not enough direction or control," would be commonly heard. Beyond this point a stage of anger would be reached, and finally people would tend to leave the scene physically, psychologically, or both. This phenomenon is familiar to all who have had experience with sensitivity training, T-groups, or encounter groups and is characteristic of the early stages of such groups when the leader quickly relinquishes control and turns all responsibility over to the group. When faced with a leaderless situation group members usually experienced a great deal of anger and anxiety before they learned how to create a new structure or to live comfortably without one.

In these workshops we also observed the reverse situation. If the leader of the workshop maintained tight organizational control and functioned more as a classroom teacher presenting ideas in lecture form, the participants at first were quite attentive but eventually a rumbling of discontent (mostly expressed out of earshot of the leader) would be heard. This discontent when translated would sound like, "There's too much structure and control here," "You're treating us like children," "You're not letting us think for ourselves," and so forth. If it was not relieved or moderated, participants would again leave the scene either physically or psychologically. Here, however, unlike in the first situation, the anger that was present would tend not to be expressed openly.

It was also observed that the conscious use of Type A and Type B behaviors by the workshop leader facilitated or impeded the movement toward change or stability. For example, at the upper level of ambiguity, Type A behavior used by the leader would bring about increased structure and reduce tension. Type B behavior could then be used to negotiate a change of direction or a new structure. In another example, when a group was operating within the confines of a highly structured situation (high certainty) and group members were behaving very passively, increased ambiguity was needed to get the group moving. Type A behavior used by the leader in this situation only maintained the status quo. When the leader switched over to Type B and began to conduct an inquiry about others' ideas and feelings, the energy level rose and the group began to move forward on its task. At times, particularly in the early stages of developing a new group, the patterns of energy and levels of ambiguity and certainty tend to be highly mixed. This is why it takes a new group a while to get itself together and develop the social or interpersonal milieu that is the basic prerequisite to effective task performance.

One key to the resolution of seemingly impossible patterns of organizational conflict and confusion appears to lie in the discovery that Type A behavior increases interpersonal conflict and that Type B behavior reduces it. Another key lies in the realization that as ambiguity rises the energy to reduce that ambiguity back to certainty rises with it. As the gap closes, energy is released until a point of rest or release is obtained. Thus we can conclude that *human energy accelerates and decelerates along the ambiguity/certainty continuum.* The ambiguity/certainty relation operates in much the same way as any natural phenomenon in which processes of tension and release may be observed. This phenomenon of tension and release is in fact well known and is commonly experienced in many physical and psychological forms such as music, drama, and biological growth, and in many fields of study such as economics, education, history, sociology, physics, and chemistry. It is simultaneously the underlying foundation of both science and art. In music, for example, its most elementary form lies in the resolution of the (ambiguous) dominant seventh chord to the (certain) major triad at the interval of a fifth lower (G^7 to C major). In zoology we observe in all forms of animal life a period of gestation (tension) followed by birth (release). In botany the tension in a bud is released with the opening of the flower.

Because the process of ambiguity and certainty (or tension and release) in a bud is released with the opening of the flower (see also Chapter 1).
turns into the other. It is never desirable to reach one or the other stage and try to hold it fast. When ambiguity is too high it must be reduced to certainty or rest, but when certainty is reached the voyage back into the unknown must begin again.

Another realization of the power of the ambiguity/certainty relation stems from its relationship to expectation and fulfillment. Expectation is hope; it is a question about a future possibility. Fulfillment is reality; it is an answer in the present or past. Expectation presents ambiguity and stimulates us to action. Fulfillment presents certainty and restores us to a state of rest. As we saw in Chapter 4, the relationship between expectation and fulfillment in both objective reality and subjective perception creates points of congruency and discrepancy. If, for example, we cannot achieve the fulfillment we seek or if our expectations remain unmet, we find ourselves in a discrepant state. This state contains sufficient energy to enable us to continue or increase our efforts, however. If we have achieved fulfillment and if our expectations have been met, we will be in a state of rest or congruence. In this state the experience of success enables us to again marshal our released energies and venture out with new expectations. Thus when points of congruency and discrepancy in any situation are identified, a strategy for the effective utilization of human energy can be devised.

The Crisis Mode and the Program Mode

Change is a fact of life in most organizations. In large business corporations many changes occur gradually and are planned as projects or programs. Occasionally, however, urgent needs arise that call for changes to be brought about with great speed. Rapid change frequently has a traumatic impact on individuals and on operating groups or departments, particularly if the change is forced. When a change is forced it brings about a rapid increase in situational ambiguity.

Ideally all changes in employee status (promotions, transfers, demotion, termination) are planned well in advance and are discussed with the individuals whose careers and personal lives are being affected. Under normal conditions, employees often have an opportunity to participate in the planning of the change that affects them: by making a selection of preferred job location, by having an opportunity to freely accept or refuse a promotion, or by deciding whether or not to exercise seniority, bumping rights, and so forth. If, however, there are no choices available and only one course of action is seen to be possible, the mutual planning process is usually aborted and the individual must undergo a forced change in status. Any forced status change involves the experience of personal loss, and loss increases ambiguity for the individual. Whenever individual ambiguity (or tension) is increased organizational tension tends to increase as well, resulting in a variety of diseconomies and disincentives. Management tends to overlook these issues, however, because when there is a heightened orientation toward achieving certainty there is a tendency to rush forward despite any diseconomies involved.

Perhaps the clearest example of the discrepancies and disincentives arising from rapid (or forced) changes of status is that of a typical situation in which management must resort to a layoff or a reduction in force. Reductions in force or layoffs have long been accepted by managers as sound business practice based on economic necessity. There are significant hidden costs involved in this practice, however, that tend to lead toward counterproductive and diseconomic results. To show why this is so, it may be worthwhile to review the commonly recognized conditions that lead managers toward the decision that a reduction in force is in fact an economic necessity.

The general predisposing factor to a layoff is the recognition that the organization is overbuilt—a situation arising when line and staff departments are larger than is necessary to achieve the goals and objectives of the organization, when costs (including wages) are rising rapidly, or when income levels are dropping. When demand for goods and/or services is slack or when all four conditions are present at once, a layoff may be required. The insatiable financial appetite of organizations under the conditions stated above first eats up profits and then begins to munch on assets. This financial appetite is so great that it will even eat unearned income and plunge an organization into a serious debt position if it is not rigorously and quickly brought under control. Thus layoffs are not economically wrong, nor do they necessarily reflect individual or organizational incompetence. They arise from great and urgent necessity even though one might argue that the conditions that require layoffs might be avoided with more effective planning.

Measures to improve general efficiency, productivity, and performance are generally adopted as ongoing projects or programs that have either moderate or lengthy time frames for the evaluation of results. Conditions that lead to a management decision that a reduction in force is necessary, on the other hand, tend to build rapidly and accelerate to crisis proportions in a relatively short time frame. Under these restricted time conditions, programmatic or project-oriented solutions do not seem feasible precisely because quick and drastic action is needed to avert what appears as (and probably is) imminent disaster, at least in economic terms.

The discrepancy in time available versus time required to effect an appropriate solution to an overbuilt situation usually triggers an organizational shift from *program mode* to *crisis mode*, from moderate toleration of ambiguity toward a high need for certainty. This shift results in some fundamental attitude changes that can be partly beneficial and simultaneously very costly and counterproductive.

Let us compare these two modes from a variety of perspectives in order to get at an underlying cost/benefit analysis of forced status change.

The *program mode* is characterized by the following:

- A moderate toleration of ambiguity
- Movement toward constructive change, development, and growth
- Varying complex strategies
- Moderate pace with a moderate error ratio
- Carefully considered responses—some opposition encouraged to gain advantage of alternative views
- Increased interdependence, with self-direction and self-starting encouraged and rewarded
- Role flexibility and freedom of movement
- Greater systemic adaptability

The *crisis mode*, on the other hand, is characterized by the following:

- A high need for certainty
- Movement toward constructive stability and order
- A simple, unified strategy
- Rapid and increasing pace with an increased error ratio

- Automatic, highly disciplined responses—no opposition accepted or desired
- Increased dependency—a waiting for commands and reduced willingness to use independent action
- Designated and defined roles with decreasing leeway for constructive action
- Greater systemic rigidity

The crisis mode of operation is also antithetical to a number of common managerial programs and practices that are seen as desirable as well as costly and difficult to implement.

Many large organizations have programs of performance appraisal to help individuals focus on positive developmental steps for performance improvement. Psychological and educational research has proven that performance evaluation that is punitive and negatively judgmental generates defensive reactions, resistance to learning and personal growth, and hostility toward the evaluator. Performance evaluations that are descriptive, positive, and that point toward realistic and achievable goals, on the other hand, are motivational and helpful to the individual. The use of performance appraisal information as a basis for layoff decisions makes it a punitive document for some organizational members and undermines the value of any performance appraisal program as a positive motivator. Thus those responsible for the effective implementation of performance appraisal programs will find their tasks much more difficult when the results of their developmental efforts are used in a negatively judgmental way. The crisis mode ushers in an era of disbelief in personal growth and a belief instead in a competitive struggle for survival. "Dog-eat-dog" then becomes the name of the game.

Problem-finding, problem-solving strategies such as the one detailed in Chapter 3 are program-mode operations *par excellence*. Effective management requires participatory planning, review of alternative strategies, internalization of commitment at all organizational levels, and a mutual effort to reach goals that are clearly thought out and attainable. But developmental programs are difficult to design and implement because many managers are reluctant to devote the amount of time it takes to accomplish these activities. A shift to crisis-mode operation thus tends to destroy the climate necessary for effective program development because it raises the level of anxiety and impossibly shortens the time frame required for action programs to be designed, implemented, and evaluated. Under crisis conditions an organization tends to develop a severe case of myopia, and as efforts toward longer- or middle-range planning are aborted there is an increased risk of situations taking one by surprise. In other words, organizations tend to lose sight of the consequences of their actions while in the crisis mode.

We might infer from the above assessment that organizations might well do everything in their power to eliminate the crisis mentality. Even in a real crisis, it is crucially important to continue to think and to try to move as slowly as possible to avoid panic. Usually we have more time than we think, and often things are not really as bad as they may seem. It is intriguing, however, to consider how many crisis-prone individuals have found their way into organizations and how many seemingly overworked individuals are only creating a lot of "sound and fury, signifying nothing."

Individuals, Organizations, and Communities

Brief reflection on the action and consciousness matrices presented in Chapters 1 and 2 reveals that each of us tends to live within psychological frameworks or orientations of different size. Some people, for example, demonstrate limited ability to tolerate ambiguity, have low interpersonal relations skills, and are competent in performing very few tasks. We might say that these individuals live within very small action and consciousness matrices. Other individuals appear to be operating at the other extreme. They can comfortably tolerate high levels of ambiguity, they are wonderful with people, and they can accomplish a vast array of tasks with consummate skill. They might be said to live in very large action and consciousness matrices. Most of us find ourselves somewhere within matrices of medium size, and the shape of our own personal matrix may not be square. Some of us are better at tasks than at interpersonal relations, and some can tolerate high ambiguity but are not task oriented at all, for example.

We might observe that organizations and communities also vary in matrix size. Some organizations are psychologically large; they operate with loose, amorphous structures, different functional roles have broad responsibilities, and the process of integration tends to be quite informal. Other organizations, even some that are physically large, may be very small psychologically. They would tend to be characterized by rigid structures, limited roles with clearly defined responsibilities, and relatively formal processes of interaction. Titles, for example, would be very important, and the use of first names would be frowned upon. Some organizations vary in psychological size at different hierarchical levels or in different locations. Thus, for example, organizational behavior that would be appropriate in the Atlanta office might be inappropriate in Milwaukee.

Communities also differ in psychological size, and these differences account for the great variation of attitudes we tend to see among those who live in large Eastern cities and those who live in the Midwest, for instance. Even within a city, variations in psychological size occur among ethnic groups and within neighborhoods.

These observable differences among individuals, organizations, and communities must be taken into account when any significant changes are being contemplated. What is perceived as a moderate change by a psychologically large individual may be seen as an intolerable burden by another. When conflict or even violence erupts, the psychologically large individual will generally experience surprise or even shock or disappointment. More realistic perception of individual capacity to tolerate ambiguity is therefore required in order to avoid conflict and to allow for the appropriate introduction of change, and the change must take place within a long enough time frame and be supported by sufficient programs of organizational or community education. Much of the disruption in our cities could have been avoided with a greater realization of the energy consequences when matrices of variable size clash at the individual, organizational, and community levels simultaneously.

This same issue seen in relation to jobs is the basis for the Peter principle (see also Chapter 5). As one moves up in a hierarchy, the positions progressively call for increased ability to tolerate ambiguity and to handle interpersonal relationships and tasks of increasing complexity. Thus if individuals do not grow with their new positions or are promoted before they are ready, they will appear (and be) incompetent because their psychological matrices in the fields of action and consciousness do not fit those required by the job or the position. Some jobs are so large (notably that of president of the United States) that only extraordinary individuals can be expected to perform well in them. Because we presently have a very limited method for identifying such competence and proving that it *does* exist in the candidates that are nominated, we had better either reduce the requirements of the job through constitutional reform, drastically improve the selection process, or risk continued marginal-to-poor performance on the part of the nation's chief executive. This is hardly a matter wherein we should continue to rely either on luck or on the accidents of history.

It is now time to turn our attention to some larger issues that arise from a deep consideration of the matrices of action and consciousness. When these matrices are assessed at their full depth, we come face to face with the ultimate concepts of being and energy, as we shall see.

9 *Energy in Human Society*

In the previous chapters I have tried to describe the ways in which human energy flows in the twofold domain of action and consciousness; in the objective reality of the world around us and also in the subjective reality of our inner awareness. I also attempted to show the linkage between consciousness and action in a general process of problem finding and problem solving, from the particular vantage point of group dynamics and interpersonal relations, and, finally, to show how human energy is underutilized in many organizations and how energy in learning may be greatly increased. In Chapters 7 and 8, I extended some of the above notions further by exploring some of the critical factors that aid and inhibit personal growth and some key issues affecting organizational development. In this final chapter, I will endeavor to apply the basic themes of this book in a way that will hopefully lead to a deeper understanding of some very perplexing human problems. I will conclude with a brief commentary on a psychological discovery that holds great promise for the future development of mankind.

AN AGE OF CRISIS

Today we face four great crises on a worldwide scale. Like the four horsemen of the Apocalypse these crises stand at the gateway to the future, guarding the secret of whether or not (or for how long) human life can continue to exist on this planet. The first crisis is that of population. Uncontrolled sexual energy can, in a relatively short time from now, turn the human race into a dehumanized plague of locusts. The second crisis is that of food. Inequality of production and distribution of food allows millions to go hungry and millions more to be continuously overfed. The third crisis is that of fuel. Without an adequate supply and distribution of basic energy resources, worldwide productivity will be drastically curtailed and national economies will crumble. As a consequence, unfulfilled human needs will create vast reservoirs of dissatisfaction and political instability may become widespread revolution. The fourth crisis is that of finance. We are now beginning to witness previously unimaginable instability in the world's money markets. The wild fluctuation in the price of gold, the lack of capital in the United States and elsewhere to create new jobs, the real possibility of the bankruptcy of several cities and states, and the tremendous increase in deficit spending by the United States government are all signs of a growing crisis in the world of finance.

As a result of these four crises and the concomitant increase of ambiguity on a worldwide scale, we are now in considerable danger of an acceleration of conflict that we can neither cope with nor contain. As we approach the year 2000 we are becoming deeply aware that we have never before been in a situation of such gravity and that the major political powers have the capacity to destroy human life on an unprecedented scale. And it does not appear that we are yet close enough to creating (or even wanting) an international government that would hold sufficient power to prevent overt or covert forms of aggression. We are thus still engaged in a nineteenth-century competitive struggle for material goods and resources with a twenty-first century technology that has given us the power to obliterate everything. Now let us turn to our situation at home.

In the United States we are beginning our third century as a nation. We stand at the crossroads, unsure of which path to take, or indeed how to move forward. We cannot go back to a simpler age nor can we stay where we are. Even with our present uncertainty, however, it is we ourselves who perhaps offer the greatest hope for the future of the world.

It now appears to be an appropriate time to reflect on our extraordinary history. We might, perhaps, regard our first century as our founding period; the time of our birth and childhood. After declaring our freedom from the British empire with immense strength of character, we entered a time of great difficulty and turmoil. After considerable internal and external conflict, including a terrible civil war, we were able at last to establish ourselves as a nation. Our second century, from 1876 to 1976, was a period of tremendous growth, analogous to the development of a human from childhood through adolescence. During this period we flexed our muscles and began to form relationships with other nations. We experienced brief love affairs and sudden battles and we have made many sacrifices to aid those in trouble. We have shown great strength and also great weakness. We have played the role of bully and have been repulsed, but we have never shown cowardice. We have had much difficulty in bringing into reality the ideas of freedom and equality that we profess, but here at last we are making progress. While the lessons of the past have been both joyful and painful they have also been a valuable and necessary part of the experience of growing up. We as a nation now appear ready to begin our adult life.

Will we behave in an adult way? Time will tell, of course, but it seems that we have much valuable experience to share with other emerging states. Because we ourselves have largely solved the problem of forming a free society from an amalgamation of cultures we may, by reflecting on our own process of growth and development, achieve a clearer perspective of the contribution we can make to others. Above all, however, it seems that we must accept and understand that newly emerging nations must of necessity go through the same difficult processes of achieving maturity that we have. As a result, perhaps we will now adopt a posture of patience and understanding. We now know we must avoid taking sides in domestic arguments (urging others to do so likewise) and use our strength to prevent as much conflict and bloodshed as possible. Hindsight gives us excellent vision into how not to interfere in the internal affairs of other countries. We can neither sell our way of life nor give it away. If others want the kind of government we have they must ask us to help them in its formulation. We can no longer assume that its value is absolute or that we are perceived in the same way by all.

As we begin to write the pages of history that will tell of the role of the United States in the next hundred years we will seek, of course, to fulfill the promise implicit in our early beginnings as a nation. We will wish to bring to further fruition those hopes and ideals that our founders expressed with such clarity of insight and firm resolution. In the course of overcoming tremendous obstacles we have so far kept faith with these ideals, and we now appear ready to face the ambiguity of the present with confidence that our founding principles are still our greatest source of strength. We have, of course, a long way to go.

Danger and Opportunity

In light of the dangers we presently face there is little wonder that people frequently observe that we live in a crisis-prone age. As it appears that this condition of crisis will continue for some time, it may be worthwhile to explore the nature of crisis in some detail. In English, the common definition of the term *crisis* is a "turning point leading to eventual disaster or recovery." In Chinese, the character that expresses this term produces a different definition —one that is filled with paradox and leads the way to deeper insight. The Chinese characters 危機 produce two English terms with no connective predicate. The two terms are *danger* and *opportunity*. Thus the English definition misses the vital concept of *opportunity* and instead stresses the alternative of disaster versus a restoration to a previous state of balance or normalcy. It does not point forward toward a new, improved situation and furthermore, it assumes that it is possible to *go back* to normalcy, which is often unlikely. In the English conception, therefore, it might appear foolhardy to risk disaster simply to maintain the status quo or get back to normal; with the Chinese conception, on the other hand, we can see the value of facing crises bravely because the opportunity presented is always accompanied by (and can only be realized by overcoming) the danger inherent in the difficult situation. The Chinese definition, therefore, calls forth an effort to accomplish a desirable goal *beyond* a previous level of attainment. It affirms that ambiguity must be experienced before certainty can be achieved.

The Chinese definition also enables us to see more clearly the tragic element of life. When one takes a great risk and experiences catastrophe because the opposing forces are too great or because uncontrollable events intervene in a fateful way, tragedy is realized as a painful loss of the sought-after opportunity. Failure to take a risk to resolve a crisis may also involve the additional tragic consequence of a lost opportunity that is not only desirable but is a practical necessity as well. Thus to fail to fight when attacked, or to fail to resist arbitrary or demagogic abuses of power, to give two examples, is to accept the tragedy of domination against one's will and the simultaneous loss of self-determination and self-esteem. It is for this reason that we can see the implicit error of placing individuals, groups, organizations, or even nations in a position of jeopardy by means of either preventing their normal development or imposing external constraints or limitations. There are enough natural constraints and limitations already, and the developmental process is slow enough without our further hampering it by preventing normal processes from taking place. When arbitrary and artificial instigations precipitate a crisis, we may expect that forces will arise that will compel us to risk danger in order to achieve a more favorable set of circumstances. On the international scene, war is the usual result of outside interference.

Success in de-escalating conflict crises at home and abroad, therefore, depends to a great extent on the willingness of individuals, organizations, and governments to reduce the levels of implicit or explicit threat to one another. To do so generally involves acting with greater moderation in domestic and international relationships, which always seems to require an increased toleration of ambiguity. The opposite approach of seeking to gain the upper hand through the use of covert and aggressive espionage or overt military force may satisfy some individuals' needs for certainty and control, but these efforts only increase the level of ambiguity for others and move us directly toward explosive conflict and bloodshed. A classic example of moderation accompanied by high toleration of ambiguity was demonstrated by the Kennedy administration in dealing with the Cuban missile crisis. The senior military officers in the United States apparently wished to solve this crisis by resorting to force—air strikes on the missile sites in Cuba. It was the diplomatic competence and political astuteness of President Kennedy and his advisers (in utilizing the tactical device of a blockade) that simultaneously reduced the level of threat and enabled the Russians to see that our resolution was unshakeable; as a result an effective de-escalation of conflict occurred.

It now appears that the mountaintop alluded to in the Allegory of the Mountain has indeed been reached and we have already begun our descent to the valley below. Some say that the age of affluence has ended; some say that the greening of America has ceased due to a sudden and unseasonable frost and as a result we may now be facing a wholly new situation. If we are required by present circumstances to descend from the pinnacle of our past material success, it is a critical time for us to consider how we are going to most effectively utilize our tremendous national energy. As adult maturity calls for both compromise and a clarification of values, we must now decide what we want, what we can afford, what we need, and what we don't need. It is clear that we will not be able to have everything; the idea of unlimited wealth arising from inexhaustible natural resources has been dispelled. Neither can we look to the government to solve all of our problems because the government, like any corporation or family, must learn to live within its means and to temper its idealistic intentions and voracious appetite for taxes with a more realistic attitude and a more modest diet. Perhaps our greatest need today is to increase our capacity to deal both creatively and constructively with conflict. It appears that we are presently wasting our vast human energy resources by engaging in unproductive confrontations and both active and passive forms of destructive behavior. As a result we are in danger of losing sight of our basic purposes and missing the opportunities that lie on the other side of the dangerous period through which we are presently passing.

Creation and Destruction

In order to forge a more satisfying and safer future we must discover a workable strategy for reducing the conflict dilemmas we constantly face. The key to such a strategy may well come from a deep understanding that all human crises arise from a fundamental crisis of human energy; *from an abundant power to create or destroy on the one hand and the lack of power either to create or to prevent destructiveness on the other.*

The original conception of creation and destruction in our civilization hinged on the notions of good and evil (or right and wrong), and these notions emerged from very ancient sources. But today the concepts of right and wrong have become so distorted and abused by centuries of rationalism that it is extremely difficult to define what these terms really mean. Destructiveness can be, and frequently is, rationalized by some individuals as "good." Legitimate reasons for social protest give some individuals all the excuse they need to commit acts of terror and violence. On the other hand, creative efforts (in the form of social change, technological innovation, modern art or music, urban development, attempts to attain racial equality, and so forth) are often labeled as bad or even evil. One result of this rationalistic confusion is that theologians find it increasingly difficult to either define or communicate any systematic or coherent form of morality. On every side we see signs of deteriorating values; the original connotation of *good* (which was creativity and constructiveness) has become passive loyalty and conformity to established frameworks, and *bad* has come to refer to those who seek to create better conditions by raising provocative or conflict-laden questions or issues.

It is indeed time to reassert the linkage of creativity and constructiveness with *good* and to recognize that both active and passive destructiveness are bad. We experience difficulty when we try to do this, however, because we often cannot agree on what constitutes creativity or destructiveness. For example, tearing down an old and useless building may be a creative act if it makes way for a new park, but it may be destructive if the "old and useless" building is a priceless architectural relic. Again we see the influence of Type A and Type B behavior and consciousness. The term *good*, being a Type A category of logic, judgment, and attribution, applies equally to *the destruction of an old and useless building* or to *the preservation of a priceless architectural relic*. Until opposing sides began to adopt Type B attitudes and become open to each other's experience and accepting of each other's viewpoints, compromise (in the form of possibly moving the building to a different location) is impossible and both sides will typically resort to legal (or even illegal) means to force their solution on the other. Attempts to bring about social change in constructive and creative ways involve an understanding of the human energy principles set forth in the previous chapters. These principles are too often neglected because of the pervasive presence in our society of a rationalistic attitude that sees only the Type A side of consciousness and action as constructive and valuable; an attitude that seeks to achieve certainty (and control) even if destructive means must be used to achieve it. This attitude is present in members of all political parties, in liberals, conservatives, and radicals, in those who want to change things, and in those who wish to maintain things as they are. Because it arises from deeply ingrained Western habits of thought and also because it is the foundation of our legal system (which supposedly provides the ultimate determination of what is right and wrong or good or bad), the rationalistic attitude is accepted as practical common sense; those who question it tend to be labeled either as naive or as impractical idealists.

The contradiction in the rationalistic attitude arises when we apply creative/destructive criteria in order to determine what is right or wrong, good or bad. This contradiction has been shown with great poignancy in the Watergate affair. The vast assemblage of legal talent required and the enormous cost involved in uncovering the coverup that arose from the rationalistic mentality of those in the oval office at that time illustrates most effectively its destructive potential. The mentality that stimulates an individual to lie publicly for the *good* of the organization—to see as *right* or correct only those choices that lead to a more secure, more certain, or more controlled situation, no matter how potentially destructive these choices may be—presents a problem of great magnitude, for the attitude that led to the Watergate problems is by no means an isolated or a rare phenomenon in our society. One way out of the dilemma created by the rationalistic viewpoint is to be found in increasing our awareness of its destructive potential and in improving our capacity to tolerate situational ambiguity and interpersonal discomfort: in other words, in developing our Type B capacity.

Perhaps one reason that it is so difficult to overcome the rationalistic mentality is that it has been taught to us from early childhood. Perhaps it might be worthwhile to take a brief look at how we might have reached our present state of affairs.

THE POWERS OF LIGHT AND DARKNESS

In very ancient times the dark night was filled with untold terrors while the light of each new day brought with it a relative degree of safety. This polarity of darkness and light, of night and day, has been observed to have had its effect on many primitive cultures. Some African tribes founded their social order and tribal rule on the duality of day and night. The chieftain was the judge, law-giver, and leader of the "forces of the day." The witch doctor or medicine man, on the other hand, had dominion over the forces of darkness and night. It was the witch doctor who guided the tribe through its struggles with the emotions, particularly fear; it was he who put on the frightening masks, rattled totems, and dispensed taboos to gain control over the forces of the night. The psychological role of the witch doctor was that of taking fear into himself. By actually becoming the fear (or the feared one) he was able to *re-present* the anxieties and fears of the people so that they could gain better control over them. When the witch doctor became fear in a representative way, he was able to gain dominion over it and greatly reduce the anxiety of all tribal members. The association of darkness with evil and goodness with light has carried down to the present day (and regrettably adds to racial misunderstanding). One may well also observe that the darkness represented ambiguity (or danger of sudden death) and the light, certainty (or the opportunity to live in a new day). Light and darkness became quite naturally the dominant powers of tribal culture, and to this day fear of the dark has an existential quality of magic, mystery, and foreboding. If you were standing in the light at the mouth of a cave, for example, and saw two large eyes staring out from the dark, you would probably not seek to go inside or even to approach too closely. And if you were *inside* and in the dark, your first concern would be for your ability to get out quickly and safely. Such is the nature of existential fear of the dark: the fear of the unknown and the unknowable.

An Emerging Civilization

As ancient peoples began to emerge from tribalism the simple notions of light and darkness began to change, and eventually they took on significant religious meaning. In the region known as the fertile crescent, which includes the river basins of the Tigris-Euphrates and also the Nile, many tribes were thrown together in what was perhaps the first great fusion of different cultures. This region spawned (among other things) the civilizations of Greece and Rome and resulted finally in the Western civilization of modern Europe and the Americas. The birthplace of the Indo-European cultures lay to the north along the external or outer curve of this fertile crescent. The Semitic cultures developed along the two points at either end of the crescent and were separated by the Arabian desert. Cultural elements distinctly recognizable as Eastern and Western were fused together in ancient Persia, whose people are believed to have had strong cultural ties with the peoples of the Indus Valley in northwest India. The Persian empire (Indo-European) dominated the entire area by about 500 B.C. Thus ancient Persia was the first major contact between ancient Eastern and Western cultures.

In ancient Persia, the Magi, or "wise men," were the custodians of the beliefs, rituals, symbols, and myths of greatest antiquity. In this early setting, good and evil, light and darkness, were fused together in a constant polarization of two equally powerful but opposing forces, and the Persian dualistic beliefs continued for many centuries into modern times. For the ancient Indo-European and Semitic peoples the problem of the power of darkness versus light was absorbed into religious practice. We are told by historians that Zarathustra (or Zoroaster), the Persian philosopher-king who lived in the seventh century B.C., revered and worshipped the god Ahura-Mazda, the supreme god of light. And among the Semitic peoples, the Hebrews developed a monotheistic consciousness and worshipped Yahweh, the one true God, who had conquered the powers of darkness and would one day free mankind from the darkness of sin by sending a Messiah. Then came the Greeks and the Romans.

As the first great thinkers of our civilization, the Greeks presented ample evidence to support the notion that the "light of the mind is the light of the world." The eyes might thus be thought of as the windows of the mind, which enabled the light to flow in and illuminate the darkness within. As a result of this conception, a basic distinction between soul and body became well developed in the writings of the Greek philosophers Plato and Aristotle, and by Roman times it was clear that the common belief within Western philosophy was that the soul was the location of the forces of good (and light) and the body the location of the forces of evil (and dark). Thus a kind of schizoid condition, or internal struggle, arose within the Western mentality that still prevails today.

At the beginning of the Christian era, Saint John the Evangelist resolved the problem of this light/dark, good/evil polarization by proclaiming the experience of his encounter with Jesus Christ and by bearing witness to the "light" that he himself had seen. Saint John opened his Gospel message with a great theme that reached to the depths of human experience since the dawn of human consciousness. To paraphrase: "It is the life of the living God that is the true light of all mankind. This light always shines and no matter how great the intensity of the darkness, it can never be mastered or overcome. The way into the light is to join into the life (family/community) of the living God through baptism in the Holy Spirit." This message meant that mankind was valued, that both body and soul were good, that there was no more need to fear the dark, and that the emotion of love was as important as the thinking powers of the intellect. While this message was clearly heard and a series of great historical events followed its dramatic announcement, however, it soon became obscured once again by the very powerful influence of the Greek and Roman body/soul dichotomy. As a result the Judeo-Christian (Semitic) conception of a community of people "living in the light of the living God" has come down to us (with no small assistance from Saint Paul) with a curious Greco-Roman twist.

So long before the Persian Magi made their way to Jerusalem to be present at the birth of Jesus, the ancient bias had already been deeply planted in the Western mentality. Light was better than darkness, mind was to be valued over body, and ideas were superior to feelings. After the fall of the Roman Empire, when Western civilization began to emerge from the so-called Dark Ages, the thirteenth-century Dominican monk Thomas Aquinas rediscovered Greek thought and formed a new synthesis that firmly wedded Christian theology to Greek philosophy. Again the ancient conception prevailed and the supposed darkness of passionate feeling continued to be seen as inferior to the light of the rational mind.

So the history of Western civilization over the past seven hundred years, for all its many accomplishments, has been laden with destructive efforts to achieve rational certainty. Both church and state engaged in bloody struggles to impose reasonable or logical frameworks on their members. Each side in any conflict saw itself, of course, as the force of light and goodness and the other side as the force of darkness or evil. As millions fought to restore the rational order upset by the unleashing of intense passions, very few if any realized that the passionate feelings had been aroused initially by the intense desires of their rulers or leaders to achieve or maintain certainty and control.

Enlightened Destructiveness

The rational world view reached full maturity with the arrival of the Age of Enlightenment. The scientific discoveries of that era held out the vision that everything could and would eventually be brought under the control of reason. The road to ultimate perfection was seen to lie straight ahead, and perfection would eventually be reached through hard work and continued scientific *progress*. As the nineteenth century ended and the twentieth century began, the forces of reason seemed to have conquered everywhere. Even the disastrous World War I, a dreadful setback for rationality, was viewed as "the war to end all wars" and was rationalized as progress.

Rationalism came to its full and tragic fruition in the unspeakable horror of consciousness and action of the German leaders (and sadly of many of the people) between the years 1933 and 1946. It was a time of implosion and explosion. The emotional and romantic German spirit described so vividly by Goethe and captured in the music of Wagner and Richard Strauss became the fuel that ignited the immense conflagration of World War II. The ambiguity of defeat in World War I enabled Adolf Hitler to marshal repressed emotional and intuitive elements in German society and forge them into a mass movement that sought to reestablish Aryan (Indo-European) supremacy through the creation of a military power that would surpass that of ancient Rome. To succeed, Hitler needed an emotional scapegoat, and the Jews became the primary victim onto which the sins of the Germans could be transferred in a cleansing and purifying act of national unification. Once the emotional fuel of hatred for the Jews was ignited to create a genocidal fire-storm, rationalism took over control of the Nazi military machine. The ultimate good was seen as victory through the destruction of the enemy. Military power, which thrives on Type A behavior and consciousness, reduced European humanity to a series of objects. As the labels changed from Jew to Czech to Pole to Norwegian to Slav to Russian, the destruction of human life continued as a rational activity out of reach of the inhibiting power of compassion or guilt.

It is this capacity to destroy life through categorization that is perhaps the most latent destructive element in rationalism, and Erich Fromm (1973) has aptly described this subversion of rational activity to wholly destructive purposes as "malignant aggression"—a social cancer. Thus rationalistic attitudes inherent in Western Type A behavior can be clearly seen to allow the most incredible justification of totally brutal destructiveness. The planned and directed atrocities of recent history, from the death camps of Buchenwald and Dachau and the slave labor camps of Siberia to the Vietnamese hamlet of My Lai, have been defended on the grounds of the legal rights of nations to eliminate political or religious dissent and to force military officers to obey even unlawful commands given by superiors. As a result of this abuse of the fundamental notions of constructiveness and destructiveness some say that Western civilization has lost its soul, and its heart and mind as well. There is little wonder that individuals, when faced with legal sanctions that favor destructive acts and simultaneously discourage or prohibit the exercise of constructive protest or deviantly constructive behavior (such as exhibited by many Vietnam war resistors), will tend to subordinate their own subjective feelings to the objective order.

Rationalism presents a formidable obstacle when used by legitimate authorities to justify inhuman acts. No normal person wishes to appear abnormal or even odd. It is far easier to simply go along with whatever is suggested by a recognized authority, especially if others are doing it, than it is to resist in a creative and constructive way. Again we are reminded of social psychologist Stanley Milgram's (1974) experiments to determine the level to which people would participate in or actually cause the torture of others. In these experiments, people were instructed to administer increasingly severe electrical shocks (the supposed victims were only faking pain) at the command of an experimenter. The ambiguity and anxiety they experienced at having to confront the leader of the experiment and refuse to carry out his orders turned out to be far more unpleasant and difficult for them than the alternative of inflicting serious physical pain on someone else. Thus fear of authority, like fear of the dark, creates a powerful norm for increasing conformity, and many will choose conformity and obedience to authority even when it is absolutely necessary that authority be questioned to bring about a more creative or constructive situation or to prevent human suffering.

It is indeed time to challenge the rational constructions of those who abuse power that is granted to them for the benefit of human society as a whole, but we cannot allow ourselves to waste energy in useless attempts to gain retribution against those who are simply assumed to be the perpetrators of injustice. It is necessary to recognize that a propensity for injustice is inherent in all of us because of the intrinsic capacity of Type A behavior (when not modified or balanced by Type B) to produce unfeeling acts of violence. Thus no matter what one's political, religious, social, or economic viewpoint there is a great necessity for increasing both the understanding and practice of Type B behavior and consciousness. As we enter the next decade this may become easier to accomplish as well as becoming simultaneously more important, for we now appear to have reached a historical watershed.

There are growing signs that the apex of Western civilization has been reached and that a new era is beginning. If this is true, the excessive rationalism of the Western world will begin to be more and more tempered and moderated by the openness and acceptance of the Eastern mentality. In the process a new cultural synthesis will develop and perhaps a new world civilization will arise. The great system theorist and biologist Ludwig von Bertalanffy (1968) writes as follows:

> I believe the "decline of the west" is not a hypothesis or a prophesy—it is an accomplished fact. That splendid cultural development which started in the European countries around the year 1000 and produced Gothic cathedrals, Renaissance art, Shakespeare and Goethe, the precise architecture of Newtonian physics and all the glory of European culture—this enormous cycle of history is accomplished and cannot be revivified by artificial means.

> We have to reckon with the stark reality of a mass civilization, technological, international, encompassing the earth and all of mankind, in which cultural values and creativity of old are replaced by novel devices. The present power struggles may, in their present explosive phase, lead to universal atomic devastation. If not, the differences between West and East probably will, one way or the other, become insignificant because the similarity of material culture in the long run will prove stronger than ideological differences.

The System's "Why"

Perhaps it is still far too early to tell if Western civilization has really ended. And perhaps too the cultural values and creativity of old will be replaced not simply by novel devices but also by new cultural values and a far greater creativity than that evinced in the past. But we can certainly see today the rush toward a similarity of material culture as multinational companies become richer and more powerful than many smaller nations and national boundaries serve less and less as cultural barriers. A large tract of downtown Boston, for example, is now owned by Kuwaiti interests, while a Japanese firm recently purchased a large Texas cattle ranch. One United States corporation in the electrical products business has found it highly profitable to play international tic-tac-toe; components manufactured in England are assembled in Brazil for sale in the Philippines. The world grows smaller daily.

What we are beginning to see as we enter the twenty-first century is not the coming triumph of the Western world view but the emergence of a world society that is a fusion of Eastern, Western, and Third-World attitudes containing for the most part, and somewhat mysteriously, a recognition of the intrinsic value of protecting the integrity of all peoples and all cultures. In other words, it appears that the ancient Greek conception of the one and the many, of ultimate diversity within unity, may eventually be realized. We seem to be heading toward a fuller realization that we must learn to live together on this planet and that the only way to do so is to develop a deep respect for pluralistic values. And this requires increased toleration of ambiguity on a worldwide scale. Therefore, if we Westerners would seek to achieve the certainty of a safe future we must at last come to terms with our own aggressive egos and learn how to relax our traditional desire for power and control. In the early days of Christianity, this effort was called "putting on a new heart and a new mind." Today we call it "developing raised consciousness and adopting new behaviors."

In 1960, Stafford Beer delivered an address to the First Systems Symposium at Case Institute of Technology (Eckman, 1961). His talk was entitled "Below the Twilight Arch—A Mythology of Systems," and he commented at length on the mythological foundations underlying systems science. Contrasting two ancient viewpoints, Beer showed clearly that the Western view sought primarily to bring order out of chaos while the opposite viewpoint proclaimed that order was already present if we would seek only to discover it. Beer claimed that instead of producing order, the Western approach often led to increased disorder; in fact, as often as not the very effort to organize resulted in the achievement of disorganization. To act intelligently in the world of the future, therefore, Western man needs to adopt a more Eastern viewpoint and begin to appreciate much more deeply the order that is already ingrained in nature. In his concluding remarks Beer said:

> Those who do not understand the system's "why" betray themselves by hatred and fear of the chaos they assume to lie outside the door; by a failure to amplify themselves and their policies by coupling each to the natural order; and by acting instead as if their job were to lay about them in the chaos with the jawbone of an ass. Such men are supported by a Hesiodic scripture some twenty-seven centuries old. May I outdo them in the authority of antiquity by quoting cybernetics from one of the Upanishads, the Hindu

scripture. The book is called the Bhagavad-Gita, and goes back 5000 years. In it the Lord Krishna declares to man:

"Action is the product of the qualities inherent in nature. It is only the ignorant man who, misled by personal egotism, says: 'I am the doer.' "

In light of the above quotation, it once again becomes important to point out that what is most needed is a balance between these two contradictory attitudes. Thus the development of a dual viewpoint leads us to the appreciation of a paradox. Because man is part of nature he must act to bring about order; at the same time, however, he must recognize the order already present. Acting to bring about order requires Type A behavior, while recognizing and appreciating the order already present requires Type B behavior and attitudes. And as we have seen, the development of an extreme attitude of either the A or the B variety creates a high potential for behaving in ways that are either actively or passively destructive. So it again becomes clear that a balance of both is needed to be creative and constructive *and to allow others to be creative and constructive as well.*

Those who do not understand the system's "why," this basic duality behind action and consciousness, tend to either "lay about themselves with the jawbone of an ass" or to sit in passive contemplation while the world passes them by. What appears to be needed, therefore, is an attitude that pulls both elements together and serves to unify opposing energy forces.

THE SOVEREIGN POWER OF MYTH

The drift into a lifeless rationalism, which has been the fate of so many institutions and organizations in our culture during the past fifty or so years, can only be offset by the infusion of a new wave of life-giving feeling and intuitive insight. Such creative forces emerge from and are provided by the sovereign power of myth. We may call myth a "sovereign power" because it holds dominion over both the Type B and Type A worlds of behavior and consciousness, although it is primarily B oriented because it takes on the elements of a descriptive story. We relate to myths as we relate to drama, by interpreting the story line in terms of our own experience; that is, we make the story come personally alive.

Myths contain the capacity to organize human experience and enable it to be interpreted in a meaningful way. Myths affect consciousness both individually and collectively, forming a coherent basis for both individual and collective action. And myths serve also as the unifying force that binds communities and cultures into a common civilization over an extended period of time. Joseph Campbell (1968), in his monumental four-volume study entitled *The Masks of God*, shows how mythic themes occur and recur throughout history. Deeply influenced by the work of Carl Jung, Campbell also shows how myths and their resultant symbols serve, at the deepest level of the psyche, as the unifying elements of the collective unconscious. Campbell says:

> The rise and fall of civilizations in the long, broad course of history can be seen to have been largely a function of the integrity and cogency of their supporting canons of myth; for not authority but aspiration is the motivator, builder, and transformer of civilization. A mythological canon is an organization of symbols, ineffable in import, by which the energies of aspiration are evoked and gathered toward a focus. The message leaps from heart to heart by way of the brain, and where the brain is unpersuaded the message cannot pass. The life then is untouched. For those in whom a local mythology still works, there is an experience both of accord with the social order, and of harmony with the universe. For those, however, in whom the authorized signs no longer work—or, if working, produce deviant effects—there follows inevitably a sense both of dissociation from the local social nexus and of quest, within and without, for life, which the brain will take to be for "meaning." Coerced to the social pattern, the individual can only harden to some figure of living death; and if any considerable number of the members of a civilization are in this predicament, a point of no return will have been passed.

If we would seek to restore meaning and purpose to life in those areas where it has been lost; if we would hope to attain the courage and strength to overcome the crises of this age, we must either direct our attention toward restoring ancient myths to their proper place or we must create new ones. Where local mythology fails and where the authorized signs and symbols no longer work, life loses its meaning and human existence becomes a pro forma exercise in futility. In our civilization, for a variety of reasons, a great many individuals go through life "coerced to the social pattern" in a manner of living death. We appear to be quickly reaching a point of no return. Let us explore this assertion more deeply.

Campbell describes four primary functions of myth. The first function is to awaken consciousness to the tremendous and fascinating mystery of the existing universe. The second function is to render an interpretive image of the mystery as it is known to contemporary consciousness in order to bring meaning to life. Thus when Shakespeare defined the function of his art as being "to hold, as 'twere, the mirror up to nature," he was also defining a function of myth. The third function is that of sustaining the moral order in terms of shaping the individual to the requirements of his or her geographically and historically conditioned social group. Finally, and we quote:

> the fourth and most vital, most critical function of a mythology, then, is to foster the centering and unfolding of the individual in integrity, in accord with d) himself (the microcosm), c) his culture (the mesocosm), b) the universe (the macrocosm), and a) that awesome ultimate mystery which is both beyond and within himself and all things.

It is obvious that we are dealing with something much deeper than the common conception of the term *myth* when it is taken to mean, as in Webster's definition, "an imaginary story without basis in historical fact." As Campbell says above, "A mythological canon is an organization of symbols, ineffable in import, by which the energies of aspiration are evoked and gathered toward a focus." If, then, as we have said previously, human energy is the bedrock underlying motivation, myth is the sovereign power that gathers and coalesces human energy, bringing it into focus for directed activity at the ultimate level. In other words, it is myth that provides us with a sense of purpose and simultaneously defines what that purpose will be.

From Myth to Reality

The ultimate explanation of the river of energy that flows from ambiguity to certainty is to be found in the inexorable movement from mythic theme to historical reality. All purposeful human activity begins as myth and slowly and inevitably becomes transformed into the reality of experience. When a myth has become fully actualized and has played itself out, or when the circumstances of reality make a particular myth appear useless or absurd, the energy forces that give it power are dissipated and we witness a familiar and curious collapse of dramatic proportions. When myths become distorted, shattered, or effectively countered by other myths, the energy required to stimulate further effort also disappears. Failure in such circumstances takes on the aspect of a self-fulfilling prophecy; the fracturing of a myth predicts oncoming disaster and then helps to bring about its occurrence by failing to provide the energy needed for eventual success.

The often expressed notion "that there is nothing so powerful as an idea whose time has come" is also a reflection on the power of myth. In these instances the personal myths of countless individuals merge and create a powerful collective force. In these situations all of the elements required to ignite the fire of a mass movement are usually present (see also Eric Hoffer quotation, p. 166).

Thus the translation of myth into reality is a process that unleashes vast creative (or destructive) power. The actualization of myths in individuals with significant creative ability can and usually does result in great art or extraordinary scientific achievement. The actualization of organizational myths is a combined process of taking the ideas of one (or a few) creative individuals and building them into a commercial enterprise of significant proportions. This process tends to occur in the space of a few years, usually less than three decades. Some notable examples of creative (mythological) organizations in recent times are Digital Equipment Corporation, the 3M company, Polaroid Corporation, and Xerox. Twenty-five years ago all four of these organizations were barely in existence. Today they are giant organizations with thousands of members.

The actualization of societal myths is a longer and more complicated process. It requires great vision, courage, and faith to build a viable society, and to build a free society of the magnitude of our own is unique in the history of the world. Theodore White (1975) expresses it well:

> There is, however, an absolutely vital political difference between the mythology of other nations and the mythology of America. Other states may fall or endure; they may change or refresh their governing myths. But Frenchmen will always remain Frenchmen, Russians will be Russians, Germans remain Germans, and Englishmen—Englishmen. Nationhood descends from ancestral loins. One can easily contemplate the British Royal Navy becoming the People's Royal Navy, its remaining salts cheering alike for Comrades Horatio Nelson, Francis Drake and Wat Tyler. But America is different. It is the only peaceful multi-racial civilization in the world. Its people come of such diverse heritages of religion, tongue, habit, fatherhood, color and folk song that if America did not exist it would be impossible to imagine that such a gathering of alien strains could ever behave like a nation. Such a stewpot civilization might be possible for city-states—a Tangier, a Singapore, a Trieste. But for so mixed a society to extend over a continent, to master the most complicated industrial structure the world has ever known, to create a state that has spread its power all around the globe—that would be impossible unless its people were bound together by a common faith. Take away that faith, and America would be a sad geographical expression where whites killed blacks, blacks killed whites; where Protestants, Catholics, Jews made of their cities a constellation of Belfasts; where each community within the whole would harden into jangling, clashing contentions of prejudices and interests that could be governed only by police.

We can see clearly from this quotation that those who resort to destructive Type A behaviors, based on logical rationalization, biased assumptions, and unfair attributions are also those who have lost the vision, courage, and faith that make America a great nation.

The enormous power generated by a demagogue such as Hitler could not have come solely from within him. Hitler's mad genius lay in collecting mythical elements in German society and forging them into a collective myth of Aryan supremacy. A similar process of exaggerated belief in supremacy occurred at the same time in both Italy and Japan, and resulting militaristic adventures fed on their own successes. Once sufficient power was developed to counter these absurd myths, however, they quickly collapsed, and today the citizens of these countries look back on this period of history as a weird nightmare. When they awoke, they suddenly wondered why they were fighting and thousands upon thousands surrendered without further struggle.

Personal myths and the concept of self. Psychologists and psychiatrists have long affirmed the importance of a healthy self-concept as a precondition of mental health. Contained within the self-concept, partially in the personal unconscious and partially linked to the archetypes of the collective unconscious (see Chapter 2), is the myth (or collection of myths) that forms the foundation from which individual expression emerges. To the extent one is conscious of the creative myth that guides one's life, and to the degree that one is effective in overcoming the obstacles necessary to translate one's personal myths into reality, to that extent one is fully alive and can achieve one's personal destiny. On the other hand, the extent to which one is unaware of one's personal mythology, and the degree to which one's own myth lies deeply buried in the unconscious, precisely determines the level of limitation that prevents one from achieving one's full potential. It is for this reason, perhaps, that those individuals in any culture who are most creative are always the ones to resist mass movements and the attempts of tyrants to assume autocratic control. While it is necessary for all individuals to align themselves with collective organizational, cultural, or social myths of their own time and place, the truly outstanding individuals always tend to do so on their own terms; thus the geniuses of every age are usually conceived to be a bit odd and hardly ever fit well into large, compact organizations where adherence to group norms is a requirement for successful participation. Thus, while alienated from organizational myths, these individuals become deeply aligned with the creative myths of their culture or civilization.

The exact opposite situation appears to be true for individuals who are basically destructive. We were all deeply shocked by the terrible horror perpetrated by the Manson family. This group was deeply motivated by destructive myths formulated in the distorted mind of their leader. Unable to become part of society, these individuals found a supportive symbiosis in their desert retreat until their destructive energies could no longer be contained and they embarked upon their senseless murderous orgy. Thus very destructive individuals are always alienated from organized society, and the danger of alienation is the deep dissatisfaction it produces in the alienated individual. If these people could live in harmless isolation forever they would pose little threat, but as they generally attempt to overcome their alienation by engaging in destructive acts they are indeed a threat to everyone. It is from this group that the assassins of our recent political history emerge. Through their destructive outbursts such people are provided with relief from their intense loneliness because, even though they remain outcasts, they force others to recognize them and pay attention to their insatiable needs.

Myths in organizations. At the foundation of all successful organizations exists a myth that is the source of that organization's energy and identity. Individuals who choose to align themselves with a particular organization must discover and adapt themselves to this myth or they cannot function in the organization successfully. This process of discovery and adaptation may be partially unconscious, yet it is just this process that provides the "we" feeling required to hold the organization together.

Organizations that have become extremely bureaucratic and are in the process of being strangled by a lifeless rationalism have lost touch with the myth (or myths) that serve as their vital source of energy. Thus these organizations become less and less productive and more and more costly to operate, and traditional management practices and controls are of little avail in correcting the enervating situation. What does help in these instances is the Type B orientation of the process of problem finding (see Chapter 3). The creation of a climate of expectancy, and the involvement of others in processes of mutual planning and need assessment, can greatly increase feelings of harmony and fulfillment—and eventually purposeful myths may be unearthed once again. When this process is utilized competently there is a marked increase in energy and emotional involvement. Those who seek only to perpetuate controlled bureaucracies, however, seem to have little understanding of such things.

Myths and society. Governments, religions, families, schools, and corporations are primary sources of support for societal myths. An effective government is one in which the leaders understand the purpose and the power of myth. Thus Theodore White appropriately identifies Richard Nixon's great failing: "The true crime of Richard Nixon was simple: he destroyed the myth that binds America together, and for this he was driven from power." In the process of selecting our presidents we must look for those who will actively support the underlying mythology of our free society. Myths to support society are also promulgated by religious and fraternal organizations. But religions lose their power when they attempt to foster their own growth and development rather than the underlying myth that gives them their purpose for existing. The family also may play a vital role in the incubation of a mythological orientation in the young. Thus the question, "What do you want to do when you grow up?" has vastly less merit than the question, "What do you want to be?" When the young concentrate on developing mental images of excellence and translate these into reality they are on their way to successful futures. Unfortunately parents do not tend to lead their young by stimulating developmental myths but choose instead to lead by exercising authority, direction, and control. Too much control and not enough imagery and excitement creates situations of conflict and resistance, and many families experience great unhappiness as a result. Instead of devoting so much time to skills training, schools as well might well formulate a mythological approach to learning and growth. Skills would develop rapidly in such a learning environment because the students would attain a vastly higher level of interest and involvement. Finally, I believe it is the purpose of a society's corporate organizations to provide career opportunities that enable individuals to feel a sense of personal worth and well-being arising from their association with the organization for which they work. Nothing is perhaps more destructive than to learn after years of faithful service that your organization's leaders are corrupt and guilty of engaging in bribes and payoffs for scurrilous favors. The desperate competition for successful achievement that compels leaders of corporations to engage in such dishonesty indicates at its depth a serious undermining of our basic social mythology.

Fortunately, all societies provide a collective myth for those who are as yet unaware of their personal myth. Thus many individuals tend to become buried in their society or culture; they are swept along with its currents and totally shaped by its values and beliefs. This collectivization of social myth provides continuity and continuing support for any culture, as well as security and comfort for its members. It is not, however, conducive to human progress, which always appears to be fostered by outstanding individuals. But those who challenge the values and beliefs of their culture risk ostracism because they hold up the mirror to reality, and perhaps nothing is more threatening than to come face to face with one's own unconscious motivations and the contradictory split that often arises between expressed beliefs and actual practice. Nondestructive challenges to any society or culture are always necessary, however, and their presence is a sign of vibrant life and healthy growth.

Myth and Antimyth

At the deepest psychological level, myth contains the elemental power that is the key to both human creativity and human destructiveness. As both creative and destructive tendencies emerge from mythological sources, there is a very fine and as yet unclear line that separates them. As we have said, there is an inexorable tendency in all myth to metamorphose into reality or actuality. The translation of myth to reality is a fundamental process that creates the tension that is the source of psychic energy. Physical energy, as we know, arises from metabolic processes that are autonomic. The origins of psychic energy are also autonomic if the mythical sources lie deeply buried within the individual's unconscious. In some as yet mysterious way physical and psychic energies become integrated in the unconscious so that an individual who is spurred to action by a particularly strong mythic urge also finds that he or she has an additional supply of physical energy to pursue a difficult quest. Extraordinary individual capacity and performance results, and one need only reflect on remarkable individuals in history to obtain a variety of examples: Joan of Arc, Leonardo Da Vinci, or Michelangelo, to name three from the past; or more recently perhaps Winston Churchill, Albert Einstein, and Pablo Picasso.

What, then, causes someone like Hitler, who also had extraordinary psychic and physical energy, to become so incredibly destructive? In the absence of scientific proof one may only speculate, and intuitively it would appear that human destructiveness arises from individuals whose guiding myth is the antithesis of the myths of others. Thus Hitler's myth was not primarily oriented toward creating a stronger, more unified Germany that could take its place in the family of nations; it was aimed instead at destroying that family, at gaining revenge for prior injustices and eventually establishing a world consisting of one nation only. It is perhaps here that the genocidal attack on the Jews found its origin. The Jewish people at that time had no physical location that they could point to as their homeland. The circumstances of the diaspora had scattered them into the midst of German society like leaven in bread. Hitler thus found himself facing an incredible ambiguity. His myth of Aryan supremacy, which required the conquest of other nations to survive, could never be aimed at a Jewish nation, because none existed. Nor could the Jews in Germany be regarded as aliens from another country; they were Germans. Their very presence was the antithesis of the myth of a unified nation of Aryans; therefore they had to be destroyed to enable the Aryan myth to flourish. We may, then, tentatively conclude that all myths are creative unless they are turned against human life itself. They then become cancerous antimyths, and grow at the expense of the health of humanity. Here again we see the wisdom behind Erich Fromm's (1973) concept of "malignant aggression."

If the above speculation is accurate we ourselves must be careful not to turn our dislike of communism or fascism into antimyths so that our whole effort is aimed at destroying these political forms. We must instead devote our energy to realizing more fully the myth of a free society—and this means maintaining the integrity of our own beliefs.

Our attempt to exercise political influence in Southeast Asia appears in retrospect to have been much more of an applied antimyth (the destruction of communism) than an attempt to extend the positive myth of a free society to another country. We exceeded the bounds of propriety and common sense, and a retrospective reflection shows that in warfare the winning side usually has a developmental mythology operating in its favor. Thus in Vietnam our antimyth of opposition to communism was not nearly as strong as the Vietnamese people's myth of unification and national development. And at the end we found out that many of the high-ranking South Vietnamese officials whom we trusted were actually working for the other side; they were, perhaps, more concerned about their nation than ours. While this may not be a popular viewpoint, I offer it only as a reflection on the ultimate weakness of any antimyth. An antimyth is very destructive and will seldom succeed in the end.

In the world of the future we are most likely to serve the cause of peaceful human growth if we come to accept the reality of a montage of mythologies. All individuals as well as all nations are psychologically entitled to pursue the actualization of their own myths as long as they refrain from building antithetical structures to block or inhibit the myths of others. As long as competition involves free choice (and is not rigged by payoffs or other subversive forms of manipulation), success will come to those whose creative energies produce the better results. If we believe in our way of life let us prove that it is best because it produces the highest standard of living, the best art and science, superior education, the lowest rate of alienation and crime, and the greatest human happiness. If we actively pursue these goals and maintain the strength to defend ourselves if attacked we have little to fear from others. It therefore is probably quite unnecessary to foment political intrigue in other nations and to pay off their leaders to purchase our products. It is clear that those among us who would resort to these means have also, like our former president, lost faith in America and the American way of life. In order to ensure a safe future for ourselves and our children, we in the West must clearly develop greater patience (characteristic of the Eastern mentality) and allow our own myths of freedom and democracy to develop naturally.

A NEW DUALITY

In the beginning of this chapter I alluded to a discovery that appeared to have great significance for mankind. It is now time to look at this discovery in relation to the primary themes expressed throughout this book, for it serves to validate the assertions I have made as well to confirm the primary orientation of the duality of Type A and B behavior and consciousness. I am referring to Carl Jung's discovery of the *principle of synchronicity* and his assertion that this principle rivals the principle of causality and stands beside it, forming, as it were, an equality, or balanced relationship. Before we elaborate on the principle of synchronicity in detail, however, some background information may be helpful.

It is perhaps a little-known fact that Jung envisioned his own work as running parallel to that of his contemporaries working in the field of relativity physics. For a time Jung met frequently with Albert Einstein, and later, when it was time for him to write down his ideas on synchronicity, he received valuable help from the physicist Wolfgang Pauli. Jung was fascinated by the physicists' efforts to release tremendous energy forces by splitting the basic structure of the atom. He conceived the human psyche to be in a way analogous to the atom, for he saw the psyche to be the unitary foundation of the self; the fundamental unity of the individual. Jung speculated that if the structure of the psyche could be opened, such a breakthrough might lead to the release of vast amounts of psychic energy heretofore unknown.

In the course of his practical work in psychiatry and psychotherapy, Jung came across the principle of synchronicity quite naturally. But he found it extraordinarily difficult to communicate this discovery because of the general lack of either an adequate preparation or a correct disposition on the part of his listeners to hear what he had to say. Although Jung discovered the principle of synchronicity in the late 1920s, because of this difficulty he did not write his essay, *Synchronicity as a Principle of Acausal Relationship*, until 1952, when he was approaching his seventy-fifth year. Even then he was not fully satisfied with his formulation of this principle; however he set forth his ideas as a way of beginning a serious dialogue and stimulating a deeper investigation into this most fascinating area.

The discovery of the principle of synchronicity was preceded by Einstein's discovery in 1905 of the theory of relativity. Einstein's famous relativity formula, $E = mc^2$, is the basic principle underlying atomic energy. While everyone knows that Einstein's theory led us into the nuclear age, it is perhaps less well known that it also reduced the principle of causality (the supposedly absolute principle of cause and effect) to the level of merely a statistically valid law. Modern physicists have identified many areas of discontinuity that are unaccounted for by the principle of causality, and the introduction of the Heisenberg uncertainty principle has also shown absolute measurement to be impossible, as Heisenberg proved that the act of measurement *itself* changes the object being measured. Relativity theory has therefore made way for a new understanding of the importance of the subjective factor in everything. The nineteenth-century scientific belief that absolute objectivity can be attained has been shattered in the twentieth century. The best approach to knowledge and reality that we can achieve within the limitations imposed by human nature and the confines of our planetary island is a simultaneous combination of objective and subjective viewpoints. This has been, however, a bitter pill for many to swallow, because the formerly unassailable conception upon which Western civilization was built is that of the absolute primacy of the law of cause and effect. It would have been less threatening to challenge any religious dogma in the early days of this century than to challenge the supremacy of the principle of causality. This principle is, of course, the very foundation of rationality, and the deep-rooted conviction of its absolute validity was what caused Jung to wait so long to attempt to introduce a *relative* counterprinciple.

It is the reduction of the principle of causality to statistical law and the introduction of the principle of synchronicity that has confirmed the validity and importance of the Type B modality of action and consciousness and opened up the possibility for the future application of relativity theory to social science. A *managerial* theory of relativity may soon emerge to provide a suitable alternative to the deep-seated Newtonian attitudes that are still so observable in our corporations and governmental bureaus. Until such time as a new management theory emerges, however, greater use of Type B behavior and consciousness is in order and will give support to a new theory. The relative inability of traditional bureaucratic management to cope with this subjective dimension, particularly when it comes to dealing with conflict brought about by such things as economic, racial, or sexual inequality, leads us to believe also that the development of a relativity theory of management is *already* overdue and is in some instances desperately needed. And we may now also begin to see that the term "participative management" is something of a misnomer. It is not just a change in the *amount* of participation in decision making that is behind the present movement toward new approaches to management practice, but a change in the *kind* of participation, a change of relationships in general. No one appreciates being treated as an object to be manipulated by the "manager," and everyone's subjective opinion is entitled to be heard if they are included in the activity taking place. In addition, those who belong to an organization have a right to know about everything that affects their status or standing in that organization. Participation is a fact of experience; denial of access is an arbitrary abuse of power.

Let us now turn our attention to examining the principle of synchronicity in some detail.

The Principle of Synchronicity

Ira Progoff (1973) tells us that Jung presented the principle of synchronicity as a means of filling a gap in the world view presented by scientists. Jung sought to show, on the basis of his own research findings, that another principle, one that included both physical and psychic phenomena, deserved to stand beside the principle of causality to provide a complete picture of reality. In this attempt he was ridiculed by many of his contemporaries, but later developments have now emerged to make his view not only plausible but of revolutionary importance.

A most important dimension of the synchronicity principle is that it brings the worlds of psychological and physical reality together. It also opens up the domain of the esoteric and gives new significance and meaning to paranormal phenomena such as extrasensory perception (ESP), psychokinesis, alterations of space-time phenomena, mental telepathy, teleportation, and levitation. Finally it sheds new light on the potential value of such subjects and techniques of prediction as astrology, *The Book of the Dead*, the Tarot, and the *I Ching* or *Book of Changes*. Jung saw in his vision of synchronicity that these subjects possessed validity not because they were themselves literal descriptions of reality but because they conveyed perceptions of reality drawn from the nonconscious and intuitive levels of the psyche. Thus they were valid symbolic representations of a dimension of human experience that lies deeply within us, of a reality that can be achieved only through indirect methods potentially known to the human psyche. Thus synchronicity provides a key to the occult that has the experience of modern science behind it.

Jung's definition of synchronicity is that of a psychologically conditioned relativity of space and time (or space-time). By using the term "synchronicity," Jung meant to indicate the simultaneous occurrence of an inner experience and a meaningfully related but coincidental external event. He tells, for example, of an acquaintance who, while in Europe, dreamed with great detail of the death of a friend in America. The death was confirmed the following morning by telegram and the details of the death (matching the dream) arrived ten days later in a letter. A comparison of the time of the dream and the death showed that the dream had occurred at least an hour before the death; therefore the dream was not a *synchronous* phenomenon but *synchronistic*. Other examples convinced Jung that synchronistic experiences tend to occur slightly before or after the actual event. Jung asserts that synchronicity consists of two factors: first, an unconscious image comes into consciousness in the form of a dream, an idea, or a premonition; and second, an objective event coincides with the content of consciousness. The origin of both events is puzzling, but their constellation in time provides clear evidence of the existence of an uncaused or acausal series of phenomena based on *meaningfully related co-incidences*. This is synchronicity, and it gives rise to further speculation about how many presumably *caused* events are in reality *acausal* phenomena.

J. B. Rhine and his associates at Duke University proved the validity of extrasensory perception in a careful scientific study that showed that suitably attuned subjects were able to consistently defy the laws of chance by correctly guessing geometric patterns printed on cards even at distances of 4000 miles (Rhine and Pratt, 1962). Jung used the Rhine experiments as partial validation for the synchronicity principle, and asserted that while meaningful coincidences are indeed thinkable as pure chance the more these events multiply and the more exact the details of correspondence are the more the probability decreases and the unthinkability increases. Recognizing that synchronistic events defy the common conception of space and time (a conception arising from our deep belief in the principle of causality), Jung expressed the belief that synchronistic phenomena had to be accounted for by a new category, which would exist along with space-time and causality as a fundamental descriptor of reality. In order to introduce this category properly, Jung turned to his friend Wolfgang Pauli for assistance.

A Synthesis of Physics and Psychology

Not too many years ago, a powerful canon of science was the supposedly correct axiom that "matter cannot be created or destroyed." Discoveries in modern physics have, of course, proved that it is not matter that is indestructible; it is energy. Recent experiments in unimaginably powerful electron accelerators have demonstrated that when two subatomic particles, an electron and a positron, collide, they annihilate each other and turn into two separate emissions of gamma radiation (indestructible energy). The discovery of radio-

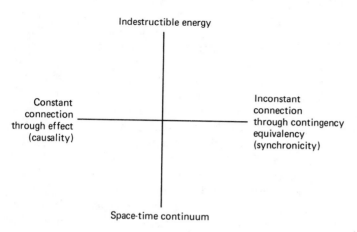

Figure 9.1

activity and the internal energy forces within atomic structure have changed the view of physicists with regard to events observable as space-time dimensions of reality. Therefore, opposite the dimension of space-time, physicists postulate the presence of indestructible energy. All objects that exist in space-time may therefore be thought of as ceasing to exist by becoming converted backward into pure energy. When Jung and Pauli discussed the principle of synchronicity they together developed a diagram, shown in Fig. 9.1, that satisfied the postulates of both modern physics and psychology. Since that time the theory of physics has continued to develop at a rapid pace, and today some scientists are asserting that all matter is simply trapped light and that human consciousness is itself a form of indestructible energy (Toben, 1975; Young, 1972). We now appear to be nearing a resolution of the centuries-old split between mind and body, spirit and matter, and psychology and physics (soft science and hard science). We quote Jung as follows:

> The synchronicity principle possesses properties that may help to clear up
> the body-soul problem. Above all it is the fact of causeless order, or rather,
> of meaningful orderedness, that may throw light on psychophysical parallelism.
> The "absolute knowledge" which is characteristic of synchronistic phenomena,
> a knowledge not mediated by the sense organs, supports the hypothesis of
> a self-subsistent meaning, or even expresses its existence. Such a form of
> existence can only be transcendental, since, as the knowledge of future or
> spatially distant events shows, it is contained in a psychically relative space and
> time, that is to say in an irrepresentable space-time continuum.*

As a result of the discovery of the principle of synchronicity it now becomes possible to construct a new diagram showing the relationship between the diagram of Jung and Pauli and the fields of action and consciousness (see Chapters 1 and 2). This diagram is shown in Fig. 9.2.

We may now construct a further hypothesis that the field of action represents the real world of space-time events. This field is governed by the principle of causality and is deeply influenced by the principle of synchronicity. The field of human consciousness, on the other hand, appears to represent the no-less-real world of indestructible psychic energy (the world of personal and collective myth). This world is governed by the principle of synchronicity and is deeply influenced by the principle of causality. Further, synchronistic events appear to operate through the conscious functions of emotion and intuition and are manifested in the physical world through highly *ambiguous* interpersonal relationships, while causal events appear to dominate the conscious functions of thought and sensation and are manifested in the physical

---

* From *The Collected Works of C. G. Jung*, ed. by Gerhard Adler, Michael Fordham, William McGuire, and Herbert Read, trans. by R. F. C. Hull, Bollingen Series XX, vol. 8, *The Structure and Dynamics of the Psyche* (copyright © 1960 by Bollingen Foundation and © 1969 by Princeton University Press): par. 948. By permission of Princeton University Press and Routledge and Kegan Paul.

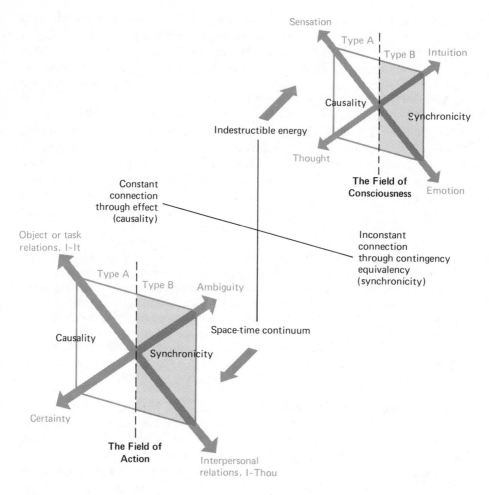

Figure 9.2

world as the task-oriented or object-related manifestations of reality that we commonly understand as *certainties*. At the deepest level of the human psyche, and simultaneously at the surface level of observable reality, we may now affirm the existence of a dualistic principle guiding human destiny.

A Mythology for the Future

In our own lifetime we appear to have reached the limits of everything. The period of geographical exploration has ended and we can now reach almost any part of the world in a matter of hours. The development (and exploitation) of our natural resources has proceeded at such a frantic pace that we can now foresee the day when we will no longer have a number of basic and critical materials. We may, therefore, be reaching the limitation of the development of material culture as we know it. We also appear to have reached, at least for the time being, a limitation in further manned exploration of outer space. Sheer physical distance plus the lack of a propulsion system that will carry us at a velocity approaching the speed of light will keep us well within our own limited solar system. And we are already fairly sure that human life is not present on any other of the planets close to us. We have indeed reached the top of the mountain whose ascent we began many aeons ago. Perhaps we naturally feel some anxiety as we contemplate our future. But when we stop to consider our situation we may discover a new frontier right before our eyes—in the exploration of ourselves and our relations with one another through the expansion of our conscious awareness. We have not nearly reached the limits of our power to love each other and to love life. We have tended to become so preoccupied with discovering the why of every object that we have largely forgotten the ultimate subject. We are now coming face to face with the necessity to look at ourselves and ask the intensely personal question, Why? When we are able to perform this act of self-realization we will be ready to begin our descent from the mountain and into the valley below. We are approaching an era that Teilhard De Chardin (1961) called the *noosphere*, an age of new consciousness and new action. In this era, Dom Aelred Graham (1971) cautions us, religion as we have known it will end and a new faith will rise like the phoenix from the ashes of the old—a combination of Western and Eastern influences. We will then perhaps cease to argue over theological and philosophical differences, for at the deepest psychological levels these arguments tend to disappear. Jung has shown us that in the archetypes of the collective unconscious we are all joined in an ultimate union. What now seems needed is a comprehensive human mythology to draw this union forth and render it consciously apparent.

An effective mythology for the future will be one that enables us to face and overcome crisis situations. Envision, if you will, improved management and better education. A management capacity to deal effectively with crisis situations will be one that creates order, not with the jawbone of an ass, but with a deep understanding of the processes from which order naturally arises. Education, for crisis resolution, calls for a deep increase of internalized understanding; therefore, we may seek to free ourselves from overly narrow specialists and try instead to develop educational approaches that will enable us to improve our competence and abilities in solving problems that are largely interpersonal in both nature and origin. This twofold combination of improved management and education can be made possible in three ways: by improving science, by creating art, and by ensuring peace.

Science. Some may ask if science and its handmaiden, engineering technology, are not two of the villains that we must encounter and overcome on our way down the mountain. It seems, however, that it is science and technology that hold the keys to the continuation of life as well as the means to end it.

More effective internal control of science and technology is needed, and this can come about through the development of a new philosophy of science, based on a generalized view of human needs, replacing the current emphasis on meeting the needs of specialized competitive interests. A growing union of depth psychology and relativity physics may in fact produce in our lifetime a new scientific mythology—a mythology of scientific humanism.

Art. It has been the function of art to create the balance necessary for human life to be lived in a fully human way. Now, however, we may have to turn our attention to the artist in addition to the art, for we seem to have reached the point where each person's life must become his or her own priceless artistic enterprise. What is it in the life of artists that enables them to produce work of such high quality in abundant quantity? Eccentric genius, romantic idealist, madman, radical reformer, are all terms used to describe outstanding artists. Sometimes these terms are used as epithets and sometimes as marks of praise; hardly anyone thinks of artists as normal, as they tend to be too nonconformist. There is now increased reason to believe that the artistic approach to life is also the most human. Contrast the banality of everyday existence in an English factory town, for example. One grows tired just thinking about living in those conditions day after endless day. Can such a life be considered human? When we are free to create or discover and live our own individual myths—when we can begin to "write and enact our own story"—we will have begun to live artistically and will become both more productive and more creative in the process. A new mythology of art, therefore, makes all of us artists.

Peace. It may well be that world peace has not yet been achieved because up to this point it has not been a complete necessity. We clearly can no longer afford the luxury of war, and we must recognize that war has in fact been a luxury for those who have in the past benefited from it. Fostering limited wars as means of maintaining the demand for military goods and hardware has also become far too risky. It appears to be those rationalistic attitudes and values that drive us and others to continue to pursue the most illogical and irrational of pathways—those that lead inevitably to our own destruction. The idea of maintaining self-defense against aggression is often a hollow stratagem for justifying the very aggression it pretends to combat. Can we overcome the terrible paranoia and anxiety that someone is waiting to club us to death when or if we relax our guard for even a moment? Can we come to a full realization of this problem before it is too late?

Perhaps we can find a remedy for many of our present Western ills if we become more familiar with the ways of the ancient East. Interest in the spiritual peace of Zen and Tao is growing rapidly in the West today. By understanding and valuing the Eastern experience, we can gradually overcome our feeling of separation from nature, a feeling that came about from the Western belief that nature was an alien adversary. Perhaps when we are able to combine the best of Eastern and Western orientations into a single mythology, we will all join together for constructive and creative purposes. War, after all, is an alienated form of work. It is, at best, a terrible waste of human energy.

Bibliography

ALLPORT, GORDON W. (1955). *Becoming: Basic Considerations for a Psychology of Personality.* New Haven, Conn.: Yale.

ARAI, SHUNZO (1971). *An Intersection of East and West.* Tokyo: Rikugei.

ARGYRIS, CHRIS (1969). "The Incompleteness of Social Psychological Theory." *American Psychologist* **24**:893–908.

ARGYRIS, CHRIS (1970). *Intervention Theory and Method: A Behavioral Science View.* Reading, Mass.: Addison-Wesley.

ARGYRIS, CHRIS (1971). *Management and Organizational Development.* New York: McGraw-Hill.

BARRETT, WILLIAM (1958). *Irrational Man: A Study in Existential Philosophy.* Garden City, N.Y.: Doubleday.

BENNE, KENNETH D. (n.d.). "Decision Making in Groups." Training document prepared by the Boston University Human Relations Center, Boston, Mass.

BENNE, KENNETH D., and PAUL SHEATS (1948). "Functional Roles of Group Members." *Journal of Social Issues* **IV**:41–49.

BENNIS, WARREN G.; KENNETH D. BENNE; and ROBERT CHIN (eds.) (1969). *The Planning of Change,* 2d Ed. New York: Holt.

BERNE, ERIC (1964). *Games People Play.* New York: Random House.

BERNE, ERIC (1972). *What Do You Say After You Say Hello?* New York: Grove Press.

BERTALANFFY, LUDWIG VON (1968). *General System Theory.* New York: George Braziller. All extracts have been reprinted by permission.

BIRDWHISTELL, R. C. (1961). "Paralanguage: Twenty-five Years After Sapir." In H. Bressin (ed.), *Lectures on Experimental Psychiatry*. Pittsburgh: University of Pittsburgh Press.

BLAKE, ROBERT R., and JANE S. MOUTON (1964). *The Managerial Grid*. Houston, Texas: Gulf.

BLOOMFIELD, HAROLD H.; MICHAEL PETER CAIN; DENNIS T. JAFFE; and ROBERT B. KORY (1975). *TM: Discovering Inner Energy and Overcoming Stress*. New York: Delacorte.

BOGEN, JOSEPH (1969). "The Other Side of the Brain: An Appositional Mind." *Bulletin of the Los Angeles Neurological Societies* **34**:135–162. All extracts have been reprinted by permission.

BOWERS, D. G. (1971). *Development Techniques and Organizational Change: An Overview of Results from the Michigan Inter-Company Longitudinal Study*. ONR Technical Report.

BROWN, BARBARA B. (1974). *New Mind, New Body Biofeedback: New Directions for the Mind*. New York: Harper & Row.

BUBER, MARTIN (1959). *I and Thou*. Translated by Walter Kaufman. New York: Scribner.

BUBER, MARTIN (1965). *The Knowledge of Man*. New York: Harper & Row.

CAMPBELL, JOSEPH (1968). *Masks of God: Creative Mythology*. New York: Viking. All extracts have been reprinted by permission.

CAMPBELL, JOSEPH (1971). *The Portable Jung*. New York: Viking. All extracts have been reprinted by permission.

CARLISLE, HOWARD M. (1973). *Situational Management: A Continuing Approach to Leadership*. New York: AMACOM, A Division of American Management Associations.

CARROLL, LEWIS (1960). Taken from *The Annotated Alice,* by Lewis Carroll, with an introduction and notes by Martin Gardner. Used by permission of Crown Publishers, Inc.

DRUCKER, PETER F. (1954). *The Practice of Management*. New York: Harper.

ECKMAN, DONALD P. (ed.) (1961). *Systems: Research and Design*. New York: Wiley. All extracts have been reprinted by permission.

FORDYCE, JACK K., and RAYMOND WEIL (1971). *Managing with People*. Reading, Mass.: Addison-Wesley.

FOULKES, FRED K. (1975). "The Expanding Role of the Personnel Function." *Harvard Business Review* **53**:71–84.

FRENCH, WENDELL L., and CECIL H. BELL, JR. (1973). *Organization Development.* Englewood Cliffs, N.J.: Prentice-Hall.

FREUD, SIGMUND (1953). *A General Introduction to Psychoanalysis.* Garden City, N.Y.: Permabooks, A Division of Doubleday.

FRIEDENBERG, EDGAR Z. (1974–1975). "Behavior Mod: Is the Pigeon Always Right?" *Ramparts* **13**:55–60.

FRIEDMAN, MEYER, and RAY ROSENMAN (1974). *Type A Behavior and Your Heart.* New York: Knopf.

FROMM, ERICH (1973). *The Anatomy of Human Destructiveness.* New York: Holt.

GALBRAITH, JAY (1973). *Designing Complex Organizations.* Reading, Mass.: Addison-Wesley.

GOLDSTEIN, KURT (1963). *Human Nature: In the Light of Psychopathology.* New York: Schocken Books.

GRAHAM, DOM AELRED (1971). *The End of Religion.* New York: Harcourt, Brace Jovanovich.

HALL, E. T. (1959). *The Silent Language.* New York: Doubleday.

HARRIS, THOMAS A. (1967). *I'm OK—You're OK.* New York: Harper & Row.

HARVEY, JERRY (1974). "The Abilene Paradox." *Organizational Dynamics* **3**:63–80.

HATT, HAROLD E. (1968). *Cybernetics and the Image of Man: A Study of Freedom and Responsibility in Man and Machine.* Nashville, Tenn.: Abingdon.

HERRICK, NEAL Q. (1975). *The Quality of Work and Its Outcomes: Estimating Potential Increases In Labor Productivity.* Columbus, Ohio: The Academy for Contemporary Problems.

HERRICK, NEAL Q., and MICHAEL MACCOBY (1972). "Humanizing Work: A Priority Goal of the 1970's." *Hearings before the Subcommittee on Labor and Public Welfare, 1972.*

HOFFER, ERIC (1951). *The True Believer.* New York: Harper & Row. All extracts have been reprinted by permission.

HOMANS, GEORGE C. (1950). *The Human Group.* New York: Harcourt, Brace & World.

INNIS, HAROLD A. (1951). *The Bias of Communication.* Toronto: University of Toronto Press.

JANIS, IRVING (1972). *Victims of Groupthink.* Boston: Houghton Mifflin.

JONGEWARD, DOROTHY, and MURIEL JAMES (1971). *Born to Win*. Reading, Mass.: Addison-Wesley.

JONGEWARD, DOROTHY, and MURIEL JAMES (1972). *Winning with People*. Reading, Mass.: Addison-Wesley.

JUNG, C. G. (1960). *The Structure and Dynamics of the Psyche*. In Gerhard Adler, Michael Fordham, William McGuire, and Herbert Read (eds.), *The Collected Works of C. G. Jung*. Trans. by R. F. C. Hull. Bollingen Series XX, vol. 8 (copyright © 1960 by Bollingen Foundation and © 1969 by Princeton University Press).

KAHN, ROBERT L., *et al.* (1964). *Organizational Stress: Studies in Role Conflict and Ambiguity*. New York: Wiley.

KEPNER, CHARLES H., and BENJAMIN B. TREGOE (1965). *The Rational Manager*. New York: McGraw-Hill.

KNOWLES, MALCOLM S. (1970). *The Modern Practice of Adult Education: Andragogy vs. Pedagogy*. New York: Association Press. All extracts have been reprinted by permission.

KNOWLES, MALCOLM S. (1972). "The Manager As Educator." *Journal of Continuing Education and Training* 2:97–105.

KNOWLES, MALCOLM S. (1973). *The Adult Learner: A Neglected Species*. Houston, Texas: Gulf.

KNOWLES, MALCOLM S. (1975). *Self-Directed Learning: A Guide for Learners and Teachers*. New York: Association Press.

KUHNS, WILLIAM (1971). *The Post-Industrial Prophets: Interpretations of Technology*. New York: Weybright and Talley.

LAING, R. D. (1960). *The Divided Self*. New York: Pantheon.

LAING, R. D. (1961). *Self and Others*. New York: Pantheon.

LAING, R. D. (1967). *The Politics of Experience*. New York: Ballantine Books.

LAWRENCE, PAUL R., and J. W. LORSCH (1969). *Developing Organizations: Diagnosis and Action*. Reading, Mass.: Addison-Wesley.

LEVINSON, HARRY (1973). *The Great Jackass Fallacy*. Boston: Harvard.

LEWIN, KURT (1948). *Resolving Social Conflicts: Selected Papers on Group Dynamics*. New York: Harper & Row.

LILLY, JOHN C. (1972). *The Center of the Cyclone: An Autobiography of Inner Space*. New York: Julian Press.

LIPPITT, GORDON L. (1969). *Organization Renewal: Achieving Viability in a Changing World*. New York: Appleton.

LUCE, GAY GAER (1971). *Body Time.* New York: Pantheon.

MCCLELLAND, DAVID (1973). "Testing for Competence Rather than for 'Intelligence.'" *American Psychologist* **28**:1–14.

MCGREGOR, DOUGLAS (1960). *The Human Side of Enterprise.* New York: McGraw-Hill.

MCLUHAN, MARSHALL (1965). *Understanding Media: The Extensions of Man.* New York: McGraw-Hill.

MCLUHAN, MARSHALL, and QUENTIN FIORE (1967). *The Medium Is the Massage.* New York: Bantam Books.

MAHLER, W. R. (1974). *Diagnostic Studies.* Reading, Mass.: Addison-Wesley.

MASLOW, ABRAHAM H. (1965). *Eupsychian Management.* Homewood, Ill.: Dorsey-Irwin.

MASLOW, ABRAHAM H. (1971). *The Farther Reaches of Human Nature.* New York: Viking.

MAYO, ELTON (1945). *The Social Problems of an Industrial Civilization.* Boston: Harvard Business School.

MILGRAM, STANLEY (1974). *Obedience to Authority.* New York: Harper & Row.

MILLER, GEORGE A.; EUGENE GALANTER; and KARL H. PRIBRAM (1960). *Plans and the Structure of Behavior.* New York: Henry Holt.

MILLS, TED (1975). "Human Resources—Why the New Concern?" *Harvard Business Review* **53**:120–134.

NEMIAH, JOHN C. (1961). *Foundations of Psychopathology.* New York: Oxford.

ORNSTEIN, ROBERT E. (1972). *The Psychology of Consciousness.* San Francisco: W. H. Freeman.

ORNSTEIN, ROBERT E. (ed.) (1973). *The Nature of Human Consciousness.* New York: Viking.

PARKINSON, C. NORTHCOTE (1957). *Parkinson's Law.* Boston: Houghton Mifflin.

PENFIELD, WILDER (1952). "Memory Mechanisms." *Archives of Neurology and Psychiatry* **67**:178–198.

PERLS, FREDERICK S. (1969). *Gestalt Therapy Verbatim.* Lafayette, Calif.: Real People Press. All extracts have been reprinted by permission.

PETER, LAURENCE J., and RAYMOND HULL (1969). *The Peter Principle.* New York: Morrow.

POLYANI, MICHAEL (1958). *Personal Knowledge towards a Post-Critical Philosophy.* New York: Harper & Row.

PROGOFF, IRA (1973). *Jung, Synchronicity, and Human Destiny.* New York: Julian Press.

RATHS, LOUIS E.; MERRILL HARMIN; and SIDNEY B. SIMON (1966). *Values and Teaching: Working with Values in the Classroom.* Columbus, Ohio: Merrill. All extracts have been reprinted by permission.

RHINE, J. B., and J. G. PRATT (1962). *Parapsychology: Frontier Study of the Mind.* Springfield, Ill.: Thomas.

ROGERS, CARL R. (1961). *On Becoming a Person.* Boston: Houghton Mifflin.

SALZMAN, LEON (1968). *The Obsessive Personality: Origins, Dynamics and Therapy.* New York: J. Aronson.

SCHEFFLER, ISRAEL (1967). *Science and Subjectivity.* Indianapolis: Bobbs-Merrill.

SCHEIN, EDGAR H. (1965). *Organizational Psychology.* Englewood Cliffs, N.J.: Prentice-Hall.

SCHEIN, EDGAR H. (1969). *Process Consultation: Its Role in Organization Development.* Reading, Mass.: Addison-Wesley.

SKINNER, B. F. (1972). *Beyond Freedom and Dignity.* New York: Knopf. All extracts have been reprinted by permission.

STEELE, FRED I. (1973). *Physical Settings and Organizational Development.* Reading, Mass.: Addison-Wesley.

TAYLOR, JACK W. (1973). "What the Behaviorists Haven't Told Us." *Personal Journal* **52**:874–878.

TEILHARD DE CHARDIN, PIERRE (1961). *The Phenomenon of Man.* New York: Harper & Row.

TEILHARD DE CHARDIN, PIERRE (1965). *The Divine Milieu.* New York: Harper & Row.

TERKEL, STUDS (1972). *Working.* New York: Pantheon.

Three Productive Years (1974). The Three Year Report of the Labor-Management Committee of the Jamestown Area.

TILLICH, PAUL (1952). *The Courage to Be.* New Haven: Yale.

TOBEN, BOB (1975). *Space-Time and Beyond.* New York: Dutton.

TOFFLER, ALVIN (1970). *Future Shock.* New York: Random House. All extracts have been reprinted by permission.

TORBERT, WILLIAM R. (1972). *Learning from Experience: Toward Consciousness.* New York: Columbia.

TOWNSEND, ROBERT (1970). *Up the Organization.* New York: Knopf.

U.S. DEPARTMENT OF HEALTH, EDUCATION, AND WELFARE (1973). *Work in America.* Cambridge, Mass.: M.I.T. Press.

UYTERHOEVEN, HUGO E. R. (1972). "General Managers in the Middle." *Harvard Business Review* **50**:75–85.

VAN ENCKEVORT, G. (1971). Personal communication.

WALTON, RICHARD (1969). *Interpersonal Peacemaking: Confrontations and Third Party Consultation.* Reading, Mass.: Addison-Wesley.

WHITE, THEODORE H. (1975). *Breach of Faith: The Fall of Richard Nixon.* New York: Atheneum. All extracts have been reprinted by permission.

YOUNG, ARTHUR M. (1972). "Consciousness and Cosmology." In *Consciousness and Reality,* edited by Charles Muses and Arthur M. Young. New York: Outerbridge and Hazard.

Index

Kahn, Robert, *et al.*, 86, 87
Kapp, Alexander, 161
Karpman triangle, 97, 98
Kelly, Walt, 109
Kennedy, John F., 7, 244
Kennedy, Robert, 7
Kepner, Charles H., 173
King, Martin Luther, Jr., 7, 18
Kipling, Rudyard, 40
Knowledge
  acquisition of, 167–174, 185
  as a dimension of individual difference,
    166
  specialization of, 5
Knowles, Malcolm S., 84, 85, 86, 136, 139,
    140, 144, 145, 146, 150, 152, 153, 154,
    161, 181

Labor relations, 119, 123
  collective bargaining, 119
Laing, R. D., 76
Land, Edwin, 177
Leadership, 55, 113
  behaviors and roles, 80, 82, 83
  role destructuring, 80, 81, 82, 83; *see
    also* Role
Leibniz, Gottfried Wilhelm, 228
Levinson, Harry, 64
Lewin, Kurt, 138, 227, 230, 231
Life positions, 96, 97
Lippitt, Gordon, 119
Locke, John, 31, 228
Louis XVI, 77

McLuhan, Marshall, 49, 115
Maccoby, Michael, 220
Magna Carta, 119
Malignant aggression, 260
Management, 3, 48, 98, 118, 125, 163, 206,
    267
Management by objectives, 64, 65, 67
Managerial Grid, The, 18
Manson family, 257
Masks of God, The (Campbell, Joseph),
    253
Maslow, Abraham, 74, 150
Mass movements, 166, 249, 255, 257
Matrix organizations, 111
Mayo, Elton, 218
Medium Is the Massage, The (McLuhan,
    Marshall), 49
Membership, 53, 58, 61, 87, 91, 92, 98, 123
  dual memberships, 124; *see also* Role
  role destructuring, 80, 81, 82, 83
  roles, 78, 80

Midas touch, 184
Milgram, Stanley, 80, 250
Mills, Ted, 218, 219
Mistrust, 11, 110
Modern Practice of Adult Education, The
    (Knowles, Malcolm S.), 139
Motivation
  attribution of, 12, 16
  external and internal theories of, 5, 181
Multispecialists, 110, 215, 216
Mutual planning, 49, 53, 55, 61, 130, 147,
    148, 152
  group action, 53
  importance of subjective perceptions,
    54, 55
My Lai, 8, 250
Myth, 27, 42, 43, 253–261
  and antimyth, 259–261
  a mythology for the future, 267–269
  organizational, 257–258
  personal, 256–257
  societal, 258–259

Nagasaki, 8
National Commission on Productivity, 219
National Quality of Work Center, 219
Needs, 49, 56–58, 61, 117, 130, 146, 148,
    152, 208
  of communities, 56, 57, 208
  of individuals, 56, 57, 142, 208
  of organizations, 56, 57, 208
  theirs and ours, 131
New England Center for Personal and Or-
    ganizational Development, 174
1984 (Orwell, George), 124
Nirvana, 40
Nixon, Richard M., 258, 261
Noosphere, 267
Normative reeducation, 138
Norms, 53, 102, 110, 155, 257
  group, 87, 90, 91, 98; *see also* Growth,
    group
  of machine theory, 106
  organizational, 12, 102

Object (or task), 18, 19, 20, 22, 23, 48
Objective, 20, 27, 202, 263
  objectivity, 54, 64, 234, 262, 263
Objectives, 46, 57, 64, 65, 130, 180
  hierarchy of, 66, 67
  setting or formulating of, 148
  theirs and ours, 131
Obsession, 191
  as excessive involvement or relation, 191

Upanishads, 40, 252
Uyterhoeven, Hugo, 108

Values, 6, 49, 58, 59, 61, 138, 146, 197, 214, 269
  clarification, 59

Walton, Richard, 92
Watergate, 246
  as a symptom of excessive rationality, 246
Western civilization, 6, 38, 41, 247, 248, 249, 250, 251, 252, 262
  the darkness of 1939, 188
  giving way before a new era, 251

principle of causality and rationality, 262
Western Electric Hawthorne Plant, 218
We/they polarization, 128, 134
Whorf, Benjamin Lee, 41
Whorfian hypothesis, 41
Winning with People (Jongeward, Dorothy, and James, Muriel), 97
Witte, Larry, 122
Wizard of Oz, The (Baum, Frank), 188
White, Theodore, 256, 258
Work in America (U.S. Department of Health, Education, and Welfare), 106, 214
World War I, 249
World War II, 2, 46, 103, 206, 249

Zarathustra (Zoroaster), 248